HUMAN RIGHTS COMPLIANCE IN EUROPE

The Local Politics of Culture and Legitimacy

Zoë Jay

BRISTOL
UNIVERSITY
PRESS

First published in Great Britain in 2025 by

Bristol University Press
University of Bristol
1–9 Old Park Hill
Bristol
BS2 8BB
UK
t: +44 (0)117 374 6645
e: bup-info@bristol.ac.uk

Details of international sales and distribution partners are available at bristoluniversitypress.co.uk

British Library Cataloguing in Publication Data
A catalogue record for this book is available from the British Library

ISBN 978-1-5292-4133-4 hardcover
ISBN 978-1-5292-4134-1 ePub
ISBN 978-1-5292-4135-8 ePdf

Cover design: Hayes Design and Advertising
Front cover image: Shutterstock/CARACOLLA
Bristol University Press uses environmentally responsible print partners.
Printed and bound in Great Britain by CPI Group (UK) Ltd, Croydon, CR0 4YY

FSC
www.fsc.org
MIX
Paper | Supporting responsible forestry
FSC® C013604

Contents

Table of Cases, Treaties, and Legislation

Case law

A. and Others v United Kingdom, App no. 3455/05 ECtHR, 19 February 2009
Airey v Ireland, App no. 6289/73 ECtHR, 9 October 1979
Arambašin v Croatia, App no. 48981/17 ECtHR, 23 June 2022
B. and Others v Croatia, App no. 71593/11 ECtHR, 19 October 2015
Basu v Germany, App no. 215/19 ECtHR, 18 January 2023
Bego v Croatia, App no. 35444/12 ECtHR, 15 November 2016
Case 'Relating to Certain Aspects of the Laws on the Use of Language in Education in Belgium', App no. 1474/62 ECtHR, 23 July 1968
Debelić v Croatia, App no. 2448/03 ECtHR, 26 August 2005
Finucane v United Kingdom, App no. 29178/95 ECtHR, 1 October 2003
Frodl v Austria, App no. 20201/04 ECtHR, 4 October 2010
Gäfgen v Germany, App no. 22978/05 ECtHR, 1 June 2010
Golder v United Kingdom, App no. 4451/70 ECtHR, 21 February 1975
Gosovic v Croatia, App no. 37006/13 ECtHR, 4 April 2017
Handyside v United Kingdom, App no. 5493/72 ECtHR, 7 December 1976
Hegediš v Croatia, App no. 41306/18 ECtHR, 23 June 2022
Hirst v United Kingdom, App no. 74025/01 ECtHR, 6 October 2005
Horvat v Croatia, App no. 51585/99 ECtHR, 26 October 2001
Jalloh v Germany, App no. 54810/00 ECtHR, 11 July 2006
Jelić v Croatia, App no. 57856/11 ECtHR, 12 October 2014
Jularic v Croatia, App no. 20106/06 ECtHR, 20 April 2011
Kelly v United Kingdom, App no, 30054/96 ECtHR, 4 August 2001
Kühnen v Federal Republic of Germany, App no. 12194/86 ECtHR, 12 May 1988
M. v Germany, App no. 19359/04 ECtHR, 17 December 2009
M. and Others v Croatia, App no. 50175/12 ECtHR, 13 November 2017
M.H. and Others v Croatia, App nos. 15670/18 and 43115/18 ECtHR, 18 November 2021
Marckx v Belgium, App no. 6833/74 ECtHR, 13 June 1979

McKerr v United Kingdom, App no. 28883/95 ECtHR, 4 August 2001
Mirošević-Anzulović v Croatia, App no. 25815/14 ECtHR, 4 October 2016
Mitzinger v Germany, App no. 29762/10 ECtHR, 9 May 2017
N.D. and N.T. v Spain, App nos. 8675/15 and 8697/15 ECtHR, 13 February 2020
Neumeister v Austria, App no. 1936/63 ECtHR, 27 June 1968
Othman (Abu Qatada) v United Kingdom, App no. 8139/09 ECtHR, 17 January 2012
Rumpf v Germany, App no. 46344/06 ECtHR, 2 September 2010
Scozzari and Guinta v Italy, App nos. 39221/98 and 41963/98 ECtHR, 13 July 2000
Skelin-Hrvoj and Đuričić v Croatia, App no. 23414/15 ECtHR, 10 June 2021
Skendžić and Krznarić v Croatia, App no. 16212/08 ECtHR, 20 April 2011
Statileo v Croatia, App no. 12027/10 ECtHR, 10 October 2014
Sürmeli v Germany, App no. 75529/01 ECtHR, 8 June 2006
The Sunday Times v United Kingdom, App no. 6538/74 ECtHR, 26 April 1979
Tyrer v United Kingdom, App no. 5856/72 ECtHR, 25 April 1978
Von Hannover v Germany, App no. 59320/00 ECtHR, 28 July 2005
Von Hannover v Germany (no. 2), App nos. 40660/08 and 60641/08 ECtHR, 7 February 2012
A. v Secretary of State for the Home Department (2004) UKHL 56
Manchester CC v Pinnock [2011] UKSC 6 [48]
Othman (Jordan) v Secretary of State for the Home Department [2008] EWCA Civ 290
R (AAA and others) v Secretary of State for the Home Department [2023] UKSC 42
R v Horncastle [2009] UKSC 14 [2010] 2 AC 373 [11]
R v Secretary of State for the Home Department, Ex parte Brind [1991] 1 AC 696 (HL)
R (Quila) v Secretary of State for the Home Department [2011] UKSC 45
R (Ullah) v Secretary of State for the Home Department [2004] UKHL 26
Wheeler v Leicester CC [1985] AC 1054, 1065
BVerfGE 6, 32, 16 January 1957 ('*Elfes*')
BVerfGE 7, 198, 15 January 1958 ('*Lüth*')
BVerfGE 7, 377, 11 June 1958 ('*Apothekenurteil*')
BVerfGE 74, 358, 26 March 1987 ('*Unschuldsvermutung*')
BVerfGE 109, 133, 5 February 2004 ('*M*')
BVerfGE 111, 307, 14 October 2004 ('*Görgülü*')
BVerfGE 101, 361, 26 February 2008 ('*Caroline II*')
BVerfGE 120, 180, 26 February 2008 ('*Caroline III*')
BVerfGE 128, 326, 4 May 2011 ('*Preventive detention*')
Constitutional Court of the Republic of Croatia, Decision U-I-745/1999, 8 November 2000

Supreme Court of the Republic of Croatia, Decision 1840/01-2, 27 October 2004

Treaties

Belfast Agreement 1998

Council of Europe, *Convention for the Protection of Human Rights and Fundamental Freedoms*, European Treaty Series No. 5, Rome, 4 November 1950

Council of Europe, *Explanatory Report to Protocol No. 11 to the Convention for the Protection of Human Rights and Fundamental Freedoms, Restructuring the Control Machinery Established Thereby*, European Treaty Series No. 155, Strasbourg, 11 May 1994

Council of Europe, *Protocol No. 11 to the Convention for the Protection of Human Rights and Fundamental Freedoms, Restructuring the Control Machinery Established Thereby*, European Treaty Series No. 155, Strasbourg, 11 May 1994

Council of Europe, Article 1, *Protocol No. 15 Amending the Convention on the Protection of Human Rights and Fundamental Freedoms*, Council of Europe Treaty Series No. 213, Strasbourg, 24 November 2013

Legislation

Bill of Rights 1689 (England), 1 William and Mary Sess 2, chapter 2

Human Rights Act 1998

Gesetz über die Konvention zum Schutze der Menschenrechte und Grundfreiheiten [Act on the Convention for the Protection of Human Rights and Fundamental Freedoms], 7 August 1952. BGBl. 1952 II, 685

Government of Wales Act 2006

Grundgesetz für die Bundesrepublic Deutschland [Constitution for the Federal Republic of Germany], 23 May 1949. BGBl. 1949 I, 1

Gesetz über den Rechtsschutz bei überlangen Gerichtsverfahren und strafrechtlichen Ermittlungsverfahren [Law on Legal Protection in the Event of Excessively Long Court Proceedings and Criminal Investigations], 24 November 2011. BGBl. 2011 I S, 2302

Northern Ireland Act 1998

Scotland Act 1998

Scottish Elections (Franchise and Representation) Act 2020

Ustav Republike Hrvatske [Constitution of the Republic of Croatia], Narodne Novine [Official Gazette], 56/1990

Ustavni zakon o izmjenama i dopunama Ustavnog zakona o Ustavnom sudu [Constitutional Act Amending and Supplementing the Constitutional Act on Constitutional Court], Official Gazette 29/2002

List of Abbreviations

AC	Appeal cases
AfD	*Alternativ für Deutschland*
BGBl	*Bundesgesetzblatt* (Federal Law Gazette)
BRD	*Bundesrepublik Deutschland*
BVerfG	*Bundesverfassungsgericht*
BVerfGE	*Entscheidungen des Bundesverfassungsgerichts* (Decisions of the Federal Constitutional Court)
CDU	*Christlich Demokratische Union Deutschlands*
CJEU	Court of Justice of the European Union
DDR	*Deutsche Demokratische Republik*
ECHR	European Convention on Human Rights
ECmHR	European Commission on Human Rights
ECtHR	European Court of Human Rights
EU	European Union
EWCA Civ/Crim	England and Wales Court of Appeal (Civil/ Criminal division)
HC/HL Deb	House of Commons/House of Lords debates
HDZ	*Hrvatska demokratska zajednica*
HRA	Human Rights Act
ICJ	International Court of Justice
ICTY	International Criminal Tribunal for the Former Yugoslavia
MP	Member of parliament
PACE	Parliamentary Assembly of the Council of Europe
SED	*Sozialistische Einheitspartei Deutschlands*
SFRJ	*Socijalistička Federativna Republika Jugoslavija*
SPD	*Sozialdemokratische Partei Deutschlands*
TP	*Travaux Préparatoires*
UDHR	Universal Declaration on Human Rights
UK	United Kingdom
UKHL	United Kingdom House of Lords
UKSC	United Kingdom Supreme Court
UN	United Nations

Acknowledgements

The process of writing (and rewriting and rewriting and rewriting) this book exposed me to ideas, methods, and ways of engaging in human rights praxis that helped me become someone who would now write a very different one. Maybe my publisher will not like me admitting that (sorry!), but I think it actually speaks to the dynamism that permeates the cultural politics of human rights, the ways we adapt, stretch, and redefine the familiar as we encounter new ideas and experiences. The governmental, judicial, and media actors I study in this book often do their adapting strategically and cynically; I can only hope my own changes and lessons learned are somehow more useful, and help me to do some good.

This book began as a doctoral thesis, completed in my home town of nipaluna (Hobart), lutruwita (Tasmania) between 2014 and 2018. The thesis was written on the land of the palawa people, whose sovereignty was never ceded. In recognition of this, and in an effort to pay the rent the settler colony owes, on the eve of submitting the final manuscript of the book I made a donation to the Aboriginal Land Council of Tasmania (https://www.givinglandback.org/). Always was, always will be Aboriginal land.

I am eternally grateful to my supervisors, Matt Killingsworth and Richard Eccleston. From teacher to supervisor to mentor to friend, Matt never wavered in his support or his faith in my ability to do this work. Richard was always generous with his limited time and unlimited ideas. Funding for the doctoral research that underpins the book was provided by the Australian Research Council (decision number DP 130104088) and the Australian European University Institute Fellowship Association Inc (AEUIFAI).

The work of converting the thesis to a book was funded by the Research Council of Finland Centre of Excellence in Law, Identity and the European Narratives (EuroStorie) (decision numbers 336676 and 353107). I am grateful to my colleagues at EuroStorie and the University of Helsinki. They made me feel welcome in Finland, read drafts, recommended literature, and provided a genuinely interdisciplinary working environment; this book is significantly better for having been written here. The students in my 'Politics of European Human Rights' course at the University of Helsinki were also instrumental in sustaining my enthusiasm for the ideas presented in this book; I am grateful for our time in class together and am excited to see where their own ideas about the politics of human rights take them.

For reading parts of the book, discussing ideas, and providing academic and administrative support I would like to thank Ben Leruth, Nicole Wegner, André Brett, Thomas Kehoe, Christian Reus-Smit, Ben Wellings, Jennifer Welsh, Aishani Gupta, Liiri Oja, Anchalee Rüland, Dennis Grube, Hannah Murphy, Terry Narramore, Catherine Goetze, Mattias Hartwig, and Bronwyn Peters. My kind and meticulous German teachers, Karin Lucas and Billy Badger, made engagement with the German language sources in this book *viel einfacher, Vielen Dank*. Tamara and Vanja Tubakovic generously assisted with translating Croatian documents, *Hvala*. Any errors in both languages (and any in English, for that matter) are of course my own.

I am especially appreciative of everyone who assisted with accessing research materials and generously answering my technical questions in Strasbourg: Mr Miroslav Papa, Permanent Representative of the Republic of Croatia to the Council of Europe; Matteo Fiori, Katarina Nedeljkovic, Ioulietta Bisiouli, Nathalie Schell, and Laura Ielciu-Erel of the Department of Executions of the Council of Europe; and the skilled and helpful librarians of the European Court of Human Rights Library.

Thank you to Zoë Forbes and the Bristol University Press team, as well as the anonymous reviewers. Zoë has guided me with kindness and insight throughout the publishing process (and of course has an excellent name) – a wonderful experience for my first book.

Parts of Chapter 4 appeared in 'Keeping Rights at Home: British Conceptions of Rights and Compliance with the European Court of Human Rights', *British Journal of Politics and International Relations*, 19(4), 2017, pp 842–60 (DOI: 10.1177/1369148117732469). Thank you to the journal editors and publisher for permission to reuse the work here.

Diligent procrastinator that I am, some of my favourite parts of writing a book were the ones where I did literally anything else. Thank you to the many friends who helped me in those pursuits and hijinks (and who were also very supportive when the time came to knuckle down): Imogen Wegman, Lydia Nicholson, Dave Huf, Evan Pitt, Anna-Maria Wilskman, Daria Krivonos, Antonio Lopez Garcia, Ali Ali, Alina Hruba, Keshia Jacotine, Nicholas Bromfield, Jakub Zahora, Felicity Gray, Ella Edwards, Mel Ross, Kat Montgomery, Em Schade, Kristof Wing, Michael Fitzgerald, and Tom Marshall. Megan Tighe and Rosanna Hunt in particular are always on standby to discuss such essential matters as where one of us saw a cute dog today. Kesherie Gurung not only read and talked through various parts of the work, but put up with an inordinate amount of text messages from me whinging about it. Our daily conversations about everything from social theory to novels to cat videos are the primary reason I am any sort of critical scholar at all; I am a better person for our friendship.

Thank you to my family – Wendy, Steve, Frances, Ruby, Cathryn, Ellis, Linda, Allison, Barbara, Elaine, Bert, Maggie, Myrtle, Flossie, Phoebe, Nala, Elmo, Worcester, Jezebel, Bear, Wally, and Jake. Humans and animals alike, they have loved me and supported me my whole life; I'll leave it to your imaginations to guess which ones have four legs.

There is no better partner in this world than Ben Rosher (Sassenach to me). He read this thing cover to cover, talked through every detail, calmed me in every moment of panic, distracted me at every opportunity. Thank you.

Finally, a word for my grandfather, Gordon Jay, who knew better than anyone in our family what it meant to move to the other side of the world at a time when it wasn't clear when we would be able to go back, and encouraged me to go anyway. This book is dedicated to him.

Introduction

For at least a decade now, the European Court of Human Rights (ECtHR) has been under siege. Far-right populist leaders from the Netherlands to Italy have declared it a 'ravening monster that, without the slightest legitimacy, overrules scores of national laws and regulations',[1] being funded to 'hand down one idiotic sentence after another'.[2] In 2018, the Danish government attempted (but failed) to curtail the Court's influence by warning that it 'should not take on the role of States Parties whose responsibility it is to ensure that Convention rights and freedoms are respected and protected at national level'.[3] And in what can only be described as a uniquely English blend of rugby metaphor and Francophobia, one British Conservative MP advised his colleagues to ignore ECtHR rulings that would prevent the government from forging ahead with its disastrous plan to deport people to Rwanda by declaring in a WhatsApp chat that 'it's time we kicked these bastards into touch. For once I won't apologise for my French.'[4]

Once widely considered to be the 'crown jewel of the world's most advanced international system for protecting civil and political liberties',[5] due in no small part to its allegedly near-perfect compliance rates, these

---

1 Thierry Baudet (2011) 'The Anti-Democratic Impulses of the ECHR', Spiked, 19 January. Available at: https://www.spiked-online.com/2011/01/19/the-anti-democratic-impulses-of-the-echr/ (accessed 31 March 2024).

2 Matteo Salvini, in ANSA.it (2015) 'Strasbourg Court "Useless" says Salvini', ANSA, 9 April. Available at: https://www.ansa.it/english/news/politics/2015/04/09/strasbourg-court-useless-says-salvini_07b1abed-c340-443f-b073-776d80562b81.html (accessed 31 March 2024).

3 Danish Chairmanship of the Committee of Ministers (2018) 'Draft Copenhagen Declaration', Copenhagen, 5 February, para 22.

4 Eleni Courea (2022) 'London Playbook: Return of the Pyjama Judges – Inside Tory WhatsApp Groups – Brussels Sues', Politico, 15 June. Available at: https://www.politico.eu/newsletter/london-playbook/return-of-the-pyjama-judges-inside-tory-whatsapp-groups-brussels-sues/ (accessed 31 March 2024).

5 Laurence R. Helfer (2008) 'Redesigning the European Court of Human Rights: Embeddedness as a Deep Structural Principle of the European Human Rights Regime', *European Journal of International Law*, 19(1): 125.

quotes illustrate the growing resistance and backlash the ECtHR faces from recalcitrant states. Although most compliance scholars are rightly sceptical of the claim to high compliance rates,[6] perceptions that the ECtHR's judgments have 'not only generally but always been complied with',[7] such that they are 'as effective as those of any domestic court',[8] form the cornerstone of Europe's mythology as the birthplace of human rights and reinforce the Strasbourg-based Court's reputation as the legitimate and pre-eminent guardian of human rights in Europe. But this reputation is increasingly threatened by claims that it has strayed from its original purpose as a minimal instrument of international law, engaging in judicial activism to impose on its member states far greater obligations than they ever signed up for. In turn, calls to restrict, or – in extreme cases – leave the Court's jurisdiction altogether, are on the rise, along with reluctance and occasionally outright refusal to obey its rulings.[9] At the same time, the overwhelming volume of cases submitted to the ECtHR each year, slow or delayed implementation of judgments, and ongoing problems with repeat violations of the same rights by the same states have left even some within the Council of Europe system wondering whether the ECtHR was ever truly capable of protecting rights within states that did not already 'want to be helped'.[10]

---

6 Darren Hawkins and Wade Jacoby (2008) 'Partial Compliance: A Comparison of the European and Inter-American Courts for Human Rights', paper delivered at the Annual Meeting of the American Political Science Association, Boston, MA, 28–31 August, p 45; Courtney Hillebrecht (2014) *Domestic Politics and International Human Rights Tribunals: The Problem of Compliance* (New York: Cambridge University Press), p 48.

7 Rolv Ryssdal (1996) 'The Enforcement System Set Up under the European Convention on Human Rights', in M.K. Bulterman and M. Kuijer (eds), *Compliance with Judgments of International Courts: Proceedings of the Symposium Organised in Honour of Professor Henry G. Schermers by Mordenate College and the Department of International Public Law of Leiden University* (The Hague: Martinus Nijhoff), p 67.

8 Barry E. Carter and Phillip R. Trimble (1995) *International Law* (2nd edn, Boston: Little, Brown), p 309, cited in Laurence R. Helfer and Anne-Marie Slaughter (1997) 'Toward a Theory of Effective Supranational Adjudication', *Yale Law Journal*, 107(2): 296.

9 Alexandra Sims (2015) 'Vladimir Putin Signs Law Allowing Russia to Ignore International Human Rights', *Independent*, 15 December. Available at: http://www.independent.co.uk/news/world/europe/vladimir-putin-signs-law-allowing-russian-court-to-overthrow-international-human-rights-rulings-a6773581.html (accessed 5 February 2018); Josie Ensor and Zia Weise (2016) 'Turkey Suspends European Convention on Human Rights Amid Fears of Further Crackdown', *Telegraph*, 21 July. Available at: http://www.telegraph.co.uk/news/2016/07/21/turkey-suspends-european-convention-on-human-rights-as-it-enacts/ (accessed 5 February 2018); James Landale (2012) 'UK Presses for European Human Rights Convention Changes', BBC News, 29 February. Available at: http://www.bbc.com/news/uk-politics-17201024 (accessed 5 February 2018).

10 Nils Muižnieks, Commissioner for Human Rights of the Council of Europe, cited in Ginger Hervey (2017) 'Europe's Human Rights Court Struggles to Lay Down the Law',

These challenges and criticisms have dealt powerful blows to the Court's democratic and procedural legitimacy and called into question its capacity to elicit compliance with its rulings. Indeed, the correlation between some states' intensifying perceptions of the ECtHR's illegitimacy and their increasing reluctance to obey its rulings is a potent reminder that, when it comes to compliance with international law, legitimacy and actors' sense of obligation are inextricably linked. The European human rights system may be celebrated for maintaining the highest rates of adherence to its obligations of any international human rights regime in the world, but the tensions between the Court and its Contracting States over the legitimate role of a supranational judiciary in protecting human rights demonstrate that this reputation for garnering compliance is far from secure.

It is in this context that this book asks: where does the sense that an international law is legitimate enough to comply with come from? In a system premised on deferring to domestic human rights protections in the first instance, and with only limited international enforcement mechanisms, this book seeks to explain why European states comply with most – but not all – of their obligations under the European Convention on Human Rights (ECHR). Building on the constructivist assumption that actors feel a 'pull towards compliance' when they believe the law is legitimate,[11] the book examines the relationship between the perceived legitimacy of the European human rights system, and states' compliance with it. The aim here is to provide answers to three interrelated questions. First, what makes state actors perceive international law as legitimate enough to comply with in the first place? Second, how do such perceptions of legitimacy translate into decisions to comply with particular judgments of the ECtHR? And third, which types of ECtHR cases are states likely to comply with or resist?

The book's central argument is that the answer to where state actors' perceptions of the legitimacy of international law come from, and how these perceptions translate into compliance, lies in domestic cultural politics. Drawing on insights from sociology and anthropology about how culture shapes knowledge and behaviour, I present a new framework for thinking about how ideas of legitimacy are the products of fluid and evolving cultural contexts, to offer a more dynamic explanation of how culture informs interactions between the ECtHR and its Contracting States and shapes variation in compliance responses. I argue that within states there are unique, local human rights cultural environments, in which identity narratives,

Politico, 20 September. Available at: https://www.politico.eu/article/human-rights-court-ilgar-mammadov-azerbaijan-struggles-to-lay-down-the-law/ (accessed 4 February 2018).

11 Thomas M. Franck (1990) *The Power of Legitimacy Among Nations* (New York: Oxford University Press), p 234.

historical experiences and national memory, and constitutional structures, practices, and traditions create specific understandings and expectations about what law and human rights are, what they should be, and what should be the respective roles of national and international actors in creating and upholding laws and rights. These cultural environments – and the politics that shape and are shaped by them – create the conditions of possibility for compliance or noncompliance with ECtHR rulings. Cultural environments orient governments and courts towards particular preferences, providing a range of ideas, strategies, and tools to determine whether a particular judgment or obligation is legitimate or acceptable, and worth complying with. Crucially, understanding culture and legitimacy as dynamic, contested, and often internally inconsistent explains not only variation in compliance across states but also within them, revealing why states with largely positive compliance records refuse or resist compliance with cases that cannot be reconciled with local sensibilities concerning what is legitimate or appropriate.

In short, I argue that notions of legitimacy are a form of what Clifford Geertz calls 'local knowledge', helping to contextualize how actors perceive international law and structuring the scope of possible responses to their compliance obligations.[12] Through a comparative analysis of three case studies – the United Kingdom, Germany, and Croatia – this study demonstrates that local, culturally embedded ideas about law, human rights, and European institutions have multifaceted and important effects on how state actors understand what counts as legitimate or illegitimate in international law. These understandings permeate states' political and judicial interactions with the ECtHR, and shape how they interpret their obligations to comply with the Court's rulings.

Examining the effects of local cultural politics of human rights on actors' perceptions of legitimacy addresses two major weaknesses in existing explanations of compliance. First, this approach responds to the failure of scholars of International Relations and International Law to provide a convincing account of where the legitimacy that ostensibly pulls states towards compliance originates. Legitimacy permeates the paradigmatic explanations of compliance, even in cases that look at face value like coercion and rational choice. But to the extent that the origins of international law and institutions' legitimacy are explored in these fields, legitimacy tends to be treated as being constructed predominantly at the international, not domestic, level.[13] This interactive and systemic dimension is important for

[12] Clifford Geertz (1983) *Local Knowledge: Further Essays in Interpretive Anthropology* (New York: Basic Books), p 215.

[13] Thomas M. Franck (1995) *Fairness in International Law and Institutions* (Oxford: Clarendon Press); Jutta Brunnée and Stephen J. Toope (2010) *Legitimacy and Legality in International Law: An Interactional Account* (Cambridge: Cambridge University Press); Christian

understanding why states comply with international law in general terms, but neglects the details of how and why particular states come to accept international law as legitimate and feel the compulsion to comply with specific obligations in the first place.

Second, the effects of domestic political and legal culture are often implicit, but not critically examined, in studies of compliance. Scholars from normative and rationalist backgrounds alike frequently examine European democracies' compliance with international and regional law by making references to these states' 'culture of rights',[14] 'rights consciousness',[15] or 'cultures of compliance'[16] as means to explain why they routinely uphold international legal commitments. These studies rarely articulate what these concepts mean in detail, or specify how such cultures generate a sense of obligation in an actor. Yet, in the words of Marie-Bénédicte Dembour, 'we do not always talk about the same thing when we talk about human rights'.[17] A 'culture of rights' in the UK will not look the same in Germany or Croatia, nor will it look the same among different political, judicial, media, social, or historical contexts within these states. The details and particularities of culture and human rights matter because it is in the processes of constructing, contesting, embedding, and disrupting their meanings and uses that we draw lines through what rights we seek to protect, who is responsible for protecting rights, and who is included or excluded from enjoying them. Moreover, the cultural politics that inform how we understand human rights cannot be assumed to automatically lead to compliance, or to be progressive at all – even, or perhaps especially, among states that are typically lauded for having strong records of compliance with their international human rights obligations.[18] Consequently, scholars who refer to 'compliance cultures' can neither explain why states with seemingly similar commitments to rule of

Reus-Smit (1999) *The Moral Purpose of the State: Culture, Social Identity, and Institutional Rationality in International Relations* (Princeton, NJ: Princeton University Press); Mlada Bukovansky (2002) *Legitimacy and Power Politics: The American and French Revolutions in International Political Culture* (Princeton, NJ: Princeton University Press); Ian Clark (2005) *Legitimacy in International Society* (Oxford: Oxford University Press).

14 Courtney Hillebrecht (2012) 'Implementing International Human Rights Law at Home: Domestic Politics and the European Court of Human Rights', *Human Rights Review*, 13(3): 297.

15 James L. Gibson and Gregory A. Caldeira (1996) 'The Legal Cultures of Europe', *Law and Society Review*, 30(1): 58.

16 Gerda Falkner and Oliver Treib (2008) 'Three Worlds of Compliance or Four? The EU-15 Compared to New Member States', *Journal of Common Market Studies*, 46(2): 296–7.

17 Marie-Bénédicte Dembour (2006) *Who Believes in Human Rights?: Reflections on the European Convention* (New York: Cambridge University Press).

18 Kate Nash (2009) *The Cultural Politics of Human Rights: Comparing the US and UK* (Cambridge: Cambridge University Press), p 19.

law and human rights principles have different approaches to protecting human rights and obeying international law, nor why states comply with most but not all of their obligations.

Elsewhere, though, International Relations scholars are developing sophisticated and compelling arguments about the nature of culture and its relationships to international political orders.[19] These works draw on scholarship from anthropology, sociology, and history to demonstrate that cultures are not coherent, bounded entities with direct causal effects on their members, but dynamic, hybrid collections of meanings and practices which shape action by contextualizing how actors interpret the world around them and providing ranges of skills and knowledge to help them move through it.[20] This book contributes to this cultural turn, adopting a dynamic understanding of culture to reveal how the cultural environments within states and among the actors responsible for complying with international law evolve and generate local ideas about law and human rights. By focusing on the cultural and historical origins of state actors' perceptions of the legitimacy of international human rights regimes, this book offers a more complete theoretical and empirical picture of how European states perceive, interpret, and act upon their compliance obligations under the ECtHR system.

Conceptualizing culture and legitimacy

This book uses dynamic understandings of both culture and legitimacy. It recognizes that culture, especially at the level of whole states and regions, is not homogeneous, universally accepted, or constant throughout history, and that it certainly does not *cause* compliance or noncompliance, at least not in a strictly linear or direct way.[21] Rather, culture *contextualizes* actors' social environments, orienting the ways actors construct meanings and providing 'repertoire[s] of actions, practices and beliefs' that actors may

---

[19] Christian Reus-Smit (2017) *On Cultural Diversity: International Theory in a World of Difference* (Cambridge: Cambridge University Press); Andrew Phillips and Christian Reus-Smit (eds) (2020) *Culture and Order in World Politics* (Cambridge: Cambridge University Press); Hendrik Spruyt (2020) *The World Imagined: Collective Beliefs and Political Order in the Sinocentric, Islamic and Southeast Asian International Societies* (Cambridge: Cambridge University Press); Lisbeth Zimmermann (2017) *Global Norms with a Local Face: Between Global Norms and Local Translation* (Cambridge: Cambridge University Press).

[20] Sally Engle Merry (2006) *Human Rights and Gender Violence: Translating International Law into Local Justice* (Chicago, IL: Chicago University Press); Jane K. Cowan, Marie-Bénédicte Dembour, and Richard A. Wilson (eds) (2004) *Culture and Rights: Anthropological Perspectives* (New York: Cambridge University Press).

[21] Christian Reus-Smit (2017) 'Cultural Diversity and International Order', *International Organization*, 71(4): 856.

put into practice or adapt across different contexts.[22] Moreover, cultural effects on how actors interpret and interact with the world are fluid; the overlapping and porous nature of cultural boundaries means local cultures are shaped by transnational and global dynamics, while those same global dynamics, in turn, are sensitive to shifts at the regional, national, and local or 'micro-political' levels.[23] The ongoing interactions within and across different political layers or communities are part of the 'active making of culture', so that understandings of rights, law, and legitimacy evolve as actors respond to new information and situations.[24]

My conceptualization of culture is especially influenced by Kate Nash's work on the 'cultural politics of human rights'. For Nash, the relationship between human rights and culture lies in the 'more or less organised struggles over symbols that frame what issues, events or processes mean to social actors who are emotionally and intellectually invested in shared understandings of the world'.[25] Human rights come to life through these struggles, constructed and enacted in particular ways at particular times through relations of power and contestation over the most just or righteous – most *legitimate* – ways to uphold them. In light of these dynamics, Nash makes a distinction between the static and essentializing term 'human rights culture', and the more open 'cultural politics of human rights', which gives space to the discourses and practices that constitute what human rights mean in varied cultural contexts.[26] I follow her lead, using the term 'cultural politics' to refer to the processes of contestation in which local elite actors participate as they struggle to meet or avoid their legal obligations, and 'cultural environment' or 'cultural context' to refer to the spaces in which the politics take place.

Local cultural contexts for human rights, then, can be understood as collections of diverse discourses, narratives, memories, institutions, norms, and practices that are frequently contradictory and subject to contestation, as well as intrinsically embedded in and connected to broader regional and international cultural orders. That this cultural knowledge is flexible and dynamic enough to be applied and adapted across different contexts is central

---

22 Sally Engle Merry (2012) 'What is Legal Culture? An Anthropological Perspective', *Journal of Comparative Law*, 5(2): 42; Susan Silbey (2001) 'Legal Culture and Legal Consciousness', in Neil J. Smelser and Paul B. Baltes (eds), *International Encyclopedia of Social and Behavioural Sciences* (Oxford: Pergamon Press), p 8627; Ann Swidler (1986) 'Culture in Action: Symbols and Strategies', *American Sociological Review*, 51(2): 273.

23 Merry, *Human Rights and Gender Violence*, p 3; Ellen Berrey (2020) 'When Liberal States Bite Back: The Micro-Politics of Culture', in Andrew Phillips and Christian Reus-Smit (eds), *Culture and Order in World Politics* (Cambridge: Cambridge University Press), p 161.

24 Merry, 'What is Legal Culture?', p 42.

25 Nash, *The Cultural Politics of Human Rights*, p 1.

26 Nash, *The Cultural Politics of Human Rights*, p 7.

to the variation within states' own compliance records – as Chapters 4, 5, and 6 show, the same basic narratives or practices can be stretched or adjusted to produce quite different compliance decisions. Nonetheless, cultures are still 'patterned and structured', meaning it is possible to identify overarching themes and structures across human rights systems while still appreciating the fluidity of the cultural politics that make and organize those patterns.[27]

Likewise, I adopt a broad conceptualization of legitimacy. The concept of legitimacy is understood here as meaning that which is considered appropriate or acceptable by an actor. It is 'a generalised perception or assumption that the actions of an entity are desirable, proper, or appropriate within some socially constructed system of norms, values, beliefs, and definitions'.[28] Within this definition, legitimacy can encapsulate more specific expectations about process (whether the entity in question was produced through appropriate methods), outcome (whether it achieved a desired result), and normative notions of justice, fairness, democracy, efficacy, and legality.[29] These concepts are viewed in this study as inherently subjective and contested, contingent on the meanings and interpretations given to them by actors – like human rights, they are the product of constant cultural politics. This is a descriptive, rather than normative, understanding of legitimacy; my focus is on the perceptions, beliefs, and expectations held by the actors being examined, as they are expressed through public discourses and narratives concerning human rights and compliance, rather than on advancing a particular argument about whether the ECtHR's rulings and the choices of its Contracting States are good or right.[30] This emphasis on how actors themselves view the ECtHR and the human rights laws it develops is key to understanding why states feel an obligation towards the Court, and how such feelings of obligation translate into actual compliance. Retaining a flexible,

---

[27] Reus-Smit, 'Cultural Diversity and International Order', p 856.

[28] Mark Suchman (1995) 'Managing Legitimacy: Strategic and Institutional Approaches', *Academy of Management Review*, 20(3): 574.

[29] Andreas Føllesdal (2013) 'Much Ado About Nothing? International Judicial Review of Human Rights in Well-Functioning Democracies', in Andreas Føllesdal, Johan Karlsson Schaffer, and Geir Ulfstein (eds), *The Legitimacy of International Human Rights Regimes: Legal, Political and Philosophical Perspectives* (Cambridge: Cambridge University Press), pp 276–7; Andrew Hurrell (2005) 'Legitimacy and the Use of Force: Can the Circle Be Squared?', *Review of International Studies*, 31(S1): 15–32; Fritz Scharpf (1999) *Governing Europe: Effective and Democratic?* (Oxford: Oxford University Press), p 6; Franck, *Fairness in International Law and Institutions*, pp 7–8.

[30] Daniel Bodansky (2013) 'Legitimacy in International Law and International Relations', in Jeffrey L. Dunoff and Mark A. Pollack, *Interdisciplinary Perspectives on International Law and International Relations: The State of the Art* (New York: Cambridge University Press), p 327; Ian Hurd (2003) 'Legitimacy and Authority in International Politics', *International Organization*, 53(2): 381.

open conceptualization of legitimacy that focuses on general perceptions and expectations is also essential for capturing the diverse influences that might inform actors' notions of what is and is not legitimate.

Opening up how we conceive of both culture and legitimacy is essential for understanding compliance patterns within the European human rights system, because of the scope given to Contracting States to determine their own approaches to compliance. Established by the Council of Europe in 1959 to interpret and monitor the European Convention on Human Rights (ECHR), the ECtHR played a central role in the postwar evolution of international law, shifting its focus to not only regulating interactions between states, but also contributing to a new form of legal accountability for the actions taken by states against their citizens. But, as Chapter 3 further explains, it was also built on the assumption that its member states were already capable of upholding human rights in accordance with their own national human rights mechanisms and traditions. The European human rights system is therefore deliberately structured to allow Contracting States substantial leeway to interpret and execute their obligations, meaning there is no one 'right' way to comply. Signatories are charged with two forms of obligation – to uphold the rights enshrined in the Convention (first-order compliance), and to remedy any violations of the Convention found by the ECtHR (second-order compliance) – but how they meet these obligations is frequently the product of negotiation and compromise. What 'counts' as compliance depends heavily on what measures Strasbourg is willing to declare sufficient, and what different state actors believe is legitimate or reasonable for an international court to ask of them.

Compliance in European democracies: a comparative approach

Examining why similar states end up with substantially different perceptions of the legitimacy of an international legal system naturally requires comparative research. This book compares the relationship between national-level perceptions of the legitimacy of the European human rights system and compliance through three Contracting State case studies: the United Kingdom, Germany, and Croatia. These cases represent different (but not exhaustive) legal, political, and historical experiences with human rights in Europe, allowing me to examine how compliance decisions are contextualized by the cultural politics of rights that play out in different state compositions.

Nonetheless, the three cases share an important similarity: all three states have what can be described as a (mostly) positive, or – to use the language of the Council of Europe – a 'good faith' relationship with the Strasbourg institutions. That is, for the most part, they accept and endeavour to meet their obligations under the ECHR. This baseline positive relationship is important for being able to identify states' compliance 'sticking points': the challenging cases, where the lines between 'legitimate' and 'illegitimate' judgments lie in the view of domestic actors, and where compliance is the result of a more deliberate decision-making and justification process.

The following additional factors guided my selection of these particular states. First, I chose the United Kingdom for its fraught relationship with the ECtHR. Despite frequently and vehemently criticizing the Court for undermining national traditions and autonomy, the UK remains one of its most compliant members. As a country that consciously and continuously frames itself as separate from Europe, the UK is a 'crucial case' for exploring the relationship between local cultural politics of human rights and compliance with the regional human rights regime.[31] Germany, with a much more 'friendly' relationship with the ECtHR, and with contrasting institutional structures and postwar human rights context to the UK, therefore presents a valuable comparative counterpoint. Croatia, with similar institutional structures to Germany (the contemporary Croatian constitution is partly modelled on the German one), but a newer signatory to the ECHR, rounds out this three-part comparative study. Croatia also has a weaker compliance record than Germany or the UK, both in terms of having a higher number of violations found (indicating noncompliance with the Convention) and a higher number of cases pending execution (indicating noncompliance with the Court), though it is by no means one of the most severe offenders in the Strasbourg system. Insights from Croatia are particularly useful as it has been largely neglected in comparative studies of the ECtHR member states, including many specifically examining Central and Eastern Europe; these studies tend to focus on former Soviet states, while Croatia is grouped with former Yugoslav and Balkan states, whose accession into European institutions has tended to be slower.[32] Yet Croatia is a rich case because it provides insight into the effects of communism, democratic transition, and

31 Harry Eckstein (1975) 'Case Studies and Theory in Political Science', in Fred Greenstein and Nelson Polsby (eds), *Handbook of Political Science*, vol 7 (Reading, MA: Addison-Wesley), pp 79–138, cited in Alexander L. George and Andrew Bennett (2004) *Case Studies and Theory Development in the Social Sciences* (Cambridge, MA: MIT Press), p 9.

32 Notable and valuable exceptions include: Ksenija Turković and Jasna Omejec (2016) 'Commitment to Reform: Assessing the Impact of the ECtHR's Case Law on Reinforcing Democratisation Efforts in Croatian Legal Order', in Iulia Motoc and Ineta Ziemele (eds), *The Impact of the ECHR on Democratic Change in Central and Eastern Europe* (Cambridge: Cambridge University Press); Christopher Lamont (2011) 'Confronting the Consequences of Authoritarianism and Conflict: The ECHR and Transition', in Antoine Buyse and Michael Hamilton (eds), *Transitional Jurisprudence and the European Convention on Human Rights: Justice, Politics and Rights* (Cambridge: Cambridge University Press); and Siniša Rodin (2012) 'Croatia', in Leonard Hammer and Frank Emmert (eds), *The*

war on domestic human rights conceptions, while still exhibiting a relatively positive overarching relationship with the ECtHR.

Structure of the book

Following this introduction, Chapter 1 outlines how existing scholarship has explained the role played by legitimacy in facilitating compliance with international law, and how these explanations undervalue the local cultural and historical contexts in which notions of what counts as legitimate or not are constructed, contested, and translated into decisions to comply with some laws but not others. This chapter also provides an overview of the types and forms compliance can take. Although this study is concerned with *why* states comply with international law, references to *how* they comply are scattered throughout the book as illustrations of the processes and outcomes that occur through cultural politics of human rights and local knowledges of legitimacy.

Chapter 2 presents the book's core theoretical contribution: how domestic politics of human rights shape state actors' notions of the legitimacy of international law. The chapter articulates a new framework for thinking about how ideas of legitimacy are produced and evolve, drawing on insights from anthropology, sociology, and the recent cultural turn in International Relations about how culture shapes knowledge and behaviour. From here, the chapter outlines the concepts of cultural politics and cultural contexts of human rights, and the methodology used to examine how state actors' notions of legitimacy constitute a form of 'local knowledge' – thematic analysis of the discourses and practices that constitute elite compliance actors' human rights cultural environments. Local cultural ideas, traditions, and institutions – and the debates and politics surrounding their construction – provide contexts that actors draw on in order to interpret, accept, contest, or reject international norms and law.

Chapter 3 provides a brief history and overview of the structures and functions of the European Court and Convention. It outlines the legal obligations that Contracting States are required to fulfil as signatories to the ECHR, along with the processes by which states are supervised in executing their obligations – what states are expected to comply with and how. By combining the historical and procedural backgrounds of the European human rights system, the chapter demonstrates how the normative underpinnings of the Convention and its supervisory institutions – their meaning, purpose, and potential – have shaped the nature of the obligations on states, and the

European Convention on Human Rights and Fundamental Freedoms in Central and Eastern Europe (The Hague: Eleven International Publishing).

means by which they are enforced and obeyed. The delicate balance the system aims to strike between effective international oversight across Europe and respecting the diverse approaches to rights protections of the Contracting States has implications for understanding the nature of compliance with the ECtHR, because the expectations held by states and the Court for what constitutes a legitimate ruling and satisfactory compliance with it are fluid and subject to debate.

Chapters 4, 5, and 6 present the case studies: the United Kingdom, Germany, and Croatia, respectively. Each of these chapters has a dual focus on how human rights and law are conceptualized, articulated, and practised within national discourses, and how these conceptualizations relate to the states' interactions and compliance with the ECtHR. Particular attention is paid to demonstrating how local narratives or stories about rights contribute to assumptions about the ECtHR in general and/or cases or interpretations of the Convention in particular. Finally, specific examples of compliance and noncompliance with ECtHR judgments reveal how domestic politics of human rights shape the way domestic actors perceive and decide to comply with or resist ECtHR judgments. From the apparently unconscionable challenge to parliamentary sovereignty of the UK prisoner voting case, to the German *Land* courts' attempts to push back against the powerful federal Constitutional Court, and the interplay of competing European and nationalist identities in Croatian war crime investigations, the cases both illustrate and expand the argument advanced in Chapter 2, highlighting the spectrum of ways state actors conceive of legitimacy and human rights, and use their conceptions as they navigate what they view as more or less onerous obligations.

The book concludes by considering the broader implications that domestic cultural constructions of legitimacy might have on relations between supranational legal institutions and their member states, and on the future of the European human rights order. Though local, culturally informed understandings of human rights and legitimacy clearly matter for understanding compliance, there is still work to be done in terms of the ongoing theorizing of the relationships between culture, politics, and law – not only in the cases studies here, but across the Strasbourg system and other international and regional rights regimes, where the cultural politics at play vary considerably from European-specific contexts. To this end, the central argument of this book – that local understandings of human rights and legitimacy can reveal why, and in what circumstances, states comply with international law – is not an end point for understanding the relationship between culture, state behaviour, and international law, but a beginning.

1

Compliance and the Origins of Legitimacy in International Law

The European Court of Human Rights (ECtHR) depends on legitimacy to elicit compliance with its judgments. But the highly variable rates of compliance across and within its Contracting States, not to mention the differences in the type and extent of legitimacy-based critiques levelled against it, show that the ways legitimacy contributes to compliance are both multifaceted and contingent. How, then, should we understand the relationship between legitimacy and compliance? Where do ideas that international law is or is not legitimate come from, and how do those assumptions translate into compliant behaviour?

The received wisdom across International Relations (IR) and International Law (IL) presents legitimacy as one of several possible explanations for compliance, alongside coercion, self-interest, institutional or public pressure, and normative argumentation; these concepts each form the basis of one of the competing approaches to compliance offered by realist-positivist, rationalist, domestic institutionalist, and constructivist and norm-oriented schools of International Relations and International Legal theory. This chapter challenges that separation, revisiting each of the explanations for compliance to show that assumptions about legitimacy run through all of them, albeit often only implicitly.

Yet while this reading highlights the pervasive role of legitimacy in underpinning different compliance explanations, it also reveals an important gap where the particular ideas, experiences, and decision-making processes of different states contribute to their understandings of legitimacy. This particularity matters: the European human rights system is deliberately designed to give Contracting States flexibility and autonomy to comply with the Convention and Court in keeping with their own domestic constitutional structures and local contexts. This is key to identifying and explaining patterns in variation within and across Contracting States' compliance records. More work therefore needs to be done to understand why and how different state actors come to view particular laws, norms, or institutions as legitimate or not, and how, in turn, these perceptions of legitimacy translate into actual decisions to comply in different contexts.

The second part of this chapter shows that when theories of compliance do address this question, they predominantly frame the origins of law's legitimacy as stemming from shared understandings produced among actors at the international level, and from within the international legal system itself. I argue that constructivist theories, while going the furthest to explore how legitimacy is constructed, privilege international dynamics between states and top-down conceptions of law and norm diffusion, at the expense of domestic dynamics within states. To the extent that domestic influences are acknowledged, the theoretical prescriptions remain vague and insufficient to explain what precisely at the domestic level makes international law culturally or politically appealing. Consequently, both International Relations and International Law neglect an important potential source of states' perceptions of the legitimacy of international law, and the local particularities that shape variation in states' compliance records. I conclude with the argument that the key to remedying this gap therefore rests in a more culturally and historically sensitive approach to legitimacy, focused on the construction and application of local conceptions of law and rights.

Compliance and other concepts

Conceptions of compliance and noncompliance as a binary have long been dismissed as unsatisfactory for capturing the range of different types or modes of compliance, as well as failing to recognize the frequent contestation surrounding what constitutes compliance with or violation of a given obligation.[1] Beyond the basic premise of 'conformity between behaviour and a legal rule or standard', or 'the act of rule following',[2] the concept of compliance has been expanded to accommodate a spectrum, not only of possible actions that 'count' as compliance or noncompliance, but also of possible intentions behind those actions.

Early enquiries into noncompliance developed concepts such as 'partial' and 'incomplete' compliance with capacity problems in mind, suggesting that states only meet part or some of their obligations because they lack the financial, institutional, or technical resources to do so fully – and would

1 Oran Young (1979) *Compliance and Public Authority: A Theory with International Applications* (Baltimore, MD: Johns Hopkins University Press), p 105.

2 Kal Raustiala (2000) 'Compliance and Effectiveness in International Regulatory Cooperation', *Case Western Reserve Journal of International Law*, 32(3): 388.

comply fully if only they could.[3] Other approaches do not assume that full compliance is always the ultimate goal, often distinguishing between 'good faith' compliance (or attempts at it), and more strategic or nefarious behaviours. Concepts such as contestation, localization, and decoupling account for the jostling over the meaning and application of norms and laws that occur as state actors try to fit international obligations into their local contexts,[4] while 'minimal compliance' recognizes that, when faced with onerous or politically sensitive obligations, states will most likely only do the bare minimum necessary for their actions to pass as compliance.[5] And in the web of overlapping domestic, regional, and international obligations that constitute the contemporary legal order, 'collateral noncompliance' helps us to understand the grey spaces between noncompliance and norm conflicts, when obeying one obligation makes it impossible – or seem impossible – to comply with another.[6]

Meanwhile, scholars of 'bad faith compliance' identify several ways in which actors strive to make their actions look like compliance while actually shirking or reducing their obligations.[7] Rather than openly refusing to comply and facing the associated costs, states turn to evasive strategies such as exploiting loopholes that technically conform to the letter of the law but violate its spirit,[8] relying on covert measures to avoid detection when they cannot find legitimate legal exemptions,[9] or 'craft[ing] arguments that could diffuse pressures to … minimise perceptions that certain actions are

3 Gergana Noutcheva (2009) 'Fake, Partial and Imposed Compliance: The Limits of the EU's Normative Power in the Western Balkans', *Journal of European Public Policy*, 16(7): 1075; Darren Hawkins and Wade Jacoby (2008) 'Partial Compliance: A Comparison of the European and Inter-American Courts for Human Rights', paper delivered at the Annual Meeting of the American Political Science Association, Boston, MA, 28–31 August, pp 1–60; Ryan Goodman and Derek Jinks (2008) 'Incomplete Internalisation and Compliance with Human Rights Law', *European Journal of International Law*, 19(4): 725–48.

4 Lisbeth Zimmermann (2016) 'Same Same or Different? Norm Diffusion Between Resistance, Compliance, and Localisation in Post-Conflict States', *International Studies Perspectives*, 17(1): 98–115.

5 Andreas von Staden (2018) *Strategies of Compliance with the European Court of Human Rights: Rational Choice within Normative Constraints* (Philadelphia, PA: University of Pennsylvania Press), pp 5–6.

6 Zoë Jay and Matt Killingsworth (2024) 'To Arrest or Not Arrest? South Africa, the International Criminal Court, and New Frameworks for Assessing Noncompliance', *International Studies Quarterly*, 68(2): 1–13.

7 Zoltán I. Búzás (2017) 'Evading International Law: How Agents Comply with the Letter of the Law but Violate its Purpose', *European Journal of International Relations*, 23(4): 857–83.

8 Búzás, 'Evading International Law', p 858.

9 Michael Poznansky (2019) 'Feigning Compliance: Covert Action and International Law', *International Studies Quarterly*, 63(1): 74.

in violation of a norm'.[10] The extreme version of bad faith compliance behaviour is 'backlash' – not only skirting an obligation, but actively seeking to reform or abolish the institution that produced it.[11] Avoiding or refusing compliance can be both a symptom and a cause of backlash, although in order to reach the threshold of 'extraordinary backlash' rather than 'ordinary resistance', the noncompliance must be systemic rather than lone or isolated cases.[12] But where evasive strategies are deployed to make noncompliance behaviour read as compliance, backlash movements thrive on public attention;[13] their members are not concerned with being caught or wearing the potential costs of noncompliance because they do not accept the legitimacy of the obligation or institution in the first place.

These conceptualizations provide a useful taxonomy for understanding some of the variations in actors' attempts to conform to – or avoid – the law. They also draw attention to the foundational role of legitimacy in matters of compliance. Whether they want to contest how an obligation is implemented, evade the costs of noncompliance, or openly criticize an international institution, different forms of compliance and noncompliance undertaken by states with the capacity to comply if they choose to occurs because they perceive the norm, judgement, or institution from which the obligation stems to be in some way illegitimate enough to refute or undermine, or at least *less* legitimately compelling than some other normative commitment or political priority. But confronted with questions about *why* states want to contest, minimize, or evade certain international obligations – especially why they do so in some circumstances but not others – scholars of the different types of compliance fall back on classical explanations, citing rationalist politics and domestic constraints, or normative commitments.

Legitimacy in competing theories of compliance

Scholars of IR and IL have proposed several explanations for why states comply with international law, from coercion to self-interest, institutional pressure, and normative preferences. Early accounts from realists and legal

[10] Jennifer M. Dixon (2017) 'Rhetorical Adaptation and Resistance to International Norms', *Perspectives on Politics*, 15(1): 83–99.

[11] Karen Alter and Michael Zürn (2020) 'Conceptualising Backlash Politics: Introduction to a Special Issue on Backlash Politics in Comparison', *British Journal of Politics and International Relations*, 22(4): 566.

[12] Mikael Rask Madsen, Pola Cebulak and Micha Wiebusch (2018) 'Backlash against International Courts: Explaining the Forms and Patterns of Resistance to International Courts', *International Journal of Law in Context*, 14(2): 210.

[13] Rochelle Terman (2020) 'The Positive Side of Negative Identity: Stigma and Deviance in Backlash Movements', *British Journal of Politics and International Relations*, 22(4): 625.

positivists suggest that states follow legal rules because of a 'coincidence of interest', and would probably behave that way regardless of the presence of law, or because of the threat of punishment – either effective state-enforced sanctions (the positivist view),[14] or through diplomatic pressure and the use of material force (the realist view).[15] Resting on Hobbesian-Austinian assumptions that law is – and can only be – an expression of state power,[16] the realist view of international law suggests that compliance is only useful insofar as it helps to maintain order in an anarchical international system, and can be ignored when there are no discernible interests or advantages at stake.[17]

For a broad school of rational choice theorists and liberal institutionalists, compliance occurs when states believe they gain more from participating in international institutions than abrogating from them. The core motivator here is a more expansive view of self-interest than that held by realists, one that emphasizes reciprocity and reputation: states consent to obey international agreements, and self-enforce them, in order to reap the rewards and predictability that come from interstate cooperation, as well as to prevent changes to the international order that might jeopardize those rewards in the future.[18] Interests are generally fixed, but rules and institutions provide a framework of expectations and incentives around which states can decide how to pursue their interests, and enhance individual or collective gains for members by limiting uncertainty.[19] In the republican-liberal variation on this theme, international institutions offer stability by strengthening adherence to democratic norms; governments rely on international commitments as a means to 'lock in' democratic institutions and shield themselves from

---

14 Hans Kelsen (1945) *General Theory of the Law and State*, translated by Anders Wedberg (Cambridge, MA: Harvard University Press), p 19; H.L.A. Hart (1961) *The Concept of Law* (Oxford: Oxford University Press), p 209.

15 Jack Goldsmith and Eric Posner (2005) *The Limits of International Law* (New York: Oxford University Press), pp 110–12; George W. Downs, David M. Rocke and Peter N. Barsoom (1996) 'Is the Good News About Compliance Good News About Cooperation?', *International Organization*, 50(3): 383–7.

16 Hedley Bull (2002) *The Anarchical Society: A Study of Order in World Politics* (3rd edn, New York: Columbia University Press), pp 124–5.

17 Hans Morgenthau (1973) *Politics Among Nations: The Struggle for Power and Peace* (5th edn, New York: Alfred A. Knopf), p 273.

18 Louis Henkin (1995) *International Law: Politics and Values* (Dordrecht: Martinus Nijhoff), p 27; Robert Keohane (1997) 'International Relations and International Law: Two Optics', *Harvard International Law Journal*, 38(2): 500; Kenneth D. Abbott and Duncan Snidal (2000) 'Hard and Soft Law in International Governance', *International Organization*, 54(3): 440; Beth Simmons (2000) 'The Legalisation of International Monetary Affairs', *International Organization*, 54(3): 574.

19 Judith Goldstein, Miles Kahler, Robert O. Keohane, and Anne-Marie Slaughter (2000) 'Introduction: Legalisation and World Politics', *International Organization*, 54(3): 387.

nondemocratic opposition.[20] Accepting the 'sovereignty costs' associated with delegating domestic authority becomes tolerable because the international regimes reduce political uncertainty and boost democratizing states' international reputations.[21]

Building on rational-institutionalist assumptions that rules constrain and influence actors' choices, domestic institutionalists contend that compliance is contingent on the strength of states' domestic institutions and local politics. States with independent judicial and parliamentary branches, free press and civil society, and democratic traditions are much more likely to adhere to international legal obligations because these institutions can exert pressure on executive governments to sign up to international regimes, and play key roles in helping to enforce and implement obligations domestically.[22] Recent scholarship in this vein also suggests that certain domestic actors with the capacity to 'choose compliance' – such as judges, government officials, and advocacy groups – can amplify the influence of international law by bolstering domestic support for politically contentious international legal requirements.[23] These 'compliance constituencies' lend political clout to international law by putting pressure on governments, but also by building normative expectations within the state and steering domestic discourses towards the idea that respecting the international rule of law is 'good'. Domestic institutionalist approaches therefore offer some valuable links between the domestic and international pressures on governments, as well as between normative and interest-driven motivations to comply, although they tend to assume domestic actors' prior support for international law without explaining how that support is built and sustained.

---

[20] Andrew Moravcsik (2000) 'The Origins of Human Rights Regimes: Democratic Delegation in Postwar Europe', *International Organization*, 54(2): 220; Anne-Marie Slaughter (1995) 'International Law in a World of Liberal States', *European Journal of International Law*, 6(3): 503–38.

[21] Emilie M. Hafner-Burton, Edward D. Mansfield, and Jon C.W. Pevehouse (2015) 'Human Rights Institutions, Sovereignty Costs and Democratisation', *British Journal of Political Science*, 45(1): 1.

[22] Oona Hathaway (2007) 'Why do Countries Commit to Human Rights Treaties?', *Journal of Conflict Resolution*, 51(4): 588–621; Courtney Hillebrecht (2014) *Domestic Politics and International Human Rights Tribunals: The Problem of Compliance* (New York: Cambridge University Press); Beth Simmons (2009) *Mobilizing for Human Rights: International Law in Domestic Politics* (New York: Cambridge University Press); Frank Schimmelfennig (2005) 'Strategic Calculation and International Socialisation: Membership Incentives, Party Constellations, and Sustained Compliance in Central and Eastern Europe', *International Organization*, 59(4): 827–60.

[23] Karen J. Alter (2014) *The New Terrain of International Law: Courts, Politics, Rights* (Princeton, NJ: Princeton University Press), p 53.

Finally, constructivists argue that states comply with international law because they have internalized its underlying normative precepts. International law reflects the ideas and values of its creators, or resonates with an actor's preconceived identity,[24] and 'exerts a strong pull towards compliance' through socialization processes among states that generate understandings of what is or is not 'appropriate behaviour'.[25] States that see themselves as democracies, as abiding by the rule of law, or committed to (a certain vision of) human rights, follow the norms and laws that they and their peers believe are necessary to maintain self- and external perceptions.[26] How constructivists suggest these understandings are produced varies: state actors may be persuaded through processes of dialogue, argumentation, or management of expectations to reach shared understandings among like-minded international actors,[27] or be socialized through acculturation and role modelling.[28] Others suggest that state actors accept international obligations because they resonate or can be adapted to resonate with domestic cultural and normative environments or identities – what Jeffrey Checkel calls a 'cultural match' – meaning their emphasis is more on self-perceptions than those of others.[29] Despite these differences, what each version of constructivism has in common is legitimacy: one way or another, compliance

[24] Jeffrey Checkel (1999) 'Norms, Institutions, and National Identity in Contemporary Europe', *International Studies Quarterly*, 43(1): 86.

[25] Thomas M. Franck (1990) *The Power of Legitimacy Among Nations* (New York: Oxford University Press), p 234.

[26] Thomas Risse and Kathryn Sikkink (1999) 'The Socialisation of Human Rights Norms into Domestic Practices: Introduction', in Thomas Risse, Stephen Ropp, and Kathryn Sikkink (eds), *The Power of Human Rights: International Norms and Domestic Change* (Cambridge: Cambridge University Press), pp 1–38.

[27] Thomas Risse (2000) '"Let's Argue!": Communicative Action in World Politics', *International Organization*, 54(1): 2; Abram Chayes and Antonia Handler Chayes (1995) *The New Sovereignty: Compliance with International Regulatory Agreements* (Cambridge, MA: Harvard University Press), pp 25–6; Emmanuel Adler (2008) 'The Spread of Security Communities: Communities of Practice, Self-Restraint, and NATO's Post-Cold War Transformation', *European Journal of International Relations*, 14(2): 195–230; Etienne Wenger (1998) *Communities of Practice: Learning, Meaning, and Identity* (Cambridge: Cambridge University Press).

[28] Ryan Goodman and Derek Jinks (2004) 'How to Influence States: Socialisation and International Human Rights Law', *Duke Law Journal*, 54(3): 621–703; Jeffrey Checkel (2004) 'International Institutions and Socialisation in Europe: Introduction and Framework', *International Organization*, 59(4): 804–15; Martha Finnemore and Kathryn Sikkink (1998) 'International Norm Dynamics and Political Change', *International Organisation*, 52(4): 887–917.

[29] Checkel, 'Norms, Institutions, and National Identity in Contemporary Europe', p 86; Andrew P. Cortell and James W. Davis (2000) 'Understanding the Domestic Impact of International Norms: A Research Agenda', *International Studies Review*, 2(1): 66; Ciaran O'Faircheallaigh (2014) 'IR Theory and Domestic Adoption of International Norms',

actors are convinced that obeying the international law or norm is good or right. As Thomas Franck famously argues, 'powerful nations obey powerless rules' when they believe the rules are legitimate, and operate 'in accordance with generally accepted principles of right process'.[30] Compliance is driven by actors' adherence to a 'logic of appropriateness', following rules because 'they are seen as natural, rightful, expected, and legitimate'.[31]

As I see it, there are two weaknesses that run through each of these theoretical explanations. First, because legitimacy has traditionally been associated with constructivist and norm-based explanations of compliance, it has typically been understood as one possible explanation among many. In fact, legitimacy is an integral driver in each explanation of compliance, albeit more implicitly in some paradigms than others. By suggesting that governments listen to their domestic compliance constituencies, domestic institutionalists recognize that international law often borrows legitimacy from more widely accepted domestic actors and institutions.[32] For rationalists, the focus on interests, reciprocity, and reputation means legitimacy tends to be accommodated as a form of functionalism: international rules and the institutions structuring them are imbued with legitimacy insofar as they are useful. Legitimacy can also be something actors want for themselves – an interest or goal they pursue in exchange for compliance, rather than something the rule itself intrinsically holds.[33] Even accounts of compliance as the product of coercion and state power implicitly include considerations of legitimacy, although realists know it better as 'prestige'.[34] As the 'everyday currency' that allows strong

International Politics, 51(2): 155–76; Harold Koh (1998) *1998 Frankel Lecture: Bringing International Law Home*, Yale Law School Faculty Scholarship Series, Paper 2102, p 642.

30 Franck, *The Power of Legitimacy Among Nations*, p 3.

31 James G. March and Johan P. Olsen (2006) 'The Logic of Appropriateness', in M. Moran, M. Rein, and R.E. Goodin (eds), *The Oxford Handbook of Public Policy* (Oxford: Oxford University Press), p 689.

32 Laurence R. Helfer (2008) 'Redesigning the European Court of Human Rights: Embeddedness as a Deep Structural Principle of the European Human Rights Regime', *European Journal of International Law*, 19(1): 125–59. Precisely how much international law can piggyback off domestic democratic legitimacy depends somewhat on how much international law is viewed as a distinct system of governance with sources and audiences distinct from domestic law. See Joseph H.H. Weiler (2004) 'The Geology of International Law – Governance, Democracy and Legitimacy', *Zeitschrift für ausländisches öffentlisches Recht und Völkerrecht*, 64: 548.

33 Hyeran Jo and Catarina P. Thompson (2013) 'Legitimacy and Compliance with International Law: Access to Detainees in Civil Conflicts, 1991–2006', *British Journal of Political Science*, 44(2): 326.

34 E.H. Carr (1946) *The Twenty Years' Crisis, 1919–1939: An Introduction to the Study of International Relations* (London: Macmillan), p 236; Robert Gilpin (1981) *War and Change in World Politics* (Cambridge: Cambridge University Press), p 30.

actors to elicit obedience without having to directly resort to force, the perceived legitimacy of military, strategic, or economic prestige reinforces existing order and power balances (although crucially the threat of coercion remains).[35] In other words, legitimacy is not *a* mechanism for understanding compliance. It is *the* mechanism, or at least one that needs to be considered in tandem with others much more closely.

Regardless of the type of legitimacy at stake – normative, functional, or mediated by power and authority – treating it as implicit or secondary underestimates the effects of various legitimacies on state actors' compliance choices by taking it for granted. Even constructivists who place legitimacy at the front and centre of their explanations tend to take acceptance of the rules as legitimate as a starting point. In assuming prior norm acceptance, though, constructivist and other accounts of compliance fail to address a key problem: where do states' decisions to accept a norm or law come from in the first place, and how do they determine whether norms, law, or institutions are legitimate, either at a particular moment or in general?

By asking 'where does legitimacy come from?', I do not mean in a linear, causal sense or what Sumi Madhok calls the 'time–space provincialism' of producing alternative timelines for the origins of human rights narratives.[36] Rather, I am interested in understanding how knowledges of legitimacy are constructed and recognized over time as a power relation.[37] By failing to account for the contexts in which perceptions of legitimacy develop and change, whose perceptions take precedence, and how they come to take precedence at the expense of others, explanations of compliance neglect a critical process in states' engagement with international law and institutions. Indeed, as Harold Koh has suggested, approaches that take norm acceptance as given 'avoid explaining the evolutionary process whereby repeated compliance gradually becomes habitual obedience', overlooking the processes of interaction with and interpretation of international law by domestic legal and political systems which is 'pivotal to understanding why nations "obey" international law'.[38] The key to understanding why states perceive particular laws as legitimate and worth complying with, then, is understanding how they construct their assumptions about what is or is not legitimate, and how these assumptions, in turn, inform governments' and courts' decisions to comply.

[35] Gilpin, *War and Change in World Politics*, p 30.

[36] Sumi Madhok (2021) *Vernacular Rights Cultures: The Politics of Origins, Human Rights and Gendered Struggles for Justice* (Cambridge: Cambridge University Press), p 13.

[37] Michel Foucault (1984) 'Neitzsche, Genealogy, History', in Paul Rabinow (ed), *The Foucault Reader* (New York: Pantheon Books), pp 76–100.

[38] Harold Koh (1997) 'Why do Nations Obey International Law?', *Yale Law Journal*, 106(8): 2603.

The second weakness is that, because all four approaches underestimate the origins of legitimacy and its attendant normative and rational preferences, none of them sufficiently explain variation within states' compliance track records. Other scholars of the ECtHR acknowledge variation in Contracting States' compliance records in general, recognizing that normative and rationalist preferences can coexist alongside international and domestic pressures in ways that lead governments and other compliance actors to pursue minimizing or evasive strategies when it comes to deciding *how* to comply.[39] But because they nonetheless rely on traditional theoretical explanations, they cannot explain when or why such variations occur.

For example, rationalist interpretations of compliance, grounded in static, ahistorical understandings of states' interests and treating legitimacy as a fixed aspiration, cannot explain variation in levels of compliance across or within otherwise similar states. If legal regimes generate stability, prosperity, and democratic legitimacy for their members, why do some states consent to participate while others decline? A suggestion to reform the ECtHR to reduce the influence of the Court relative to states may seem an absurd way to maintain regional stability and legitimacy to a German government, but make perfect sense to a British government. By framing legal regimes as fixed, ahistorical institutions that constrain states' choices, and states as strategic utility-maximizers, rationalists overlook the social, political, and normative dynamics that interact with or shape interests and thus might lead states to comply with, or reject, law in seemingly irrational situations.[40]

Similarly, domestic institutionalists struggle to account for the fact that domestic actors and institutions often lead the charge *against* compliance, rather than putting pressure on governments to uphold their international commitments. What drives the British media's Eurosceptic fervour or the UK Parliament's refusal to debate the prisoner voting cases? Why are the German and Croatian constitutional courts generally willing and able to engage in productive dialogue with the ECtHR while subnational courts defy or ignore it? This is a challenge for constructivists too. Framing compliance as the product of states' supposed identities as supporters of liberal democracy and human rights, or their 'rule of law cultures', without unpacking what those identities and cultures mean in different contexts, does not explain why members of the same political party refer to Britain's longstanding commitment to the rule of law to justify compliance and noncompliance in

39 Hillebrecht, *Domestic Politics and International Human Rights Tribunals*, p 11; von Staden, *Strategies of Compliance with the European Court of Human Rights*, pp 5–6.

40 Martha Finnemore and Stephen J. Toope (2001) 'Alternatives to "Legalisation": Richer Views of Law and Politics', *International Organization*, 55(3): 743–58; Christian Reus-Smit (ed) *The Politics of International Law* (Cambridge: Cambridge University Press, 2004), pp 19–20.

equal measure, including in the case of prisoner voting in the same ruling and set of obligations.

It is not enough to defer to a 'prevailing human rights culture', or 'preference-led behaviour' in the abstract,[41] because these alone cannot account for shifting patterns and variation in both perceptions of the legitimacy of rulings and institutions, *and* in concrete compliance actions. The ways institutional structures, conceptions of what it means to have a 'human rights culture', and political understandings of what is currently expedient intersect with specific cases produce and reflect dynamics of power, prioritizing some narratives or ideas over others, sometimes naturalizing them until they are taken for granted, and shaping the outcomes that appear to be rational decisions at particular moments in time. Domestic institutionalists and constructivists alike therefore underestimate the relationship between the domestic actors lobbying for or against compliance, and the broader cultural and normative influences that shape those actors' preferences and behaviour. In order to better understand these dynamics, then, we need approaches to compliance that accommodate variation within and across current explanations' static conceptions of institutions, interests, identity, and culture. We can start by opening up how we understand where legitimacy comes from.

Legitimacy and obligation in international law

Relatively few scholars have directly attempted to account for where actors' perceptions that a norm or law is legitimate come from, or how those perceptions translate into decisions to comply. Yet, as the constructivist emphasis on the logic of appropriateness and notions of doing what is right demonstrates, legitimacy is intrinsically linked to compliance. It 'implies a willingness to comply with rules or to accept a political order even if this goes against specific interests at specific times'.[42] Those who have addressed the link between legitimacy and compliance head on tend to frame it as the sense of obligation actors feel to comply with the law, and suggest that the obligation stems from forces inherent to the law itself.

Legitimacy as 'internal' to law

As one of the first scholars in either IL or IR to address the relationship between legitimacy and compliance explicitly, Thomas Franck attributed

[41] Von Staden, *Strategies of Compliance with the European Court of Human Rights*, pp 149–50.

[42] Andrew Hurrell (2005) 'Legitimacy and the Use of Force: Can the Circle Be Squared?', *Review of International Studies*, 31(S1): 16.

legitimacy and the subsequent compulsion actors feel towards obeying international law to properties intrinsic to the law or law-making process itself. Specifically, Franck asserts that legitimacy 'accommodates a deeply held popular belief that for a system of rules to be fair, it must be firmly rooted in a framework of formal requirements about how rules are made, interpreted and applied'.[43] He suggests that law needs four 'objective factors' in order to be considered legitimate: determinacy, symbolic validation, coherence, and adherence.[44] Rules that are most likely to be legitimate and to exert a strong compliance pull must be clear, as well as perceived as fair or sensible (determinacy); validated and signposted by symbols, rituals, and cues such as treaty-signing ceremonies (symbolic validation); connected to, and consistent with, other rules in the same system or community (coherence); and they must adhere to a nexus of secondary rules about the standards and sources of rules that establish what constitutes fair process (adherence).

Similarly, for Jutta Brunnée and Stephen Toope, a legal norm's adherence to eight criteria of 'legality' is 'crucial to generating a distinctive legal legitimacy and a sense of commitment'.[45] Borrowing from the domestic legal theory of Lon Fuller, Brunnée and Toope suggest that, in order for a norm to count as legal, it must be general, promulgated (so actors know what the law is), nonretroactive, clear, noncontradictory, realistic, constant, and finally, congruent (with broader social norms and understandings).[46] When international law meets these requirements, it generates a sense of obligation – what Fuller calls 'fidelity'[47] – to both specific laws and to the rule of law in general.[48] This claim is important, because it suggests that being a *legal* norm carries greater weight of obligation than being a social or moral norm. It means that legal norms possess unique characteristics that attract a stronger sense of obligation and willingness to comply than other norms or sources of obligation. In other words, in this view, law produces its own compliance pull.

Brunnée and Toope connect their emphasis on legitimacy stemming from internal characteristics of law to the broader social influences of international politics by stressing that the creation and application of legality criteria is

---

[43] Thomas M. Franck (1995) *Fairness in International Law and Institutions* (Oxford: Clarendon Press), pp 7–8.

[44] Franck, *The Power of Legitimacy Among Nations*, pp 44 and 49.

[45] Jutta Brunnée and Stephen J. Toope (2010) *Legitimacy and Legality in International Law: An Interactional Account* (Cambridge: Cambridge University Press), pp 6–7.

[46] Brunnée and Toope, *Legitimacy and Legality in International Law*, p 6; Lon L. Fuller (1977) *The Morality of Law* (rev ed, New Haven, CT: Yale University Press).

[47] Lon L. Fuller (1958) 'Positivism and Fidelity to Law – A Reply to Professor Hart', *Harvard Law Review*, 71(4): 630.

[48] Brunnée and Toope, *Legitimacy and Legality in International Law*, p 21.

an inherently dynamic social process. In addition to meeting the legality criteria, they argue, legal norms must be based on shared understandings that produce social legitimacy, and continuously reinforced through practice. Specifically, legal norms emerge and garner legitimacy when they are grounded in social norms, which are themselves grounded in collectively held understandings about how actors perceive themselves, each other, and the world. Shared understandings and extant social norms therefore provide the context necessary for actors to perceive particular norms as legitimate. In order for the norms to possess 'legal legitimacy' – to be called law – they must also meet the legality criteria. Finally, the general social legitimacy and specific legal legitimacy of the norm must be continuously maintained and reinforced through practice and engagement; actors must use and uphold the legal norms they value, lest alternative norms and social interactions change expectations or preferences, and erode the norm's existing legitimacy. Participation and interaction with the norm are especially important for facilitating actors' sense of obligation because they make the relationship between actors and the law 'reciprocal' – that is, engagement in the process of creating and sustaining legal norms allows actors to feel a sense of connection to the law, and thus enhances the law's legitimacy.[49]

This recognition of the socially constructed nature of law is the core strength of Brunnée and Toope's interactional theory. It acknowledges that international law is firmly embedded in, and given meaning by, dynamic social processes. Law does not have to be hierarchical, imposed from above by lawmakers (or sovereign states) on their subjects; rather, being able to engage and reason with laws creates a sense of ownership and responsibility towards the legal system. Importantly, this means Brunnée and Toope are able to engage with the political processes that create law, generate legitimacy, and lead to compliance without relying on arguments about state consent, coercion, or interest as used by positivist and rationalist scholars. Hence, interactional theory is particularly useful for explaining why actors comply with law that seemingly contradicts their interests, because it demonstrates how obligation can be internalized through continuous social interactions.

Yet this focus on the 'internal morality of the law'[50] – the idea that laws can possess inherent qualities that instil legitimacy and exert a compliance pull – does not explain why those particular qualities are attached to the law over others, nor how the actors creating and obeying the law came to recognize them as important. Legitimacy is an inherently subjective quality though, one that is 'relational between actor and institution, and defined

[49] Brunnée and Toope, *Legitimacy and Legality in International Law*, pp 53–4.

[50] Fuller, *The Morality of Law*, p 96.

by the actor's *perception* of the institution'.[51] Subjectivity or perception is a core principle of the Weberian concept of legitimacy: social action and specifically willingness to obey are oriented by 'a *belief* in the existence of a "legitimate order"'.[52] Actors' notions of legitimacy – what is or is not an appropriate rule to follow and why – are dependent on pre-existing social and cultural ideas, built up and reinforced over time, about what counts as fair, effective, or democratic. Because legitimacy is attached to rules and institutions by the actors creating and using them, and those actors create rules with particular goals and normative preferences in mind, legitimacy is, as Andrew Hurrell argues, 'quite literally meaningless outside of a particular historical context and outside of a particular set of linguistic conventions and justificatory structures. To paraphrase Ronald Dworkin, legitimacy has no DNA.'[53]

Consequently, theories that ground legitimacy and obligation within the law or legal order itself suffer from what Christian Reus-Smit calls a 'problem of interiority' – they cannot account for the legitimacy of particular aspects of the law or legal system without 'fall[ing] back on assumptions about the legitimacy of the normative system in general'.[54] Franck himself acknowledges that it is 'only by reference to a community's evolving standards of what constitutes right process that it is possible to assert meaningfully that a law, or an executive order, or a court's judgment, or a citizen's claim on a compatriot, or a government's claim on a citizen, is *legitimate*', though he provides no insight into how the international community's 'evolving standards' might emerge or change over time.[55] To this end, the argument that legitimate laws exert a compliance pull only tells a small part of the compliance story because it cannot explain why Franck's 'objective factors' came to be recognized as legitimate to begin with.

Brunnée and Toope also concede that legal obligation is a social construct and that their particular legality criteria are embedded in the liberal understandings of law, legitimacy, and statehood that are specific to the contemporary international system. In articulating their theory, Brunnée and Toope are clear that their goal is not to explain where such understandings of legitimacy come from, but to explain their effect on 'the

51 Ian Hurd (2003) 'Legitimacy and Authority in International Politics', *International Organization,* 53(2): 381 [original emphasis].

52 Max Weber (1964) *The Theory of Social and Economic Organisation*, translated by Talcott Parsons (New York: Oxford University Press), p 124 [original emphasis].

53 Hurrell, 'Legitimacy and the Use of Force', p 29; Ronald Dworkin (2004) 'Hart's Postscript and the Character of Political Philosophy', *Oxford Journal of Legal Studies*, 24(1): 1–37.

54 Christian Reus-Smit (2003) 'Politics and International Legal Obligation', *European Journal of International Relations*, 9(4): 593.

55 Franck, *The Power of Legitimacy Among Nations*, p 26.

contemporary practice of international law'.[56] Nonetheless, the origins of actors' contemporary ideas about what law is and should be are essential for understanding how feelings of legitimacy and obligation are formed and lead to compliance, because they provide insight into how actors might interact with the law, and whether they are likely to accept and obey it. Actors' decisions and preferences at any given moment are almost always influenced, at least partially, by previous experiences and ideas they already hold. Given the pains to which Brunnée and Toope go in order to stress the importance of social interactions and continuous practice in establishing and maintaining both law and actors' sense of obligation to it, their reluctance to engage with the history that led to those interactions is an unfortunate oversight.[57]

Legitimacy as 'historically and socially contingent'

In order to avoid legal scholars' overreliance on pre-existing acceptance of particular values and properties to explain legitimacy, some constructivist and English School accounts have looked to the broader social structures and processes that shape international communities' understandings of law and legitimacy. Here, legitimacy is a product of context, a diverse set of principles that are interpreted, applied, contested, and mediated differently in distinct historical environments and political cultures.[58] For Reus-Smit in particular, this means that a 'satisfactory account' of obligation in international law must view politics as 'historically and socially contingent'.[59] In this view, 'expressions of politics and institutional rationality are milieu-specific', meaning that the particular rules, ordering principles, and ideas that actors value as legitimate and worth adhering to have evolved over time in specific historical contexts.[60] How actors understand and apply legitimacy, and the obligations they will accept or resist, are therefore also 'historically and socially grounded'.[61] In order to understand why an actor feels the 'pull towards compliance' of a given law or legal order, it is necessary to look at the broader historical experiences and social structures that lead actors to privilege particular notions of what 'counts' as legitimate over others.

56 Jutta Brunnée and Stephen J. Toope (2011) 'History, Mystery, and Mastery', *International Theory*, 3(2): 348.

57 Christian Reus-Smit (2011) 'Obligation Through Practice', *International Theory*, 3(2): 344.

58 Mlada Bukovansky (2002) *Legitimacy and Power Politics: The American and French Revolutions in International Political Culture* (Princeton, NJ: Princeton University Press), p 24; Ian Clark (2005) *Legitimacy in International Society* (Oxford: Oxford University Press), p 13.

59 Reus-Smit, 'Politics and International Legal Obligation', p 594.

60 Reus-Smit, 'Politics and International Legal Obligation', p 613.

61 Reus-Smit, 'Politics and International Legal Obligation', p 594.

Still, though, accounts that locate legitimacy in 'milieu-specific' social understandings remain very broad, focusing on the shared values and practices that shape entire epochs and international orders. Seeking to explain the fundamental institutions, forms of sovereignty, and conceptualizations of justice that underpin different international societies, for example, Reus-Smit highlights the necessity of appreciating the cultural and historical contexts in which these variations have evolved, rather than treating them as given, in order to comprehensively understand the nature of different international orders.[62] To this end, Reus-Smit is not concerned 'with the legitimacy of particular international regimes, or the rules they comprise, but with the social validity of modern international law as an institutional practice'.[63] Ian Clark similarly argues that the processes of 'working through' concepts of legitimacy and related principles such as stability, morality, and legality make legitimacy fundamentally indeterminate and susceptible to the contours of the politics of different international societies throughout history.[64] These are valuable arguments that shed light on how modern conceptions of international law have evolved and why modern states have come to recognize it as generally binding and obligatory. Nonetheless, the emphasis on the social and political structures and interactions that create broad collective understandings about international law means this approach rests on similar arguments to other constructivist accounts that overemphasize internationally constructed shared understandings. It cannot necessarily pinpoint the more precise influences that inform individual actors' normative preferences and decisions within international orders, or the internally held or domestic understandings actors might bring with them to social interactions. Arguments concerned with the macro-level socially and historically constructed rationalities of contemporary international law therefore offer some useful insight into general, collectively agreed ideas about international law being obligatory and legitimate, but their ability to explain how independent actors develop perceptions of legitimacy within wider social structures remains limited. To this end, as Reus-Smit notes, 'it is difficult to escape the conclusion that the "local" understandings of historical actors must play a key role in the identification of "their law"'.[65]

[62] Christian Reus-Smit (1999) *The Moral Purpose of the State: Culture, Social Identity, and Institutional Rationality in International Relations* (Princeton, NJ: Princeton University Press), pp 5 and 11.

[63] Reus-Smit, 'Politics and International Legal Obligation', p 611.

[64] Clark, *Legitimacy in International Society*, p 256.

[65] Reus-Smit, 'Obligation through Practice', p 346.

Conclusion

Theoretical understandings of the links between legitimacy and compliance are rich, but incomplete. Although current theories can draw attention to broad patterns of compliance, they remain limited in their ability to pinpoint why states decide to comply with particular cases, and to unpack the political dynamics that influence which cases states will obey and which they will resist. They further struggle to account for the varied and local sources of state actors' feelings of legitimacy and obligation, because they overemphasize the role of collective or shared understandings of legitimacy held among the international community in enabling international law and institutions to generate their own compliance pull. A gap remains where the unique decision-making and belief-forming processes of different states and their constituent parts lie, which holds the key to more nuanced insights into the nature of states' compliance with international law.

In order to address the specific question of how states come to perceive international law as legitimate, and which types or aspects of the law they are likely to accept or not, we need to shift the focus from the general to the particular, and from the international community to the domestic. Closer examination of the domestic side of compliance – not only of contemporary institutions or of static cultural matches but the specific discourses, traditions, and cultural and historical experiences that inform them – can complement and enrich existing theories of legitimacy-based compliance by offering an additional layer to constructivist explanations of how ideas and norms shape state behaviour. In the next chapter, I make the case for a localized account of the origins of legitimacy, turning to insights from sociology and anthropology about culture to explain how the 'unshared' understandings of legitimacy orient actors' assumptions about international law and human rights, and provide a toolkit of actions to help actors translate those assumptions into compliance.

2

Legitimacy as Local Knowledge: Human Rights in Cultural Context

The dominant paradigms of both International Relations (IR) and International Law (IL) currently offer only partial explanations of how the notions of legitimacy that supposedly pull states towards compliance are produced and maintained. They say very little about the origins of legitimacy: where the beliefs that international law and legal systems are legitimate come from. To the extent that these literatures do explore how legitimacy is constructed and generates obligation (or 'pull' or 'fidelity'[1]), they focus on collective ideas produced at the international level, on the 'shared understandings' held among actors and hashed out through processes of deliberation, persuasion, managerialism, and socialization.[2] In doing so, they neglect or underspecify the equivalent processes occurring in domestic contexts – the understandings and assumptions about what is legitimate or not that are produced in local political and legal cultural

---

[1] Lon L. Fuller (1958) 'Positivism and Fidelity to Law – A Reply to Professor Hart', *Harvard Law Review*, 71(4): 630–72.

[2] Jutta Brunnée and Stephen J. Toope (2010) *Legitimacy and Legality in International Law: An Interactional Account* (Cambridge: Cambridge University Press), pp 53–4; Harold Koh (1997) 'Why do Nations Obey International Law?', *Yale Law Journal*, 106(8): 2599–659; Thomas Risse (2000) '"Let's Argue!": Communicative Action in World Politics', *International Organization*, 54(1): 1–39; Abram Chayes and Antonia Handler Chayes (1995) *The New Sovereignty: Compliance with International Regulatory Agreements* (Cambridge, MA: Harvard University Press); Thomas Risse, Stephen C. Ropp, and Kathryn Sikkink (eds) (1999) *The Power of Human Rights: International Norms and Domestic Change* (Cambridge: Cambridge University Press); Ryan Goodman and Derek Jinks (2004) 'How to Influence States: Socialisation and International Human Rights Law', *Duke Law Journal*, 54(3): 621–703; Jeffrey Checkel (2001) 'Why Comply? Social Learning and European Identity Change', *International Organization*, 55(3): 553–88.

environments, and which may differ from, or even openly contradict, ideas at the international level. Yet without an account of the *un*shared understandings of legitimacy, theories of compliance are unable to explain variation: why states comply with most, but not all, of their obligations within a legal system, and which types of cases those states are likely to obey or resist.

This chapter explains how state actors' perceptions of the legitimacy of international law are shaped from the domestic side. I argue that the process by which actors formulate their own ideas about the legitimacy of international law, and how ideas translate into decisions to obey or resist legal obligations, can be accounted for by better appreciating the domestic traditions, historical experiences and memories, and cultural narratives that inform states' interactions with the international laws, norms, and institutions with which they are confronted. Culture, Jürgen Habermas writes, is 'the stock of knowledge from which participants in communication supply themselves with interpretations as they come to an understanding about something in the world'.[3] Building on insights from anthropology and sociology about how culture shapes knowledge and behaviour, I argue that local cultural environments shape state actors' assumptions about human rights and the legitimate ways to protect them. These cultural environments are diverse – heterogeneous and dynamic, with fluid, contested boundaries – but they nonetheless play crucial roles in informing state actors' understandings of the international laws and legal systems with which they interact. The relationship between a state and international legal norm or regime is shaped by the state's historical experiences with, and cultural knowledge of, human rights, as these frameworks help to determine how state actors decide or are persuaded that particular norms or laws are legitimate at a particular moment in time. Local cultural contexts are essential for understanding this relationship, because the discourses, practices, traditions, and ideas that constitute ideas about rights and law provide insight into how state actors interpret the role and importance of complying with international law.

Culture and compliance

Compliance theories in both IR and IL make frequent references to culture as a factor influencing compliance, but struggle to articulate how it does so beyond vague descriptions. States with strong human rights records are

[3] Jürgen Habermas (1987) *The Theory of Communicative Action*, vol 2: *Lifeworld and System: A Critique of Functionalist Reason*, translated by Thomas McCarthy (Boston, MA: Polity Press), p 138.

described as having a 'culture of rights'[4] or 'rights consciousness',[5] while willingness to comply with international legal commitments is explained as a product of some states' 'cultures of compliance'.[6] This pattern appears across theoretical lines. Constructivists suggest that international norms are more easily received into domestic spheres when there is a 'cultural match' between the norm and the pre-existing domestic environment,[7] while the emphasis that domestic institutionalists place on local institutions and actors in facilitating compliance hinges on the assumption that those institutions embody the 'democratic traditions' or 'rule of law culture' that motivate them to lobby governments to meet human rights commitments.[8] In both approaches, the domestic culture is treated as static, something which existed prior to the introduction of the international norm or law and which is either receptive to it or is not. Neither approach explains what having a rights consciousness or compliance culture means to different actors within states, or how exactly such cultures translate into compliance decisions. Consequently, countries like Germany and the United Kingdom are equally described as having strong 'rule of law cultures',[9] despite having very different conceptions of what it means to be a rule of law state and very different relationships with the European human rights system. Culture can therefore be useful for understanding variations in legitimacy and compliance, but only if the specific dynamics within cultures are unpacked.

The treatment of culture as a static explanation for compliance is part of a broader tendency in mainstream IR and IL to view culture in monolithic terms. In a trilogy exploring the relationship between cultural diversity and international order, Christian Reus-Smit argues that mainstream IR in particular is grounded in an outdated understanding of culture, one

4 Courtney Hillebrecht (2012) 'Implementing International Human Rights Law at Home: Domestic Politics and the European Court of Human Rights', *Human Rights Review*, 13(3): 297.

5 James L. Gibson and Gregory A. Caldeira (1996) 'The Legal Cultures of Europe', *Law and Society Review*, 30(1): 58.

6 Gerda Falkner and Oliver Treib (2008) 'Three Worlds of Compliance or Four? The EU-15 Compared to New Member States', *Journal of Common Market Studies*, 46(2): 296–7.

7 Jeffrey Checkel (1999) 'Norms, Institutions and Identity in Contemporary Europe', *International Studies Quarterly*, 43(1): 87.

8 Courtney Hillebrecht (2014) *Domestic Politics and International Human Rights Tribunals: The Problem of Compliance* (New York: Cambridge University Press); Andreas von Staden (2018) *Strategies of Compliance with the European Court of Human Rights: Rational Choice within Normative Constraints* (Philadelphia, PA: University of Pennsylvania Press), p 43.

9 von Staden, *Strategies of Compliance with the European Court of Human Rights*, p 201; Julia Rackow (2015) 'From Conflict to Cooperation: The Relationship between Karlsruhe and Strasbourg', in Katja S. Ziegler, Elizabeth Wicks, and Loveday Hodson (eds), *The UK and European Human Rights: A Strained Relationship?* (Oxford: Hart Publishing), p 399.

that treats cultures 'as coherent entities: bounded, integrated, and distinct wholes'.[10] This understanding is out of step with research from disciplines such as anthropology, sociology, and history, as well as critical IR scholarship, which present more nuanced conceptions of culture as heterogeneous, interconnected, and dynamic. Framing culture in this outdated form risks reinforcing stereotypes and essentialized portrayals of 'national character'.[11] Such approaches effectively reduce culture to a black box which explains everything, and nothing. Even if researchers do not intend to make essentialist claims, theoretical arguments which make broad references to cultural resonance or dissonance without specifying what they mean by culture or how it works simply shift the burden of defining culture onto the audiences of the research, reinforcing the default conception implicitly. Differences in what it means to have a rule of law culture across supposedly similar European democracies provide a key illustration of how underspecifying culture's effects can undermine attempts to explain variation in compliance, as well as in international politics more broadly.

The static conception further implies that culture is a problem to be solved, something that constitutes national identities but can ultimately be smoothed over by a coherent international order, either through international institutions or balances of power.[12] But this assumption – reflected in narratives of universalism in the liberal world order or the common normative ambitions of European integration – is at odds with the principles of subsidiarity and deference to national authority that are built into international and regional human rights institutions. Static understandings of culture cannot engage with the politics that emerge from the tensions between national autonomy and supranational oversight, overlooking not only how understandings of rights and perceptions of legitimacy might be shaped by culture at the domestic level, but how domestic and international understandings of the legitimacy of international law interact and co-constitute each other.[13] In doing so, Reus-Smit argues, IR 'obscures the politics of culture', that is:

---

10 Christian Reus-Smit (2018) *On Cultural Diversity: International Theory in a World of Difference* (Cambridge: Cambridge University Press), p 5; Andrew Phillips and Christian Reus-Smit (eds) (2020) *Culture and Order in World Politics* (Cambridge: Cambridge University Press).

11 Sally Engle Merry (2006) *Human Rights and Gender Violence: Translating International Law into Local Justice* (Chicago, IL: Chicago University Press).

12 Phillips and Reus-Smit, *Culture and Order in World Politics*, p 5.

13 Jane K. Cowan, Marie-Bénédicte Dembour, and Richard A. Wilson (eds) (2004) *Culture and Rights: Anthropological Perspectives* (New York: Cambridge University Press), p 6; Marie-Bénédicte Dembour (2004) 'Following the Movement of a Pendulum: Between Universalism and Relativism', in Jane K. Cowan, Marie-Bénédicte Dembour, and Richard A. Wilson (eds), *Culture and Rights: Anthropological Perspectives* (New York: Cambridge University Press), p 74.

> how cultural meanings and practices are constantly amplified or silenced, mobilised or suppressed. So long as this politics is obscured, we have no way of grasping the processes through which cultural formations are produced and reproduced, or comprehending the relationship between these processes and the constitution, institutionalisation, and exercise of political power.[14]

Recent IR scholarship on culture has therefore sought to engage more directly with the political processes of culture and their consequences. International legal scholars, too, are increasingly attuned to the specific ways pluralist legal orders structure culture and how the law and its practitioners legitimize particular forms of variation within legal cultures and systems.[15] This is important work, albeit work predominantly focused on large-scale global orders, empires, and civilizations.[16] But as Ellen Berrey argues, when IR scholars 'cleave off internal domestic politics, including micro-level cultural politics, from a conception of international order', they overlook the ways in which cultural dynamics shape the international.[17] Thus, in order to understand how culture informs perceptions of legitimacy and shapes variable compliance choices from local, domestic angles, we need a conceptualization of it that embraces the pluralities, inconsistencies, and fragments that constitute cultures, and the politics and contestation through which cultural meanings or practices are made.

---

14 Reus-Smit, *On Cultural Diversity*, pp 187–8.

15 Arnulf Becker Lorca (2020) 'Universal and European: Cultural Diversity in International Law', in Andrew Phillips and Christian Reus-Smit (eds), *Culture and Order in World Politics* (Cambridge: Cambridge University Press), p 209; Miia Halme-Tuomisaari (2010) *Human Rights in Action: Learning Expert Knowledge* (Leiden: Brill); Nico Krisch (2008) 'The Open Architecture of European Human Rights Law, *Modern Law Review,* 71(2): 183–216.

16 Ayşe Zarakol (2020) 'The Ottomans and Diversity', in Andrew Phillips and Christian Reus-Smit (eds), *Culture and Order in World Politics* (Cambridge: Cambridge University Press), pp 49–70; Victoria Tin-bor Hui (2020) 'Cultural Diversity and Coercive Cultural Homogenisation in Chinese History', in Andrew Phillips and Christian Reus-Smit (eds), *Culture and Order in World Politics* (Cambridge: Cambridge University Press), pp 93–112; Hendrik Spruyt (2020) *The World Imagined: Collective Beliefs and Political Order in the Sinocentric, Islamic and Southeast Asian International Societies* (Cambridge: Cambridge University Press); Andrew Phillips and J.C. Sharman (2015) *International Order in Diversity: War, Trade and Rule in the Indian Ocean* (Cambridge: Cambridge University Press); Peter J. Katzenstein (ed) (2010) *Civilisations in World Politics: Plural and Pluralist Perspectives* (Abingdon: Routledge).

17 Ellen Berrey (2020) 'When Liberal States Bite Back: The Micro-Politics of Culture', in Andrew Phillips and Christian Reus-Smit (eds), *Culture and Order in World Politics* (Cambridge: Cambridge University Press), p 162.

Culture in action: sensibilities, repertoires, and toolkits

Research from sociology and anthropology offers more useful and multifaceted understandings of what culture is and how it operates in social life. Wary of the problems that stem from treating local culture as a barrier to progress – as primitive rather than modern, parochial rather than cosmopolitan, and resistant to diversity and change – social theorists have all but abandoned conceptions of 'culture as a unity rather than an aggregate'.[18] Instead, they emphasize the plurality of variation, contestation, overlapping, and intersecting that occurs within and across cultural lines, and the porous, dynamic nature of their boundaries.[19]

To this end, cultures are not coherent, 'superorganic' civilizations,[20] but rather 'shreds and patches remaking themselves'.[21] Viewed in this way, cultures are neither identifiable by universally recognized narratives and practices, nor neat spatial or social boundaries, but rather, as Akhil Gupta and James Ferguson argue, through the processes 'that go into the construction of space as place or locality in the first instance'.[22] This conception is especially valuable for discussing culture in the context of states and nations, international and regional communities, where political boundaries of inclusion and exclusion – state borders, institutional memberships, national identities – rarely, if ever, map onto neatly contained cultural or social spaces.

But if culture is defined by its hybridity, how exactly does it shape action? Cultural specialists offer several explanations, most of which suggest that culture serves to contextualize knowledge and practice by shaping actors' notions of what can be done, and providing skills, methods, or styles to undertake action. For Clifford Geertz, the answer is semiotic: cultures are public, intersubjective collections of symbols which produce systems of meaning, or 'webs of significance' that people themselves have spun.[23] Culture, in this view, helps to frame an actor's sensibilities or ways of thinking about and understanding the world. Specific elements of social life – religion,

---

[18] Sally Engle Merry (2012) 'What is Legal Culture? An Anthropological Perspective', *Journal of Comparative Law*, 5(2): 41.

[19] Merry, 'What is Legal Culture?', p 42.

[20] A.L. Kroeber (1917) 'The Superorganic', *American Anthropologist*, 19(2): 163–213.

[21] H.P. Glenn (2004) 'Legal Cultures and Legal Traditions', in M. Van Hoeck (ed), *Epistemology and Methodology of Comparative Law* (Oxford: Oxford University Press), p 32; David Nelken (2012) 'Using Legal Culture: Purposes and Problems', *Journal of Comparative Law*, 5(2): 6.

[22] Akhil Gupta and James Ferguson (1997) 'Beyond "Culture": Space, Identity, and the Politics of Difference', *Cultural Anthropology*, 7(1): 8.

[23] Clifford Geertz (1973) *The Interpretation of Cultures: Selected Essays* (New York: Basic Books), p 5.

art, science – are both reflections of, and contributors to, these systems. Law, too, is a system of symbols and meanings, 'not just a bounded set of norms, rules, principles, values, or whatever from which jural responses to distilled events can be drawn, but part of a distinctive manner of imagining the real'.[24] The symbolism and intersubjectivity of culture mean that, in Geertz's conception, culture is not something that determines specific actions, but an environment providing a foundation for interpreting the meanings and consequences of actions. Thus, 'culture is not a power, something to which social events, behaviours, institutions, or processes can be causally attributed, it is a context, something within which they can be intelligibly – that is, thickly – described'.[25]

Crucially, this means that law and legal cultures are best understood when they are interpreted as highly localized and context-specific 'texts'.[26] Geertz famously describes law as 'local knowledge', contextualized not only by factors such as place and time but by the particular language of ideas, practices, and ways of thinking familiar to that community – in other words, 'vernacular characterisations of what happens connected to vernacular imaginings of what can'.[27] What matters here is the idea that legal sensibilities differ across, as well as within, cultural communities. From different legal cultures stem different assumptions about the meanings of concepts such as justice, rights, and obligation, and about the purpose of different institutions in maintaining them. These assumptions are not directly constitutive of identities in the way IR scholars have historically understood the concept, as a coherent set of fundamental values.[28] Rather, legal sensibilities provide what Geertz calls 'orienting notions', diverse collections of symbols and practices that set the scene for thinking through problems and providing 'a more or less handy way into understanding the social institutions and cultural formations that surround them and give them meaning'.[29] In order to understand how ideas about the legitimacy of law might translate into obedience, then, it is necessary to explore how those ideas came to be part

24 Clifford Geertz (1983) *Local Knowledge: Further Essays in Interpretive Anthropology* (New York: Basic Books), p 173.

25 Geertz, *The Interpretation of Cultures: Selected Essays*, p 14.

26 Geertz, *The Interpretation of Cultures: Selected Essays*, p 14.

27 Geertz, *Local Knowledge*, p 215.

28 Emanuel Adler (1997) 'Seizing the Middle Ground: Constructivism in World Politics', *European Journal of International Relations*, 3(3): 319–63; Alexander Wendt (1999) *Social Theory of International Politics* (New York: Cambridge University Press); John Gerard Ruggie (1998) 'What Makes the World Hang Together? Neo-Utilitarianism and the Social Constructivist Challenge', *International Organization*, 52(4): 863.

29 Geertz, *Local Knowledge*, pp 186–97.

of the local knowledge, and how they are understood and applied by those who use them.

A second insight into how culture shapes action offered by culture specialists is the understanding of culture as a 'repertoire of actions, practices and beliefs'.[30] Susan Silbey, for instance, argues that law (or any other social institution) provides a collection of 'cultural materials with which people produce and experience legality as a structure of social action'.[31] Similarly, James Ferguson writes of a 'cultural style', suggesting that culture produces a range of 'surface practices' without necessarily articulating a 'total way of life' that comprehensively defines how to think and act.[32]

Building on the idea that culture helps to construct shared meanings, Ann Swidler explores how the symbols, narratives, and world views that constitute a culture translate into 'strategies of action'.[33] Like Geertz, Swidler cautions against conceptions of culture and action that suggest the relationship is one of direct cause and effect, where distinct, tangible values can be siphoned out of a cultural space to explain why actors make certain choices. The 'reigning model used to understand culture's effects on action', she writes, 'is fundamentally misleading. It assumes that culture shapes action by supplying ultimate ends or values towards which action is directed, thus making values the central causal element of culture.'[34] Such an approach overstates the predetermined control of culture over agents' values and choices, and risks making sweeping, essentialist claims about culture by treating its constituent elements as concrete, universal concepts rather than contested, evolving, and adaptable.

Instead, culture provides what Swidler calls a 'toolkit': a broad range of skills, habits, ideas, and practices that can be used by actors in many different ways to interpret and move through the world.[35] In this view, cultural values do not *cause* actions, but inform an actor's sense of what is possible, desirable, or practicable. This model offers a particularly valuable way to understand variation and inconsistency within a culture because it highlights the variety

30 Merry, 'What is Legal Culture?', p 42.

31 Susan Silbey (2001) 'Legal Culture and Legal Consciousness', in N.J. Smelser and P.B. Baltes (eds), *International Encyclopedia of Social and Behavioural Sciences* (Oxford: Pergamon Press), p 8627.

32 James Ferguson (1990) 'Cultural Style as Inscription: Toward a Political Economy of the Styled Body', paper presented at the meetings of the American Ethnological Society, Atlanta, cited in Gupta and Ferguson, 'Beyond "Culture"', p 19.

33 Ann Swidler (1986) 'Culture in Action: Symbols and Strategies', *American Sociological Review*, 51(2): 273.

34 Swidler, 'Culture in Action', p 273.

35 Swidler, 'Culture in Action', p 273; see also Ulf Hannerz (1969) *Soulside: Inquiries into Ghetto Culture and Community* (New York: Columbia University Press), pp 186–8.

of possible actions and pathways actors might take to achieve their goals and live their lives. Swidler points to how people depend on family and friends for different forms of support at different points in time, or to the range of skills a merchant uses to sell their products in a market – not every skill is necessary or appropriate in every transaction, but they form a corpus of habits and expertise that the merchant knows they can rely on as needed.

Thus, Germans do not value freedom of the press specifically or solely because of the Nazi regime's restrictions of it, or because of a specific normative hierarchy where some other value such as privacy sits below press freedom. Rather, politicians, journalists, human rights activists, or other individuals can construct and draw on postwar narratives about working through the past and the inviolability of rights to explain why (they believe) it is important to uphold press freedoms now. Similarly, British judges interpret and apply common law according to principles of so-called pragmatism and gradual development, but the fact that this is a different approach to the more doctrinal methods of continental legal systems becomes most important culturally when it is framed as incompatible or irreconcilable by actors seeking to pin down a 'British' or 'English' culture that is distinct from a continental European culture. The toolkit/repertoire approach is therefore useful for understanding how perceptions of legitimacy translate into feelings of obligation and actual decisions to comply with or resist law, because it shows how the symbols, meanings, and stories of culture can be mobilized by actors reacting to particular circumstances and making particular choices. Legal sensibilities inform what people within a cultural context might think about law and human rights, while the toolkit shows how those sensibilities might be applied in practice.

Finally, culture specialists view culture and the repertoires of action they help to construct as dynamic and changeable. Because cultures are unbounded and contain diverse narratives, symbols, and ways of thinking or acting, they are also constantly shifting and evolving.[36] In contrast to static conceptions of culture, dynamic approaches suggest that processes of negotiation, contestation, and construction are a core part of how ideas or practices come to be recognized and then maintained as part of a culture.[37] It is in the debates and discourses, and processes of change that culture is often most visible – through battles for legitimacy, or the flexibility of narratives and rituals to be applied and adapted to new contexts.

[36] Cowan et al, *Culture and Rights: Anthropological Perspectives*, p 28; Sally Engle Merry (2004) 'Changing Rights, Changing Culture', in Jane K. Cowan, Marie-Bénédicte Dembour, and Richard A. Wilson (eds), *Culture and Rights: Anthropological Perspectives* (New York: Cambridge University Press), pp 41–2.

[37] Gupta and Ferguson, 'Beyond "Culture"', p 16.

Moreover, dynamic understandings of culture emphasize the interconnectedness of cultures with each other and with other social processes, historical contexts, and power relations.[38] The fluid, hybrid nature of local cultures means they are not only subject to contestation from within, but are 'embedded in national and transnational processes and particular historical trajectories'.[39] Thus, local legal cultures shift in response to the emergence of new international legal instruments, while global events such as migration, violence, or globalization contribute to changes in local conceptions of human rights by forcing widespread reassessments of local systems (as is often the case after periods of war or regime change), or by stretching the meanings and applications of rights beyond the ways they are typically expected to be used. In turn, global spaces are sensitive to shifts at the national and local level – such as when international courts are persuaded by arguments for a margin of appreciation in ways that alter the trajectory of the court's case law.

The key to cultural analysis, then, is to examine the 'active making of culture'[40] – how certain ideas take hold or become dominant among a community, who advocates or contests them, the institutions in which they become embedded, and the particular historical and political contexts in which these processes occur. Kate Nash calls this the 'cultural politics of human rights': the 'more or less organised struggles over symbols that frame what issues, events or processes mean to social actors who are emotionally and intellectually invested in shared understandings of the world'.[41] Struggles over what human rights mean matter because how they are understood is foundational to how they are enacted, and both how they are understood and how they are enacted are 'constructed in relations of power … always open to political challenge and contestation, whilst at the same time, caught up in the inertia of repetition'.[42] An approach that engages cultural politics in this way is therefore essential for thinking through the relational influences of legitimacy and compliance, because it shows not only how actions are influenced by cultural tools, but how those actions reverberate in their historical and political context. The internal struggles and debates over meaning and application of cultural symbols not only help with the reception of international norms and laws by connecting them to power and practice; they also underpin the

[38] Merry, *Human Rights and Gender Violence*, p 3; Merry, 'Changing Rights, Changing Culture', pp 41–2.

[39] Merry, 'What is Legal Culture?', p 42.

[40] Merry, 'What is Legal Culture?', p 42.

[41] Kate Nash (2009) *The Cultural Politics of Human Rights: Comparing the US and UK* (Cambridge: Cambridge University Press), p 1.

[42] Nash, *The Cultural Politics of Human Rights*, p 8.

legitimating processes and interpretations of those laws that push local actors to obey them.

Background knowledge and cultural validation

The conception of culture as expressing intersubjective meanings through texts and practices resonates with critical constructivist research on norm contestation. In contrast to earlier constructivist scholarship, which focused on the diffusion of norms assumed to hold relatively stable, agreed-upon definitions, critical constructivists start from the premise that the meanings and interpretations of norms are not fixed and universal, but 'works-in-progress'.[43] Actors prescribe meanings to norms 'in use', applying attributes and interpretations of norms' definitions, purposes, and virtues as they interact with or implement them.[44] The meanings are subject to change, depending on the contexts in which the norms are applied, and who applies them. The assumption that the meanings and applications of norms are intersubjective and contestable is relevant to understanding variation in compliance within and across states, because it recognizes that there are unique national, local, and individual perspectives and understandings at play when actors interpret and interact with international norms.

Norm contestation literature's emphasis on the 'localization' of international norms and the means by which actors can adapt and reinterpret norms to suit local needs and preferences has important ramifications for understanding compliance and legitimacy. There are two competing strands of thought on how exactly contestation relates to legitimacy, though. One strand implies that contestation indicates a failure of norm diffusion or socialization, where the original integrity of the international norm is compromised to make it more palatable to domestic audiences.[45] At its worst, this form of contestation may be linked to more defiant opposition, regression, or backlash against

[43] Mona Krook and Jacqui True (2010) 'Rethinking the Life Cycles of International Norms: The United Nations and the Global Promotion of Gender Equality', *European Journal of International Relations*, 18(1): 104.

[44] Antje Wiener (2004) 'Contested Compliance: Interventions on the Normative Structure of World Politics', *European Journal of International Relations*, 10(2): 190.

[45] Ryan Goodman and Derek Jinks (2008) 'Incomplete Internalisation and Compliance with Human Rights Law', *European Journal of International Law*, 19(4): 725–48; Gergana Noutcheva (2009) 'Fake, Partial and Imposed Compliance: The Limits of the EU's Normative Power in the Western Balkans', *Journal of European Public Policy*, 16(7): 1065–84; Cristina G. Badescu and Thomas G. Weiss (2010) 'Misrepresenting R2P and Advancing Norms: An Alternative Spiral?', *International Studies Perspectives*, 11(4): 354–74; Thomas R. Eimer, Susanne Lütz, and Verena Schüren (2016) 'Varieties of Localisation: International Norms and the Commodification of Knowledge in India and Brazil', *Review of International Political Economy*, 23(3): 455.

unwelcome incoming norms, which are seen as fundamentally incompatible with local preferences.[46] This approach recognizes that domestic contexts can shape whether actors view international norms and the institutions promoting them as legitimate, but only in the negative sense that contestation or backlash implies an absence of legitimacy. It says little about how or why such an absence may occur in the first place, implicitly reinforcing the broad references to 'domestic salience' of classical constructivist norm diffusion.[47]

The other strand suggests that the process of contesting the meaning of international norms can in fact enhance norms' legitimacy. In this view, contestation over the application of norms allows actors to directly participate in interpreting and applying them according to their own needs.[48] Norms that can survive heated contestation and evolve to meet actors' shifting needs are stronger and more likely to be complied with or internalized because they offer greater flexibility than norms with rigid prescriptions and obligations. This ties in with Brunnée and Toope's argument about the reciprocal nature of socially constructed interactional law being able to stimulate obligation and compliance more effectively than hierarchical law in which actors feel they have no active stake.[49]

The legitimizing function of contestation emerges through what Antje Wiener calls 'cultural validation'.[50] Recognizing that formal validation (through treaties and other official documents or procedures) and social recognition (shared understandings) of the meaning of norms alone are insufficient to understand why norms are viewed as legitimate or not, Wiener suggests that the actual interpretations or meanings-in-use of norms

---

46 Diana Panke and Ulrich Petersohn (2012) 'Why International Norms Disappear Sometimes', *European Journal of International Relations*, 18(4): 719–42; Ryder McKeown (2009) 'Norm Regress: US Revisionism and the Death of the Torture Norm', *International Relations*, 23(1): 11; Karen J. Alter and Michael Zürn (2020) 'Conceptualising Backlash Politics: Introduction to a Special Issue on Backlash Politics in Comparison', *British Journal of Politics and International Relations*, 22(4): 563–84; Nicole Deitelhoff (2020) 'What's in a Name? Contestation and Backlash against International Norms and Institutions', *British Journal of Politics and International Relations*, 22(4): 716; Alan Bloomfield (2016) 'Norm Antipreneurs and Theorising Resistance to Normative Change', *Review of International Studies*, 42(2): 310–33.

47 Andrew P. Cortell and James W. Davis (2000) 'Understanding the Domestic Impact of International Norms: A Research Agenda', *International Studies Review*, 29(1): 66.

48 Antje Wiener (2014) *A Theory of Contestation* (Heidelberg: Springer); Nicole Deitelhoff and Lisbeth Zimmermann (2019) 'Norms Under Challenge: Unpacking the Dynamics of Norm Robustness', *Journal of Global Security Studies*, 4(1): 5; Nicole Deitelhoff and Lisbeth Zimmermann (2020) 'Things We Lost in the Fire: How Different Types of Contestation Affect the Robustness of International Norms', *International Studies Review*, 22(1): 52.

49 Brunnée and Toope, *Legitimacy and Legality in International Law*, p 7.

50 Antje Wiener (2008) *The Invisible Constitution of Politics: Contested Norms and International Encounters* (Cambridge: Cambridge University Press), p 4.

are also constituted by actors' 'invisible' cultural and historical contexts.[51] These contexts provide 'background knowledge', the social and institutional 'facts' or constitutive rules that underpin and give order to social interactions and decision making.[52] Actors carry their individual and local assumptions, beliefs, past experiences, and expectations with them, relying on this background or 'normative baggage' in social interactions to interpret and give meaning to new norms, rules, and practices.[53] Culture therefore represents 'the sum of background experiences gathered through interactions over time and expressed through the cultural validation of norms in day-to-day life'.[54] Practice theory also works with a similar conception of background knowledge, suggesting that underlying cultural ideas and discourses are made material and given meaning through particular ways of doing,[55] although practice scholars stress that practices are part of an interdependent system of social, individual, and material influences and cannot be reduced to individual background knowledge alone.[56] Critical constructivist and practice theory thus share with sociological and anthropological perspectives the conception of culture as a landscape of possible actions and interpretations, and the need to engage with local or personal sources of knowledge as well as shared social sources.

But the critical constructivist conception of background knowledge remains fundamentally passive. Wiener and Puetter argue that actors only fall back on their background knowledge to fill in gaps 'in the absence of shared social recognition and collective deliberation'.[57] Not only is

---

51 Wiener, *The Invisible Constitution of Politics*, pp 63–4.

52 Antje Wiener and Uwe Puetter (2009) 'The Quality of Norms is What Actors Make of it: Critical Constructivist Research on Norms', *Journal of International Law and International Relations*, 5(1): 6; Jennifer Milliken (1999) 'The Study of Discourse in International Relations: A Critique of Research and Methods', *European Journal of International Relations*, 5(2): 231; John R. Searle (1995) *The Construction of Social Reality* (New York: Free Press), p 28.

53 Wiener and Puetter, 'The Quality of Norms is What Actors Make of it', p 6.

54 Wiener, *A Theory of Contestation*, p 45.

55 Emanuel Adler and Vincent Pouliot (2011) 'International Practices', *International Theory*, 3(1): 7; Vincent Pouliot (2008) 'The Logic of Practicality: A Theory of Practice of Security Communities', *International Organization*, 62(2): 267; Iver Neumann (2002) 'Returning Practice to the Linguistic Turn: The Case of Diplomacy', *Millennium: Journal of International Studies*, 31(3): 631–2; Andreas Reckwitz (2002) 'Toward a Theory of Social Practices: A Development in Culturalist Theorising', *European Journal of Social Theory*, 5(2): 249; Ludwig Wittgenstein (1967) *Philosophical Investigations* (3rd edn, Oxford: Blackwell), p 43.

56 Christian Bueger and Frank Gadinger (2015) 'The Play of International Practice', *International Studies Quarterly*, 59(3): 453.

57 Wiener and Puetter, 'The Quality of Norms is What Actors Make of it', p 6; Wiener, *A Theory of Contestation*, p 39.

individual background knowledge secondary to shared knowledge in this view, but actors only draw on it when their understandings or experiences 'are so clearly opposed that they actually *clash*'.[58] The implication, then, is that cultural knowledge, and variation in the interpretation of norms across cultural actors, only matters after the dominant social interpretation has been established, and can be mitigated through more robust shared social interactions. Yet cultural knowledge and skills play far more constant roles in actors' lives than this. The relationship between social recognition/shared understanding and cultural validity/vernacular is not sequential, but reciprocal.[59] Actors certainly do rely on forms of background knowledge to interpret ambiguous norms at the implementation stage, but they also carry that knowledge with them at other stages of norm interaction, and with other forms of social interaction and meaning construction. Local cultural knowledge shapes how actors generate shared understandings and practices in the first place, and is – as Merry's work on the dynamic interaction between local and international conceptions of human rights shows – shaped in turn by ongoing social interactions.[60] Recognizing that local knowledge orients all of actors' interpretations and interactions, not just those where other knowledge is unavailable, is crucial for explaining how they interpret the legitimacy of norms (and laws, institutions, and entire organizing structures), because it provides the scope to understand how local–national notions of legitimacy are produced and applied, both independently and in relation to broader shared understandings.

---

58 Wiener, *A Theory of Contestation*, p 41.

59 Holger Niemann and Henrik Schillinger similarly argue that while Wiener's theory of contestation starts from the assumption that norms are inherently contested, by treating cultural background knowledge as secondary to social recognition the theory accidentally produces 'a de facto reaffirmation of an understanding of norms as defined by fixed meanings'. Any contestation on the basis of cultural diversity therefore appears as a deviation from the original shared understanding, rather than part of the process of producing meaning and legitimacy in the first place. To avoid reinforcing the assumption that shared understandings come first, we need a framework that shows how diversity and dynamic contestation, both within and across cultures, are constant features of actors' engagements with society, not simply a fallback in the absence of shared understanding. Holger Niemann and Henrik Schillinger (2017) 'Contestation "All the Way Down"? The Grammar of Contestation in Norm Research', *Review of International Studies*, 43(1): 40–1 and 47.

60 Merry, *Human Rights and Gender Violence*; see also Lisbeth Zimmermann's model of 'interactive feedback loops': Lisbeth Zimmermann (2017) *Global Norms with a Local Face: Between Global Norms and Local Translation* (Cambridge: Cambridge University Press), p 53.

Cultural contexts, legitimacy, and the push towards compliance

An understanding of culture as fluid, disaggregated, and as an active source of knowledge offers more comprehensive ways of thinking about how actors develop and apply their ideas about legitimacy with respect to international law and human rights norms. When culture is understood as a porous and dynamic collection of overlapping and contradictory ideas, habits, traditions, and practices, it becomes easier to understand the variations and apparent inconsistencies within states' own compliance records. There are many different ways for actors within a state to understand what human rights are and which institutions should protect them in which ways. Exploring the battles over meanings and processes of constructing particular narratives can shed light on why a state with a generally strong compliance track record might baulk in response to particular obligations, or why the international obligations that spark debates over the legitimacy of a law or legal system may be triggered by different issues at different times across states with otherwise similar structural conditions. Moreover, by adopting a sociological-anthropological understanding of culture as a repertoire or toolkit, it becomes possible to see more precisely how domestic cultural influences inform perceptions of legitimacy and translate into specific compliance decisions. Culture does not tell actors the 'right' way to respond to a legal obligation; it provides a range of ideas and practices that shape actors' realms of possibility.

Building on the insights of dynamic culture approaches, I argue that within states there exist unique local human rights cultural environments, which play crucial roles in shaping state actors' understandings of the international laws and legal systems with which they interact. I follow Kate Nash's lead by making a distinction between the term 'human rights culture', which reduces culture to a bounded, essentialist idea, and 'cultural politics of human rights', which opens up the political practices and discourses that underpin our understandings of what human rights and legitimacy mean in particular cultural contexts.[61] Thus, I use 'cultural politics' to refer to the processes of contestation and power that shape local elites' expectations of rights and legitimacy, and 'cultural environment/context' to refer to the particular locations and moments in which these cultural politics occur (which in this book primarily means the cultural milieu within a given state). Where I occasionally use the term 'human rights culture', I do so to convey specific actors' conceptions of their own cultural context as coherent or universal, for instance if a politician appeals to a particular formulation of their own

[61] Nash, *The Cultural Politics of Human Rights*, p 7.

culture as different from another, or if a common narrative situates rights in an uncritical articulation of national identity or legal tradition.

These cultural environments, and the politics that sustain and change them, produce loose but nonetheless broadly familiar bodies of local human rights knowledge – they both shape and are shaped by a state's historical and contemporary experiences with rights and its legal and political mechanisms for protecting rights, creating vernacular and local elite expectations about what rights are, how they should be upheld, and whom they are for. Moreover, like all cultures, they are dynamic, heterogeneous, and interconnected. Local human rights cultural contexts are sensitive to change from both above and below, shifting in response to contestation and adaptation from within the state as well as reacting to external influences from the international community. Understanding the local cultural politics of human rights is therefore essential for understanding the varied legitimacies of international law, because the discourses, practices, traditions, and arguments that constitute cultural environments at home reveal how state actors perceive the meanings, purposes, and impacts of international law and human rights.

The perceptions of legitimacy that emerge from local cultural contexts translate into decisions to comply with or resist legal obligations through two processes. First, they structure (non)compliers' realms of acceptability. Oriented by their local rights knowledge,[62] actors within particular cultural contexts formulate 'legitimacy criteria', notions about what is reasonable or tolerable to be asked by a law or legal institution, and what are reasonable options for responding. By legitimacy criteria I do not mean some standardized checklist or rules for what counts as legitimate or not 'in our culture', but rather a conceptual shorthand for culturally resonant reference points. The state actors involved in making and justifying compliance decisions – governments, legislatures, and courts – participate in cultural politics over the meaning and suitability of the obligation in question, searching for interpretations of local principles and narratives that allow them to position compliance as a tool or source of motivation to help maintain their understanding of what rights mean in 'their culture'.

These referents or criteria create the conditions of possibility for certain compliance choices. Generally, where actors interpret the obligation in a way that aligns with local expectations (or at least, does not directly contradict them), compliance is more likely. Conversely, if the obligation cannot be reconciled with local sensibilities, the likelihood that domestic actors will attempt to contest, minimize, evade, or openly reject it will increase. These evaluations are relational, and often strategic – what is considered acceptable in one context may not be so in another. Cultural sensibilities inform

62 Geertz, *Local Knowledge*, p 186.

actors' decisions about the costs and benefits of both rational and normative trade-offs, and about what type of (non)compliance strategy might work to satisfy the obligation in the eyes of the international community while saving face at home.

Even in the face of negative evaluations and overt resistance, local understandings of legitimacy reveal why state actors often comply with laws that prove to be domestically contentious. This is where the second process comes in – an active making and justification of specific compliance decisions. Domestic actors produce and reinforce their legitimacy criteria by constructing compliance narratives that are grounded in local knowledge. Local motivations become all the more important when an obligation is perceived as contentious, for instance when the timing is politically inconvenient, or when the international institution requiring compliance lacks enough legitimacy to generate its own consistent fidelity. Here, state actors construct narratives from familiar ideas about what is right or appropriate at home to remind or cajole themselves into complying with the international obligation. Thus, a government may be unconvinced by arguments of commitment to the rule of law or to particular human rights norms from the international community (top-down socialization or persuasion), but still ground its decision to comply with a case in rule of law terms because they value their particular local conceptions of the importance of rule of law. In short, actors are frequently driven to comply, and construct their sense of obligation and legitimacy towards law, by internal rather than external motivations. The local cultural politics of human rights show that – in contrast to the dominant explanations of the relationship between legitimacy, obligation, and compliance – what states often feel is not a *pull* towards compliance exerted by the law itself, but a *push*.

The combination of these two processes – legitimacy criteria and the compliance push – provides the key to understanding variation in compliance: why states comply with most, but not all, of their obligations, and which obligations states are more likely to comply with or resist. When assessing the legitimacy of international law, state actors are engaged in a constant process of debating and deciding whether the law is legitimate – or legitimate enough – so that it can be accepted, or whether it clashes so fundamentally with local legitimacy criteria that it should be rejected entirely. States that baulk at some of their obligations despite general track records of compliance are more likely to do so when they cannot reconcile what is being asked of them with their own sensibilities. Understanding what those sensibilities are and when states might be more or less receptive requires detailed, historicized interpretation of not only the specific actors and institutions making compliance decisions, but the cultural contexts in which they operate.

Interpreting the cultural politics of human rights

Methodologically, demonstrating the link between cultural politics and compliance requires two steps: first, examining how a cultural politics of human rights contextualizes and constructs local knowledges of legitimacy, and second, analysing how those local knowledges inform decisions to comply with or resist contentious European Court of Human Rights (ECtHR) rulings. The first step is interpretive, developing an iterative thematic analysis of how human rights are constructed and used in national political and legal discourses. Comparative case studies of the UK, Germany, and Croatia – chosen for their different legal and political traditions and different compliance records, but also for their largely 'good faith' relationships with the Council of Europe – allow for examination of patterns and variation across different European states. Within these case studies, an interpretivist approach is valuable for exploring the hybrid, shifting patterns and contested meanings that play out within domestic cultural environments.[63] As Geertz writes, 'cultural analysis is (or should be) guessing at meanings, assessing the guesses, and drawing explanatory conclusions from the better guesses'.[64] My aim here is to offer a 'thick description' of the key ideas, narratives, practices, and institutions that emerge from domestic actors' discussions of human rights and law, to set the scene in which the cultural politics that underpin compliance practices play out.

I focus on discourses surrounding human rights and law in three elite-level fields: government and politics; the judiciary; and the media. This produces a narrow, tightly curated set of stories about national human rights histories in each country, carefully selected by powerful elites and much more sanitized than the broader, fluid processes of meaning making and contestation in local cultural environments at large.

But this approach has two key advantages. First, political leaders tend to build their arguments and language on norms and narratives that resonate with the broadest possible audiences – or at least with the broadest possible voter base.[65] Political leaders' articulations of certain narratives in certain ways reinforces those narratives' dominant position in mainstream discourses, shaping public perceptions of how human rights work in familiar, albeit contested, circulations. Judges and courts, though independent and not seeking electoral support, ground their arguments in the relevant precedents, principles, and doctrines of their legal system and thus are the actors most

[63] Cecelia Lynch (2014) *Interpreting International Politics* (New York: Routledge).

[64] Geertz, *The Interpretation of Cultures: Selected Essays*, p 14.

[65] Thomas Banchoff (1999) 'German Identity and European Integration', *European Journal of International Relations*, 5(3): 269.

deeply embedded in discourses surrounding the content and normative purposes of the law. National media outlets are neither agents of democratic states nor responsible for implementing states' international legal obligations, but they are often the primary sources through which political and judicial actors communicate their decisions and justifications concerning human rights. The media therefore plays a key role in shaping which and whose ideas about human rights law receive mainstream attention. As Nash puts it, 'news media tend not to originate justifications for human rights but rather to *translate* the justifications of other actors into media products, representing them in the mediated public as "neutral" information or in strongly worded and emotive arguments explicitly intended to influence the public and government officials'.[66]

The second advantage of focusing on cultural politics among elite actors is that it is states – or the governments, judiciaries, and legislatures that comprise them – that are primarily responsible for responding to international legal obligations, including the judgments of the ECtHR. Focusing on human rights narratives as they are used and understood at this level ensures that rights discourses are not only broadly familiar to general domestic audiences, but that the discourses are most likely to both influence and be articulated by the actors making compliance decisions.

In each of the three country case studies, the materials I use to examine the local cultural politics of human rights and legitimacy are divided into three 'archives': one for materials related to how governments and politicians conceptualize human rights (policy documents, governing and election manifestos, parliamentary debates, and speeches and statements to the press or elsewhere in public); one for materials related to how judiciaries and judges conceptualize human rights (judgments, dissenting opinions, extrajudicial speeches, and judges' academic writings); and one for materials related to press coverage of ECtHR cases and related issues (primarily online articles from the major national newspapers in each country because these are available most consistently). I did not constrain the materials to a particular time period, partly in order to keep open possibilities for encountering variations in the content and presentation of local human rights discourses, and partly to accommodate the different timelines of compliance and noncompliance in the selected ECtHR cases in each country. I analysed the material thematically,[67] looking for recurring patterns in how and by whom the ECHR and ECtHR, as well as human rights and international law more generally, are discussed in the political, judicial,

66 Nash, *The Cultural Politics of Human Rights*, p 68.

67 Virginia Braun and Victoria Clark (2022) *Thematic Analysis: A Practical Guide* (London: Sage).

and media fields to draw out the core narratives and counternarratives that constitute elite actors' ideas about what rights are, and how and by whom they should be protected.

The second step of this study involved analysing how the local knowledges that become apparent through the first step inform state actors' decisions to comply with or resist contentious ECtHR rulings. Here, I traced the details of selected ECtHR cases and the state's response to the judgment alongside the broader domestic human rights cultural context, to identify whether and how perceptions about what counts as legitimate inform the state's compliance actions. I supplemented the political-legal-media archives for each country with compliance documents from the Council of Europe – progress reports, evaluations from the Committee of Ministers and so on. Each of the three country case study chapters features examples of both compliance and noncompliance with ECtHR rulings. I selected these cases because they sparked a significant degree of contention or debate within the respondent state (either publicly or among compliance actors – for example, significant disagreement among different judges about a technical point of law which affects the state's compliance but does not necessarily appeal to mainstream media). The specific issues, points of law, and ways of implementing or refusing to implement judgments vary in each case, making it possible to tease out how the cultural threads and narratives underpinning local conceptions of rights and legitimacy can be used in different ways and to different ends. The relationship between theory and case studies in this book is an abductive one: I move back and forth between them to draw out the empirical nuances of specific cases and the ways these dynamics contribute to a broader, more reflexive framework for understanding compliance. To this end, the case studies each shed light on the core argument – that cultural politics inform perceptions of legitimacy and compliance – but also test its potential and limits, illustrating how the cultural politics particular to each case stretch and fold in different ways and in response to different contexts.

By analysing how the local cultural contexts identified in step one influence state actors' compliance decisions, I am not trying to determine a strictly causal relationship in a positivist sense, where a coherent local human rights culture provides a concrete answer about why the state complied (for example, 'commitment to a rule of law tradition = compliance'). Rather, I am interested in the ways state actors operate within their local cultural environment, engaging with, drawing on, or contesting discourses and practices of human rights in the process of deciding whether and how to meet their international legal obligations. This better suits the fluid, interpretive understandings of culture's effect on behaviour developed by anthropologists; culture, as Jeffrey Alexander writes, 'is not a thing but a dimension, not an object to be studied as a dependent variable but a thread that runs through, one that can be teased out of every conceivable social form'.[68] Most importantly, treating cultures as dynamic, disaggregated environments that provide repertoires of possible interpretations and actions helps us to account for variation. As governments and courts come up against what they consider to be contentious cases and onerous obligations, we can observe how they engage local culturally informed understandings of what is legitimate or not, moulding and adapting recognizable ideas and practices to inform their decisions to comply with or resist contentious ECtHR rulings in different contexts. What we find empirically will vary from case to case, but a methodological and theoretical approach that embraces the fluidity of cultural politics allows us to know where to look for those variations, and to tease out potential patterns across Europe.

Three sites of cultural politics

Drawing on the results of my thematic analysis of the political, judicial, and media discourses surrounding human rights and the ECtHR in the UK, Germany, and Croatia, I suggest that there are three main sites where the cultural politics of human rights play out. These are spaces where especially powerful patterns of contestation over the meanings and uses of human rights occur, and which emerge relatively consistently across the three states. These are not the only sites and moments where cultural politics of human rights play out, but they provide guideposts for observing where and over what issues cultural politics and legitimacy construction regularly occur within and across European states.

The first site concerns states' historical experiences with, and national memories of, human rights. What matters here is not the factual historical events per se, but how events and figures are remembered in historical memory and national narratives. Memory politics in contemporary European societies is increasingly intertwined with human rights and law, as past atrocities are remembered as the ultimate human rights abuses, and the 'proper way of remembrance' becomes inseparable from 'normative worldviews of human rights that promote "facing the past", "duty to remember", and "justice for victims" as its pillars'.[69] These memories and narratives can shape states' collective attitudes towards human rights and law by, for example, crafting an identity as a rights-respecting state, or providing a historical turning point from which the community hopes to distance itself. Law plays a role in these politics by legally defining the

[68] Jeffrey Alexander (2003) *The Meanings of Social Life: A Cultural Sociology* (Oxford: Oxford University Press), p 7.

[69] Lea David (2020) *The Past Can't Heal Us: The Dangers of Mandating Memory in the Name of Human Rights* (Cambridge: Cambridge University Press), p 1.

shape of historical memory. Processes of 'setting legal frames on how "our story" can be remembered' depoliticize normative expectations, not only through specific memory laws, but by legitimizing legal institutions as valuable protectors of rights and memory while delegitimizing nonlegal critiques or counternarratives.[70] As Daniel Levy and Natan Sznaider write, memory politics do not directly *cause* a specific culture; rather 'they produce a continued negotiation process between "international law" (ie finding the criteria for degrees of wrong doing) and "normative ethics" (based on questions of reason and morality)'.[71] But in global and European contexts of what Lea David calls 'memory standardisation', local narratives of human rights and history can take on increasingly homogeneous and hegemonic forms, often leaving little room in mainstream conceptions of what is right or legitimate for adaptation, contestation, or refusal outside the constraints of the dominant memory.[72] The cultural politics that play out in relation to memory and human rights thus do not 'emerge without the exercise of power over what to remember and how'.[73] Examining the intersections between memory and law is therefore an essential component of understanding the cultural contexts in which narratives about how and by whom human rights should be protected take shape.

The second dimension consists of the state's human rights institutions and constitutional traditions. Institutions and constitutional structures do not only reflect pre-existing cultural ideas or establish rules to neutralize cultural contestation and fix meanings in place; rather, they organize understandings of rights.[74] As dynamic bodies imbued with particular powers of interpretation, institutions have the capacity to define norms and values as human rights or not, authorizing their protection and implementation in certain ways, and conditioning the actors operating within them to think of the institutions' roles and legitimacy in certain ways. But culture structures the institutions in return, underpinning the power dynamics that 'validate particular perspectives, creating hierarchies of subordination and obscuring or excluding recognition of differences and inequalities'.[75] Ulf Hannerz describes this as a two-way process of 'channel[ling] the cultural flow at the same time as it is being, in part, culturally produced'.[76] One

70 Maria Mälksoo (2015) '"Memory Must Be Defended": Beyond the Politics of Mnemonical Security', *Security Dialogue*, 46(3): 223.

71 Daniel Levy and Natan Sznaider (2004) 'The Institutionalisation of Cosmopolitan Morality: the Holocaust and Human Rights', *Journal of Human Rights*, 3(2): 144.

72 David, *The Past Can't Heal Us*, p 1.

73 Mälksoo, 'Memory Must Be Defended', p 225.

74 Reus-Smit, *On Cultural Diversity*, p 34.

75 Nash, *The Cultural Politics of Human Rights*, p 7.

76 Ulf Hannerz (1992) *Cultural Complexity: Studies in the Social Organisation of Meaning* (New York: Columbia University Press), p 14.

of the clearest examples of how this dimension works in practice – as demonstrated throughout the case study chapters – is the way institutions and constitutional principles such as parliamentary sovereignty or doctrinal methods of interpretation structure and reinforce particular notions of rights via traditions of political or legal constitutionalism. Indeed, constitutionalists have long recognized that different constitutional traditions and institutions produce different ways of thinking about norms. As James Tully writes, the inherent diversity – what he calls the 'strange multiplicity' – of culture means that constitutional actors 'bring very different and often conflicting traditions of interpretation, conceptions and weightings of constitutional and democratic considerations to bear on a case at hand'.[77] Understanding the place of institutions in directing the 'flow' of culture is therefore a core component of understanding the cultural context of rights more broadly.[78]

The third site, domestic actors' interactions with the international actors and institutions creating international law, is crucial for thinking through the interconnectedness of local and global cultures. Regional and international legal institutions are created in particular historical and political contexts,[79] which exert additional legitimacy pressures on the systems in ways that are distinct from (and indeed, often contradictory to) pressures concerning 'pure' legal legitimacy. For the Strasbourg human rights system, this means not only considering its functions as a human rights court and status as part of the international legal order, but also its relationship to the European integration project. The European Convention and Court of Human Rights may not be as deeply embedded in debates about integration and supranationalism as the European Union, but they are nonetheless built on the same postwar democratization and common heritage narratives.[80] Part of understanding the influence of the cultural politics of rights on compliance with the ECtHR, then, is understanding public discourses about European institutions and issues of European identity and scepticism.

Finally, it is worth noting that cultural politics of human rights shape domestic actors' perceptions of legitimacy dynamically not only over time and in response to new contexts, but also in response to different objects

---

77 James Tully (1995) *Strange Multiplicity: Constitutionalism in an Age of Diversity* (Cambridge: Cambridge University Press), p 11; James Tully (2008) 'The Unfreedom of the Moderns in Comparison to Their Ideals of Constitutionalism and Democracy', *Modern Law Review*, 65(2): 206.

78 Hannerz, *Cultural Complexity*, p 14.

79 Merry, 'Changing Rights, Changing Culture', p 41.

80 Gráinne de Búrca (2011) 'The Road Not Taken: The European Union as a Global Human Rights Actor', *American Journal of International Law*, 105(4): 649–93; Marco Duranti (2017) *The Conservative Human Rights Revolution: European Identity, Transnational Politics, and the Origins of the European Convention* (Oxford: Oxford University Press).

within the constitutional or international order. For this reason, it is useful to make a distinction between three different layers of legitimacy: international law and regimes as a general legal system; specific institutional instruments and bodies such as treaties or courts; and the particular human rights norms and legal clauses or interpretations with which states must comply in a given case. I adapt this three-level distinction from scholars of backlash against international courts, who differentiate between the legitimacy of an institution and the legitimacy of its individual rulings or obligations, as well as between the 'ordinary resistance' that makes up the normal processes of interpreting and applying international law and the 'extraordinary backlash' which comes with mainstream public attention and explicit aims to undermine or abolish the institution.[81] The legitimacy of an institution as a whole is not typically threatened by individual frustrating or (allegedly) illegitimate cases, although individual rulings are more likely to be tainted if they are made by an institution perceived to be inherently illegitimate.[82] But the reverse may also be true, so that a series of controversial rulings that clash with local politics and cultural sensibilities may accumulate to generate or exacerbate perceptions of illegitimacy at higher levels. Support for the Convention does not automatically equate to support for the Court, and compliance with one ruling does not guarantee compliance with another. The basic foundations or 'orienting notions' underpinning local perceptions of the legitimacy of norms, institutions, and the legal order may be broadly similar among the state actors in a given country, but the ways they play out in practice will differ depending on the particular laws or institution to which those notions are being applied, and by which state actors (government ministers, members of parliament, judges). In turn, the new applications and interpretations these actors develop feed back into local cultural debates, as well as up to international ones, contributing to the ongoing 'active making of culture' by producing alternative or additional meanings and possibilities for action regarding the interpretation, application, and legitimacy criteria for

[81] Mikael Rask Madsen, Pola Cebulak, and Micha Wiebusch (2018) 'Backlash against International Courts: Explaining the Norms and Patterns of Resistance to International Courts', *International Journal of Law in Context*, 14(2): 202; Ximena Soley and Silvia Steininger (2018) 'Parting Ways or Lashing Back? Withdrawals, Backlash and the Inter-American Court of Human Rights', *International Journal of Law in Context*, 14(2): 238; Alter and Zürn, 'Conceptualising Backlash Politics', p 566.

[82] Pamela Slotte and Martin Scheinin (2011) 'Captain, Fire Brigade or Icebreaker? Political Legitimacy as a Rationale in Human Rights Adjudication', in Tage Kurtén and Lars Hertzberg (eds), *Legitimacy: The Treasure of Politics* (Frankfurt am Main: Peter Lang), p 103; Ian Clark, Sebastian Kaempf, Christian Reus-Smit and Emily Tannock (2018) 'Crisis in the Laws of War? Beyond Compliance and Effectiveness', *European Journal of International Relations*, 24(2): 319–43.

rights. This is the cultural toolkit in action – actors can maintain changing, disparate, and even seemingly incongruous positions simultaneously because different contexts necessitate different ways of developing and applying cultural tools over time. Ultimately, understanding how perceptions of legitimacy vary within and across layers – from systems to organizations to laws and norms – requires a culturally contingent approach.

Conclusion

Research on compliance is aware of the relevance of domestic cultural influences on the acceptance and implementation of international law, but needs a firmer grasp on how exactly it works. This chapter harnessed insights from culture specialists in anthropology and sociology to show how ideas about legitimacy are produced at the domestic level, arguing that states' unique cultural and historical experiences with human rights and law inform their decisions to comply with or resist legal obligations. Thus, building on the work of Clifford Geertz, Kate Nash, and others, I argue that legitimacy is local knowledge, and that knowledge is shaped by cultural politics. Ideas about right and wrong, fairness, and justice shape and are shaped by actors' and communities' human rights cultural contexts, and orient their views on what rights are, whom they are for, and how and by whom they should be protected. These ideas about what is or is not legitimate in the realm of human rights law are fluid, diverse, and contested, but the making of them produces patterns and possibilities for action in the form of narratives, traditions, practices, norms, and sensibilities that shed light on why states obey or resist their human rights obligations.

Framing the construction of legitimacy this way unlocks questions of compliance unanswered by approaches that place legitimacy in the international legal system itself through intrinsic qualities and socially produced shared understandings (or overlook it entirely). Specifically, insights from culture specialists tell us more about unshared understandings of legitimacy, and by extension, variation in compliance. By understanding cultures as repertoires or toolkits of possible meanings and actions, rather than a set of fixed values, anthropologists and sociologists of culture show how actors can draw on the same source material to interpret law and human rights in different ways across varied contexts, or different source material to interpret like contexts. The cultural contexts of human rights do not tell actors what to do, but they do structure their understandings of legitimacy, from which actors develop criteria to interpret, apply, and contest or accept international human rights and legal norms. It is here in the ongoing processes of legitimizing – the making and remaking of cultural symbols, the historical and political contexts in which they occur – that actors find justificatory narratives and motivations to push themselves towards compliance. This push – not the pull of an ungrounded legitimacy inherent to international law itself – helps to explain why states baulk in the face of some culturally confronting cases but find ways to accept others, and thus fills the gap left by constructivists and domestic institutionalists alike when they defer to states' unspecified 'compliance cultures'. To this end, states' local cultural politics of human rights – when understood as dynamic, heterogeneous, and an ongoing part of actors' engagement with rights from the outset – can clarify why, and in what circumstances, states are likely to comply with international human rights judgments, by providing a context for understanding how local perceptions of the legitimacy of international law and human rights are constituted, and in turn how these perceptions translate into action.

3

A History of Compliance and Obligation in the European Human Rights System

When the original ten member states of the Council of Europe drafted and adopted the European Convention on Human Rights (ECHR) in 1950, they did so as 'European countries which are like-minded and have a common heritage of political traditions, ideals, freedom, and the rule of law'.[1] Building on the belief that the few remaining or recovering democracies in Western Europe were already defined by their strong human rights credentials and commitment to democratic principles, the drafters of the Convention sought to entrench the rights they believed reflected a definitive statement of those principles as a means to buttress democratic Europe from the threats to their common heritage posed by totalitarianism. To this end, the ECHR of 1950 reflected a relatively traditional, liberal conception of rights as political freedoms, and sought to protect only the most essential rights necessary to preserve the democratic traditions and respect for the rule of law already well established throughout Western Europe.

The belief that European democracies share a common history, culture, and set of values remains a core normative underpinning of the contemporary European human rights system, providing a foundational narrative intended to unify otherwise diverse nations and to legitimize the supranational oversight of national human rights protections by the European Court of Human Rights (ECtHR). Yet the assumption that participants in the European human rights system share an identical or universal conception of human rights, and of the role of the European system in defending it, has given rise to considerable friction throughout the Strasbourg system's

[1] Council of Europe, *Convention for the Protection of Human Rights and Fundamental Freedoms*, European Treaty Series No. 5, Rome, 4 November 1950, Preamble.

history. Since their inception, the European Convention and Court have been shaped by, and contributed to, ongoing attempts to balance international judicial oversight and the creation of consistent human rights standards across Europe with national autonomy and the diverse domestic frameworks and cultural contexts in which human rights are protected.

This chapter provides an overview of the Strasbourg system's normative and historical origins, drawing attention to the particular human rights norms and legal rules with which Contracting States to the ECHR and Court are expected to comply. It situates the Strasbourg system in postwar Europe's historical, political, and cultural context, and identifies some of the key pressure points or political tensions that arise from the challenge of balancing the unique human rights needs of 46 different states in one coherent system. In keeping with more extensive histories and critiques of the ECHR, the chapter suggests that the debates over the creation, evolution, and purpose of the European human rights system reveal that, beyond the broad, generalized expression of their commitment to these values, the ECtHR and its different member states often hold profoundly divergent, even conflicting, understandings of what the rights enshrined in the Convention mean in practice.[2] This contestation over the purpose and meaning of the Convention rights has permeated Strasbourg's core functions and processes, producing a particular set of obligations and requirements for compliance that are themselves frequently fluid and contested. To this end, the chapter concludes by suggesting that understanding compliance with the ECtHR is contingent on an understanding of the dynamics between Europe's uncommon national and international human rights mechanisms.

The origins of the European human rights system

The immediate impetus for a European instrument of human rights protection lay in European leaders' fear of a return to the atrocities of the Second World War era. In the wake of the devastating experiences of fascism, Nazism, and the Holocaust, and confronted with the supposed imminent threat of communism – from both the rapidly expanding Soviet Union and burgeoning socialist movements within democratic states – the few remaining or recovering democracies in Western Europe were acutely aware of the fragility of their democratic institutions and traditions. The first steps towards modern international human rights law were being taken at the United Nations (UN) in the form of the 1948 Universal Declaration on Human Rights (UDHR), but the declaratory nature of the UDHR and the

2 Marie-Bénédicte Dembour (2006) *Who Believes in Human Rights?: Reflections on the European Convention* (New York: Cambridge University Press), p 233.

inclusion of nondemocratic regimes in the UN's membership left European elites concerned about its enforceability and in want of a stronger guarantee.[3]

It was in this context that proposals for a pan-European convention and court for protecting human rights were first made at the Congress of Europe in The Hague in 1948.[4] These proposals were realized in the form of the Council of Europe, the first interstate institution for European integration, whose statute was signed by ten founding states on 5 May 1949.[5] It was in the Council of Europe's dual decision-making institutions, the Consultative Assembly (comprised of parliamentary representatives from each of the member states) and the Committee of Ministers (comprised of foreign ministers and their deputies), that drafts of the Convention were first debated, and then agreed on. Yet, while there was a strong, if begrudging, consensus among the Council of Europe states that Europe needed an international human rights instrument,[6] no such agreement existed regarding the shape the instrument should take, or the particular rights it ought to protect.[7] The Convention that was adopted in 1950, and the Commission and Court established to protect it, are consequently the products of several compromises between actors who were reluctant to have too many obligations imposed on them by an international institution, and those who wanted stronger oversight for national human rights protections.

Drafting the European Convention on Human Rights

Delegates at early negotiations of the Hague Congress and inaugural meetings of the Council of Europe clung to the belief that European democracies

---

3 European Movement, 'Examination of Criticisms', *European Convention of Human Rights*, INF/5/E/R, 1949, cited in Ed Bates (2010) *The Evolution of the European Convention on Human Rights: From its Inception to the Creation of a Permanent Court of Human Rights* (New York: Oxford University Press), p 53.

4 Marco Duranti (2017) *The Conservative Human Rights Revolution: European Identity, Transnational Politics, and the Origins of the European Convention* (New York: Oxford University Press), pp 96–162.

5 The Statute of the Council of Europe was signed on this date by the governments of Belgium, Denmark, France, Ireland, Italy, Luxembourg, the Netherlands, Norway, Sweden, and the United Kingdom. Although not founding members, Greece and Turkey signed the Statute three months later, on 9 August 1949, and therefore became members of the Council early enough to participate in the drafting of the ECHR.

6 A.W.B. Simpson (2004) *Human Rights and the End of Empire: Britain and the Genesis of the European Convention* (Oxford: Oxford University Press), p 710; Bates, *The Evolution of the ECHR*, pp 77–9.

7 Danny Nicol (2005) 'Original Intent and the European Convention on Human Rights', *Public Law*, Spring: 155.

already possessed strong human rights credentials.[8] Many of the founding member states of the Council of Europe claimed to be home to centuries-old democratic traditions, and viewed themselves as birthplaces for key human rights milestones such as Magna Carta and the Declaration of the Rights of Man and Citizen, and for the development of modern conceptions of liberty and justice. To this end, the founding members of the Council of Europe already believed themselves to be, in the words of the eminent international lawyer Hersch Lauterpacht, 'faithfully and permanently wedded to the tradition of human rights and freedom'.[9]

Early campaigns led by the group of organizations advocating European integration, the European Movement, also reflect a widespread sentiment that, due to this human rights heritage, European integration entailed a civilizing mission, bringing the particular conception of justice and human rights held by members of the European Movement and the Council of Europe's founding states to the rest of Europe, and indeed the world.[10] The final document of the Hague Congress, *Message to Europeans*, suggested that Europe's 'mission' was to 'unite her peoples in accordance with their genius of diversity' and to 'revive her inventive powers for the greater protection and respect of the rights and duties of the individual of which, in spite of all her mistakes, Europe is still the greatest exponent'.[11] In reality, western Europe's claims to expound a universal conception of rights dripped with the hypocrisies of excluding communist states in the east from their plans for a 'pan-European' union, and of drafting a human rights convention that allowed its Contracting States to exclude their occupied and colonial territories, deliberately denying rights to numerous minoritized and racialized individuals and communities both within and beyond geographical Europe.[12]

According to the European Movement, Europe's immediate history with totalitarianism was an aberration, caused by dictators abandoning democratic and moral values, and which could not be stopped by the weak parliamentary and judicial institutions of interwar regimes.[13] The centralized, authoritarian governments and planned economies of communist regimes, too, posed a clear threat to European democracies' pluralist, rule-of-law-abiding societies

[8] Congress of Europe (1948) *Message to Europeans*, The Hague, London, Paris: International Committee of the Movements for European Unity, 10 May; ECHR Preamble.

[9] Hersch Lauterpacht (1950) *International Law and Human Rights* (London: Stevens and Sons), p 445.

[10] Duranti, *The Conservative Human Rights Revolution*, pp 164–212 and 404.

[11] Congress of Europe, *Message to Europeans*.

[12] Sumi Madhok (2021) *Vernacular Rights Cultures: The Politics of Origins, Human Rights and Gendered Struggles for Justice* (Cambridge: Cambridge University Press).

[13] Duranti, *The Conservative Human Rights Revolution*, p 5; Bates, *The Evolution of the ECHR*, p 46.

and, most importantly, their precious liberal markets.[14] In order to defend the 'common heritage' of western European democracies, an international convention would need to provide a clear assertion of the fundamental rights and freedoms protected throughout national systems, serving as a reminder of the ideas that defined European democracies' common heritage and buttressing them against the corrosive influence of totalitarianism.

Thus, the primary ambition of the drafters of the Convention was to create a 'system of collective security against tyranny and oppression',[15] designed to preserve western European democracies' existing human rights protections rather than impose new obligations on them. Crucially, states themselves would bear the bulk of the responsibility for preserving individual rights, while the Convention would 'sound the alarm' to prevent states from descending into totalitarianism,[16] thereby 'halting the progress of evil before it is too late'.[17] Still, as historians have documented, there remained a large minority for whom the ECHR held the potential to become a more extensive and substantive bill of rights for Europe, not to mention a basis for deeper European integration.[18] One of the key drafters of the Convention, the French parliamentarian, Pierre-Henri Teitgen, was an especially fervent advocate of building on the 1950 Convention in order to gradually realize a more comprehensive pan-European human rights infrastructure, though this ambition was initially thwarted by the need to produce a convention that would be acceptable to – and therefore enforceable upon – all the states involved.

Division over the purpose and potential of the Convention is also evident in the process of deciding which rights to include and in what form. Arguing that western Europeans already shared a common understanding of the rights they sought to entrench,[19] representatives from France, Ireland, Italy, and Turkey believed a general enumeration of the rights, without detailed definitions, would suffice.[20] For the Netherlands, Norway, Denmark,

---

14 The second stanza of the *Message to Europeans* describes 'disunited Europe' as 'overladen with barriers that prevent the circulation of her goods'. Congress of Europe, *Message to Europeans*.

15 David Maxwell-Fyfe, in Council of Europe (1975) *Collected Edition of the 'Travaux Préparatoires' of the ECHR* ['*TP*'], ed A. Robertson (The Hague: M. Nijhoff, 1975–85), Vol I, p 120.

16 Pierre-Henri Teitgen, in *TP*, Vol I, p 292.

17 Jacques Camille Paris, Secretary General of the Council of Europe, in *TP*, Vol II, p 304.

18 Bates, *The Evolution of the ECHR*, pp 105–7; Nicol, 'Original Intent and the ECHR', p 155.

19 *TP*, Vol IV, p 14.

20 Belgium and Luxembourg also favoured general enumeration, but only if a court were established to provide guidance and interpretation for the rights. Sweden did not commit to a preference. *TP*, Vol IV, p 178.

Greece, and especially the United Kingdom, however, precise definitions were essential in order to ensure signatories understood exactly what they were agreeing to. Precision, the British argued, would not only ensure that signatories were not confronted with any unexpected and unwanted obligations, but would also facilitate more effective enforcement by providing detailed explanations of what obeying the rights entailed, making them 'more difficult to violate'.[21] In the end, the British were successful in securing extensive definitions of the Convention rights, a victory intended to retain the Convention as a reiteration of the human rights status quo in Europe, and to limit its potential to expand and impose new obligations on its signatories. Likewise, proposals to include social and economic rights alongside civil and political rights were eventually overruled by conservatives and Christian democrats concerned about the growing popularity of left-wing and socialist movements in their own countries.[22] The rights to property, education, and free elections – whose potential applications were too divisive for the states involved to resolve in the first draft of the Convention – were only attached to the Convention after its creation, as part of the first nonbinding Additional Protocol.[23] Negotiations over the drafting of the Convention thus reveal a lack of consensus between delegates who hoped to produce a broad statement of rights with the potential to evolve, and delegates who wanted to enshrine the minimum number of rights – and therefore the minimum obligation on Contracting States – necessary to bolster core democratic values in the face of antidemocratic threats.

Ultimately, advocates of the more traditional international pact won out; the final draft of the Convention included 13 precisely defined rights and freedoms relating predominantly to the core civil and political activities necessary to sustain democratic, pluralist societies.[24] The Convention adopted by the Council of Europe in 1950, and which entered into force in 1953, thus reflected a 'classical liberal understanding of European human

[21] *TP*, Vol IV, p 106.

[22] Marco Duranti (2012) 'Curbing Labour's Totalitarian Temptation: European Human Rights Law and British Postwar Politics', *Humanity: An International Journal of Human Rights, Humanitarianism & Development*, 3(3): 362.

[23] Bates, *The Evolution of the ECHR*, p 68; Nicol, 'Original Intent and the ECHR', pp 163–4

[24] These are: 1) Right to life; 2) Prohibition of torture; 3) Prohibition of slavery and forced labour; 4) Right to liberty and security; 5) Right to a fair trial; 6) No punishment without law; 7) Right to respect for private and family life; 8) Freedom of thought, conscience, and religion; 9) Freedom of expression; 10) Freedom of assembly and association; 11) Right to marry; 12) Right to an effective remedy; 13) Prohibition of discrimination. The Convention also includes general obligations on Contracting States to uphold these rights, and sets out the circumstances in which the limitation of, or derogation from, particular Convention rights is acceptable.

rights' as civil liberties intrinsically guaranteed to all individuals (save where the state expressly imposes limitations to maintain democratic order and prevent rights abuses against other individuals), as well as a predominantly conservative and Christian democratic – rather than progressive or socialist – conceptualization of morality.[25] Nonetheless, contestation over a minimalist or comprehensive rights document highlights the fact that the particular Convention and supporting institutions that emerged in the 1950s were not inevitable.[26] Moreover, it demonstrates that notions of what would provide an effective, efficient, and legitimate international human rights instrument varied among actors, a theme that has continued to inform the evolution of the Convention system throughout its life.

The creation of the European Court of Human Rights

The matter of establishing a European court to interpret the Convention was likewise heavily contested. Proposals for a judicial body to interpret and defend the Convention were made from the very beginning of the process of creating a regional human rights system, although the ECtHR was not established until 1959, by which time it had been subjected to several compromises. In the meantime, the European Commission on Human Rights (ECmHR or Commission), a political body tasked with investigating claims of human rights violations by Contracting States and issuing non-binding reports, had already been established in 1954. It was the Commission, rather than the Court, that bore the responsibility to monitor states' adherence to the Convention in its early years, though reforms to the Court in 1998 rendered the Commission defunct as its role was absorbed into that of the new permanent, full-time Court.

Two key debates dominated negotiations over the creation of a European court. The first concerned whether an international court was necessary at all. Those who viewed the Convention simply as an antitotalitarian device (notably representatives from the UK) were deeply reluctant to become subject to an international body that might create new, unexpected obligations or undermine national traditions through judicial activism.[27] They believed that proposals for a court constituted an unnecessary imposition on the sovereignty and proven human rights records of states who were perfectly capable of upholding the Convention themselves.[28] For the few very

---

[25] Duranti, 'Curbing Labour's Totalitarian Temptation', p 364; Duranti, *The Conservative Human Rights Revolution*, pp 129–32.

[26] Nicol, 'Original Intent and the ECHR', p 171.

[27] Elizabeth Wicks (2000) 'The United Kingdom Government's Perceptions of the European Convention on Human Rights at the Time of Entry', *Public Law*, Autumn: 438–55.

[28] *TP*, Vol I, p 244.

serious cases that might need international intervention, the Commission would suffice.[29] The Committee of Ministers of the Council of Europe would further ensure compliance with the Convention through diplomatic and public shaming methods. On the other side, French, Italian, and Irish delegates suggested that an independent judicial, rather than political, institution would provide the legitimacy and authority necessary to ensure the Convention's efficacy.[30] Advocates of both perspectives were equally concerned with producing a system that could be enforced, though they differed on how that might best be achieved.

The second impasse concerned the right of individuals to petition the Commission and Court directly. Proposals to allow individuals to access their rights under international instruments had been made before, in the early stages of drafting the UDHR, but were ultimately rejected.[31] The inclusion of the right of individual petition in the European system would therefore be the first time that direct recourse for individuals was granted in international law. Again, though, Greek, Dutch, and British representatives worried about the implications of this novel proposal for state authority, expressing concern that the Court would be overrun by vexatious applicants – or worse, communists! – seeking to undermine national courts and governments.[32] In the end, both the jurisdiction of the Court and the right of individual petition were included in the Convention system as optional features for Contracting States to adopt if they saw fit. And given that when the Convention was first opened for signature only three states – Ireland, Denmark, and Sweden – accepted the individual petition protocol, and only two – Ireland and Denmark – accepted the jurisdiction of the Court, concerns that these features would transform the Convention system into an overbearing supranational court of appeal were easily assuaged.

The Court that emerged from these negotiations, like the Convention before it, predominantly reflected the role of providing only limited oversight preferred by the British, Dutch, Greek, and Scandinavian delegations, rather than the more ambitious constitutionalizing goals of continental advocates. In its first decade, the then part-time Court heard only a handful of cases, almost all of which it ruled on in a manner that favoured the Contracting States rather than individual applicants.[33] The bulk of the cases brought to Strasbourg were investigated by the Commission, whose findings were merely

[29] *TP*, Vol I, p 244.

[30] Teitgen, in *TP*, Vol II, p 174. See also Bates, *The Evolution of the ECHR*, pp 72–3.

[31] Bates, *The Evolution of the ECHR*, pp 84–5.

[32] *TP*, Vol IV, p 252.

[33] Bates, *The Evolution of the ECHR*, pp 8–10 and 173–84. The first case in which the Court found a violation of the Convention was not heard until 1968. *Neumeister v Austria*, App no. 1936/63 (ECtHR, 27 June 1968).

advisory for Contracting States. In the few cases referred by the Commission to the Court for further review, the Court also read the Convention in a relatively narrow, or literal manner, deferring to states and cementing its position as a limited guardian of rights that were otherwise well known and firmly entrenched within the Contracting States' national systems, at least for the first decade of its existence.

The evolution and expansion of the European human rights system

After a quiet initiation period playing a minimal role in protecting human rights, the Court embarked in the 1970s on what would eventually be recognized as a radical divergence away from its previous approach. Two factors in particular were vital in facilitating this shift and contributing to the evolution of the Convention system's influence over human rights in Europe. First, the expansion of the membership of the Council of Europe, first to southern and central Europe in the 1960s and 1970s, and then to former communist states in the 1990s, along with the acceptance of the (still optional) jurisdiction of the Court and right of individual petition by both existing and new members, considerably increased the number of applications submitted to the Commission. Second, the Commission became more willing to refer cases to the Court.[34] Together, these factors provided the Court with a swell of new opportunities to interpret the Convention and enhance its jurisprudence. It was in this era, then, that the Court made the landmark rulings that formed the basis of the dynamic or evolutive interpretation, and the concepts of subsidiarity and the margin of appreciation, that now define Strasbourg's approach to applying Convention rights.[35]

The drastic increase in the workloads of the Commission and Court triggered by their expanded membership and the evolving conception of the nature of the Convention rights necessitated reform of the system. The Convention institutions were established in an era in which only a handful of cases were anticipated to ever reach Strasbourg, yet by the 1990s the Commission was receiving nearly 10,000 applications per year.[36] Though the (at this point, 40) members of the Council of Europe were initially divided over the best way to achieve reform, the strain on the existing

[34] Bates, *The Evolution of the ECHR*, p 145.

[35] See *Marckx v Belgium*, App no. 6833/74 (ECtHR, 13 June 1979), *Golder v United Kingdom*, App no. 4451/70 (ECtHR, 21 February 1975), *Tyrer v United Kingdom*, App no. 5856/72 (ECtHR, 25 April 1978), *The Sunday Times v United Kingdom*, App no. 6538/74 (ECtHR, 26 April 1979), *Handyside v United Kingdom*, App no. 5493/72 (ECtHR, 7 December 1976), *Airey v Ireland*, App no. 6289/73 (ECtHR, 9 October 1979).

[36] Bates, *The Evolution of the ECHR*, p 453.

system was great enough that compromise was struck relatively quickly.[37] The reforms introduced in 1998 by Protocol 11 were therefore primarily aimed at streamlining the process of reviewing cases. The original two-tier system with the Commission referring cases to the part-time Court was abolished, and the two institutions were replaced with a single, full-time Court.[38] The process of monitoring states' compliance with the ECtHR's judgments remained with the Committee of Ministers. As well as making the review process more efficient, Protocol 11 introduced new obligations for states by making the jurisdiction of the new ECtHR and the right of individual petition compulsory (rather than optional and renewable every three years) for all signatories to the Convention. As in 1950, the British attempted to oppose this proposal, concerned about compulsory obligations circumventing national decision making and political leverage, though they were alone in their opposition this time and in the end accepted the new protocol.[39] The creation of the new Court in 1998 thus represents the birth of the contemporary European human rights system, though the process of reform is ongoing. A series of 'high level conferences' between 2010 and 2015 mark the latest attempt to reform the Strasbourg system. Aimed at allowing the Court to more actively point out the causes of violations and possible solutions in its proceedings, as well as encouraging states to take greater responsibility for their Convention obligations and compliance, the conferences reflect the ongoing tensions and compromises that characterized the Strasbourg system's origins.[40]

As the ECtHR has grown in size and consolidated its jurisprudence, it has increasingly shifted away from its initial role as a last defence against totalitarianism towards being a more active arbiter of rights. In doing so, however, the Court has also gradually accrued greater authority on European rights standards relative to its Contracting States, such that it is now a leading constitutional institution for upholding human rights in Europe. This, in turn, has fuelled tensions between the Court and states that preferred its more traditional status as a limited instrument of international law. To this

[37] Council of Europe, *Explanatory Report to Protocol No. 11 to the Convention for the Protection of Human Rights and Fundamental Freedoms, Restructuring the Control Machinery Established Thereby*, European Treaty Series No. 155, Strasbourg, 11 May 1994, p 1; see also Bates, *The Evolution of the ECHR*, p 456.

[38] Council of Europe, *Protocol No. 11 to the Convention for the Protection of Human Rights and Fundamental Freedoms, Restructuring the Control Machinery Established Thereby*, European Treaty Series No. 155, Strasbourg, 11 May 1994.

[39] Bates, *The Evolution of the ECHR*, pp 457–60.

[40] European Court of Human Rights (no date a) *History of the Court's Reforms*. Available at: https://www.echr.coe.int/documents/d/echr/Reforms_history_ENG (accessed 29 September 2024).

end, the need to reconcile national authority with international oversight that characterized the Convention's foundation remains a central feature of the modern Court, both in terms of how the Court reviews cases, and how the Council of Europe supervises state compliance with its judgments.

Key features and processes of the ECtHR

The contemporary ECtHR continues to reflect the lack of consensus over the best approach to protecting human rights that define its history. In particular, the two competing forces of maintaining state autonomy, on one hand, and guaranteeing effective international oversight, on the other, are clearly reflected in the structure, functions, and core interpretative principles of the Strasbourg institutions. The balance struck between these two forces has important consequences for understanding compliance within the European system, as it demonstrates that the meanings of Convention rights, and what constitutes satisfactory compliance with them, is often contested between the ECtHR and its member states.

Evolutive interpretation and the ECHR as a 'living instrument'

First among the principles that define the modern ECtHR's work is the notion that the ECHR is a 'living instrument', to be interpreted 'in the light of present day conditions'.[41] This principle, first referenced in the ECtHR's case law in the 1978 case, *Tyrer v United Kingdom*, forms the basis of the ECtHR's dynamic or evolutive approach to interpreting the Convention.[42] Evolutive interpretation emphasizes the purpose, objectives, or 'spirit' of the Convention, rather than reading it in a purely literal (formalist) manner or in light of the original meaning of the text intended by the Convention's founders.[43] To this end, it allows the ECtHR the flexibility necessary to adapt the Convention to new circumstances and keep pace with rapidly changing

41 *Tyrer v United Kingdom*, para 31.

42 The terms 'dynamic' and 'evolutive' interpretation are used interchangeably by the ECtHR and in academic literature, as well as occasionally the term 'teleological method'.

43 The ECtHR recognizes the record of the proceedings in which the Convention was drafted, the *Travaux Préparatoires*, as a legitimate source of law, but they have a subordinate status to other interpretive aids such as the Vienna Convention on the Law of Treaties and the existence of consensus or emerging trends across Europe on the meaning of a right, and the Court rarely cites the *Travaux* in its rulings. In any event, the *Travaux* do not always reveal a clear intention or consensus on a given aspect of the Convention. Nicol, 'Original Intent and the ECHR', p 155; Jean-Paul Costa (2011) 'On the Legitimacy of the European Court of Human Rights' Judgments', *European Constitutional Law Review*, 7(2): 176–9.

human rights standards across Europe.[44] Moreover, dynamic interpretation has enabled the Court to expand the scope of the Convention beyond that envisaged by the Convention's founders, and in doing so, expand the Court's own jurisdiction and authority to evaluate the relationship of the Convention to new areas of law, policy, and society.[45] In this way, the ECtHR has played a critical role in transforming the Convention from reflecting a predominantly classical liberal conception of rights as negative freedoms and political rights towards a broader conception that increasingly includes social rights and stronger positive obligations.

In order to develop the Convention in line with evolving understandings of rights in Europe, the ECtHR uses two supporting concepts. The first is the notion that the Convention must guarantee 'not rights that are theoretical and illusory but rights that are practical and effective'.[46] This doctrine ensures that the Convention is interpreted and applied in a manner that guarantees substantively meaningful and useful rights for individuals, grounding relatively abstract human rights principles in considerations of individuals' actual circumstances and practical needs. Second, the ECtHR looks for what it calls 'European consensus', that is, consistency or uniformity across the national systems of Europe on a particular norm or issue.[47] The Court uses comparative analysis to determine whether a standard is common throughout Europe (or at least indicates an emerging trend). Consensus is thus a key guiding principle for interpreting the Convention, as it allows the Court to read new rights and obligations into the Convention system while maintaining the underlying historical assumption that the Convention exists to protect well-established and widely shared human rights norms. Together, these concepts provide an important basis for testing and justifying new or evolved interpretations, and by extension for legitimizing the ECtHR's rulings.

Dynamic interpretation is not without criticism, however, particularly from actors who view the ECHR as a traditional international treaty that

[44] Kanstantsin Dzehtsiarou (2011) 'European Consensus and the Evolutive Interpretation of the European Convention on Human Rights', *German Law Journal*, 12(10): 1732; Alastair Mowbray (2005) 'The Creativity of the European Court of Human Rights', *Human Rights Law Review*, 5(1): 61; George Letsas (2013) 'The ECHR as a Living Instrument: Its Meaning and Legitimacy', in Andreas Føllesdal, Birgit Peters, and Geir Ulfstein (eds), *Constituting Europe: The European Court of Human Rights in a National, European and Global Context* (Cambridge: Cambridge University Press), pp 106–41.

[45] Wayne Sandholtz (2017) 'Expanding Rights: Norm Innovation in the European and Inter-American Courts', in Alison Brysk and Michael Stohl (eds), *Expanding Human Rights: 21st Century Norms and Governance* (Cheltenham: Edward Elgar Publishing), p 157.

[46] *Airey v Ireland*, para 24.

[47] Dzehtsiarou, 'European Consensus and the Evolutive Interpretation of the European Convention on Human Rights', pp 1733–4.

should be interpreted narrowly, and actors who are wary of relinquishing too much influence to an international institution. Lord Hoffman of the UK Supreme Court contends that although 'the practical expression of concepts employed in a treaty or constitutional document may change', such change nevertheless 'does not entitle a judicial body to introduce wholly new concepts … into an international treaty which makes no mention of them, simply because it would be more in accordance with the spirit of the times'.[48] More subtle critiques suggest that the ECtHR does not always sufficiently explain or justify its evolutive decisions, raising questions about the transparency and procedural legitimacy of the Court's interpretive methods, and highlighting the importance of European consensus and the notion of upholding existing, commonly held rights in tempering the Court's work.[49]

Nonetheless, concerns about reading new rights and concepts into the Convention reflect the broader tension apparent throughout the Convention's history between its originally conceived purpose as an antitotalitarian pact and its potential to evolve into something stronger. It also has important consequences for compliance with the ECtHR's rulings because it means the Court has the capacity to create new, sometimes unpredictable, obligations for states.[50] Although acceptance of the ECtHR's jurisdiction implies that states anticipate some evolution in their obligations, disagreement over the boundaries of this evolution mean dynamic rulings can create friction between states and the Court, and foster resentment or reluctance to comply. As such, though dynamic interpretation is a central feature of the Court's approach to protecting human rights, it also serves as a vector for contestation over the purpose of the Convention, the meaning of specific rights and norms, and the respective roles of national and international bodies in determining those meanings.

Subsidiarity and the margin of appreciation

If the notion of the ECHR as a living instrument expands the interpretive authority of the ECtHR, the principle of subsidiarity provides a state-oriented counterpoint. Subsidiarity, along with its practical legal expression, the doctrine of the margin of appreciation, remains the bedrock of the European human rights system. At its core, the principle of subsidiarity assumes that, although Strasbourg plays a crucial role in maintaining a minimum human rights standard and safety net, it is ultimately national

48 Lord Hoffman (2009) 'The Universality of Human Rights', Judicial Studies Board Annual Lecture, 19 March, pp 21–2.

49 Mowbray, 'The Creativity of the European Court of Human Rights', p 61.

50 Sandholtz, 'Expanding Rights', p 158.

authorities who are best equipped to guarantee individual rights in the first instance.[51] In light of this principle, the margin of appreciation is applied by the Court to grant states (some) flexibility to determine how they apply Convention rights in accordance with national human rights provisions and traditions.[52]

Although the principles of subsidiarity and the margin of appreciation were not explicitly included in the text of the Convention when it was drafted, both have evolved into central features of the Strasbourg human rights system through the Court's case law. The ECtHR clearly outlined its understanding of its subsidiary position in the *Belgian Linguistics* case in 1968, asserting that the Court:

> cannot assume the rôle of the competent national authorities, for it would thereby lose sight of the subsidiary nature of the international machinery of collective enforcement established by the Convention. The national authorities remain free to choose the measures which they consider appropriate in those matters which are governed by the Convention. Review by the Court concerns only the conformity of these measures with the requirements of the Convention.[53]

As for the margin of appreciation, the clearest articulation of the doctrine comes from *Handyside v United Kingdom* in 1976. Here, the Court noted that the Convention leaves 'the task of securing the rights and liberties it enshrines' to its Contracting States '[b]y reason of their direct and continuous contact with the vital forces of their countries', suggesting that national authorities are subsequently 'in principle in a better position' than the ECtHR to determine the human rights requirements within their state.[54] As with dynamic interpretation, the Court looks for European consensus when determining how wide a margin to grant to states. Where there is a clear and consistent understanding of an issue throughout national systems, the Court is less likely to tolerate state practices that fall outside the scope of that

[51] Alastair Mowbray (2015) 'Subsidiarity and the European Convention on Human Rights', *Human Rights Law Review*, 15(2): 313–41; Samantha Besson (2016) 'Subsidiarity in International Human Rights Law – What is Subsidiary about Human Rights?', *The American Journal of Jurisprudence*, 61(1): 69–107.

[52] Costa, 'On the Legitimacy of the European Court of Human Rights' Judgments', p 180; Steven Greer and Luzius Wildhaber (2013) 'Revisiting the Debate about "Constitutionalising" the European Court of Human Rights', *Human Rights Law Review*, 12(4): 674.

[53] *Case 'Relating to Certain Aspects of the Laws on the Use of Language in Education in Belgium' ('Belgian Linguistic Case')*, App no. 1474/62 (ECtHR, 23 July 1968).

[54] *Handyside v United Kingdom*, App no. 5493/72 (ECtHR 7 December 1976), para 48.

consensus. By contrast, in the absence of 'a uniform European conception of morals', the Court is much more likely to display leniency and flexibility.[55]

Crucially, though, the margin of appreciation does not give states 'an unlimited power' to apply (or neglect) the Convention as they please.[56] The Court plays a vital supervisory role, both in terms of granting wider or narrower margins in the first place, and in determining whether states' actions are compatible with the Convention. As the Court asserted in *Handyside*, the domestic margin of appreciation 'goes hand in hand with a European supervision'.[57] Likewise, the subsidiarity principle is intended to entrust the primary responsibility for upholding the Convention to national human rights protections. The ECtHR is not subsidiary to sovereign political will, but to the national judiciaries, parliaments, and public authorities with the local knowledge and experience necessary to integrate the Convention rights into their domestic structures effectively.[58] This understanding of the principle is deliberately formulated to ensure the Convention rights are protected at both the national and international levels, and to overcome the lack of state accountability for rights abuses facilitated by traditional conceptions of sovereignty by providing multiple layers of oversight.

Yet this understanding of subsidiarity and the margin of appreciation doctrine has given rise to tensions over the circumstances in which they should be applied. The ECtHR has stressed that Contracting States only enjoy the leeway to determine how to apply the Convention themselves insofar as the ECtHR agrees that they are doing so in line with European standards.[59] In this view, the ECtHR remains the ultimate authority on Convention standards, and retains the right to determine how wide a margin it will grant to states in a given case. As former President of the ECtHR, Dean Spielmann puts it, 'the margin of appreciation is something that is *allowed* to States *by the Court*'.[60] In practice, the Court is increasingly deferential to states, retreating from the expansionist path it first began to set in the 1970s. Seemingly anxious to maintain the legitimacy it garners

[55] *Handyside v United Kingdom*, para 48.

[56] *Handyside v United Kingdom*, para 49.

[57] *Handyside v United Kingdom*, para 50.

[58] Dean Spielmann (2014) 'Whither the Margin of Appreciation?', UCL Current Legal Problems Lecture, London, 20 March, p 4.

[59] *Handyside v United Kingdom*, para 49; Robert Spano (2014) 'Universality or Diversity of Human Rights? Strasbourg in the Age of Subsidiarity', *Human Rights Law Review*, 14(3): 87–502.

[60] Dean Spielmann (2013) 'Allowing the Right Margin: The European Court of Human Rights and the National Margin of Appreciation Doctrine: Waiver or Subsidiarity of European Review?', speech at the Max Planck Institute for Comparative Public Law and International Law, Heidelberg, 13 December [original emphasis].

from the support of its Contracting States, the Court has made considerably more references to the margin of appreciation in its case law since the 2012 Brighton Declaration calling for greater subsidiarity.[61] It also exhibits more judicial restraint and offers wider margins to the original member states in western Europe than to their newer, eastern counterparts,[62] a practice that plays straight into the narratives of human rights exceptionalism pushed by western European states when they try to minimize or downplay their human rights obligations.

For states, subsidiarity and the margin of appreciation are the practical expression of their autonomy. For the most part, this view has been subtler than (just) traditional understandings of sovereignty as the birthright of independent states; rather, it reflects the original aim of the Convention to maintain human rights as they are already understood and upheld within national communities. Recently, however, subsidiarity has been relied on by state governments seeking to restrict the influence of the ECtHR and limit their obligations under the ECHR. The new Protocol 15, which entered into force in August 2021, introduced an explicit reference to subsidiarity and the margin of appreciation in the Convention preamble.[63] The amendment is the product of a decade of heated debate over the meaning and application of subsidiarity. In a speech delivered in the lead up to the High Level Conference at Brighton in 2012, then-UK Prime Minister David Cameron stressed his determination to 'rebalance' the relationship between the ECtHR and states.[64] In 2018, an early draft of the declaration from the High Level Conference at Copenhagen further raised eyebrows by calling for 'better balance … based on shared responsibility' and stronger emphasis on national implementation over the 'subsidiary role of the Court'.[65] This language was toned down in the final Copenhagen Declaration, which reaffirmed the

[61] Mikael Rask Madsen (2018) 'Rebalancing European Human Rights: Has the Brighton Declaration Engendered a New Deal on Human Rights in Europe?', *Journal of International Dispute Settlement*, 9(2): 199.

[62] Janneke Gerards (2018) 'Margin of Appreciation and Incrementalism in the Case Law of the European Court of Human Rights', *Human Rights Law Review*, 18(3): 495–515; Øyvind Stiansen and Erik Voeten (2020) 'Backlash and Judicial Restraint: Evidence from the European Court of Human Rights', *International Studies Quarterly*, 64(4): 770.

[63] Council of Europe, Article 1, *Protocol No. 15 Amending the Convention on the Protection of Human Rights and Fundamental Freedoms*, Council of Europe Treaty Series No. 213, Strasbourg, 24 November 2013.

[64] David Cameron (2012) Speech on the European Court of Human Rights, delivered to the Parliamentary Assembly of the Council of Europe, 25 January. Available at: https://www.gov.uk/government/speeches/speech-on-the-european-court-of-human-rights (accessed 9 August 2017).

[65] Danish Chairmanship of the Committee of Ministers (2018) 'Draft Copenhagen Declaration', Copenhagen, 5 February.

States Parties' 'deep and abiding commitment to the Convention' and lauded the Convention system's 'extraordinary contribution to the protection and promotion of human rights and the rule of law in Europe'.[66] Meanwhile, some states have found more subtle ways to reinforce the practice of subsidiarity to their advantage by appointing judges they believe to be deferential to national autonomy.[67] Still, the emphasis on subsidiarity and rebalancing the relationship between the Court and States Parties, from Brighton to Copenhagen, has contributed to concerns among observers of the Convention system that the proposals were political manoeuvres designed to constrain the Court and reassert states as the primary arbiters of rights protections.[68] This pushback – evident from the UK to the Netherlands, Switzerland, and Denmark, to Russia[69] – has important implications for compliance, because it suggests that, as the Court continues to evolve and impose new obligations through its dynamic interpretation, it is likely to face greater resistance to complying with its judgments from some states.

Compliance with the ECtHR: obligations and procedures

State obligations under the Convention and Court

State obligations under the European human rights system begin with the general duty to uphold the rights enshrined the European Convention on Human Rights. Contracting States are obliged to 'secure to everyone within their jurisdiction the rights and freedoms defined in Section I of this Convention'.[70] However, the Convention does not specify how the

---

66 Committee of Ministers (2018b) High Level Conference: Continued Reform of the European Human Rights Convention System – Better Balance, Improved Protection, 'Copenhagen Declaration', Copenhagen, 12–13 April. See also Committee of Ministers (2012b) High Level Conference on the Future of the European Court of Human Rights, 'Brighton Declaration', Brighton, 19–20 April.

67 Stiansen and Voeten, 'Backlash and Judicial Restraint', p 771.

68 See, for instance, the speech delivered by Sir Nicolas Bratza, then-President of the ECtHR, at the opening of the Brighton Conference, in N. Bratza (2012) Council of Europe, Proceedings of the High Level Conference on the Future of the European Court of Human Rights, Brighton, 19 April, p 22.

69 Philip Leach and Alice Donald (2015) 'Russia Defies Strasbourg: Is Contagion Spreading?', *EJIL Talk!* (blog), 19 December. Available at: https://www.ejiltalk.org/russia-defies-strasbourg-is-contagion-spreading/ (accessed 30 June 2017); Janneke Gerards (2016) 'The Netherlands: Political Dynamics, Institutional Robustness', pp 327–60 and Tilmann Altwicker (2016) 'Switzerland: The Substitute Constitution in Times of Popular Dissent', pp 385–411, both in Patricia Popelier, Sarah Lambrecht, and Koen Lemmens (eds), *Criticism of the European Court of Human Rights – Shifting the Convention System: Counter-Dynamics at the National and EU Level* (Cambridge: Intersentia).

70 Article 1, ECHR.

rights contained within it must be secured, leaving Contracting States to determine how best to meet their Convention obligations in accordance with national constitutional structures and traditions. For some states, this entails incorporating the Convention rights into domestic legislation in the form of a bill of rights; for others, the Convention is signed, ratified, and obeyed according to the state's standard procedures for adopting international treaties. Although executive governments are typically responsible for signing treaties (sometimes with the permission of the national legislature), and for representing the state throughout proceedings before the ECtHR, the obligation to uphold the ECHR is considered binding on all the branches of state – executive, legislature, judiciary, as well as administrative authorities and the civil service – an obligation designed to facilitate the permeation of Convention rights throughout national human rights structures.[71] It is also worth noting that the obligations established under the Convention represent a minimum standard of human rights protection; states must uphold the Convention, but are also encouraged to provide further human rights protections domestically.[72] To this end, the general human rights obligations established by the Convention represent 'a floor, rather than a ceiling' of human rights protection.[73]

States that fail to live up to their general obligation to uphold the ECHR can be taken to the ECtHR by individuals or other states who believe their rights under the Convention have been breached. In cases where the Court finds a violation of the ECHR, the respondent state is subsequently confronted with three additional obligations. The first is to desist from the action, policy, or law causing the violation. Second, the state must restore the applicant to their situation prior to the violation or, where such restoration is not possible, to provide 'just satisfaction' – reparations, compensation, or damages.[74] The Court interprets its just satisfaction competence very broadly, and considers itself 'free to award damages whenever these are claimed by the applicant'.[75] Third, respondent states are required to undertake general

[71] Committee of Ministers (2015a) High Level Conference on the Implementation of the European Convention on Human Rights, Our Shared Responsibility, 'Brussels Declaration', 27 March; Alice Donald and Philip Leach (2016) *Parliaments and the European Court of Human Rights* (Oxford: Oxford University Press), p 24.

[72] Helen Keller and Alec Stone Sweet (eds) (2008) *A Europe of Rights: The Impact of the ECHR on National Legal Systems* (New York: Oxford University Press), p 6.

[73] David Feldman (2005) 'The Impact of the Human Rights Act 1998 on English Public Law', keynote address delivered at the conference European Influences on Public Law: 5 Years of the Human Rights Act 1998 in English Law and Recent Developments in France, British Institute of International and Comparative Law, London, 7 October, p 7.

[74] Article 41, ECHR.

[75] Tom Barkhuysen and Michiel L. van Emmerik (2005) 'A Comparative View on the Execution of Judgments of the European Court of Human Rights', in Theodora Christou

measures to prevent any repetition of the identified breach. The principle of subsidiarity allows states considerable flexibility and freedom in terms of determining how best to comply with specific ECtHR judgments, although they are expected to do so in good faith and are monitored by the Committee of Ministers.[76]

How national authorities comply with ECtHR judgments – and what is considered satisfactory compliance by both respondent states and the Committee of Ministers – therefore varies considerably, depending particularly on the circumstances of the case and the institutional structure, political and legal culture, and resources of the respondent state. However, standard measures to ensure compliance typically include legislative or policy reform, or education for relevant state authorities to facilitate cultural change and greater awareness of their practical human rights obligations. Thus, while the Strasbourg system imposes multiple obligations on its Contracting States, including both the general requirement to protect human rights as a matter of course and more specific obligations arising from individual judgments delivered by the ECtHR, these obligations are balanced with an appreciation of, and trust in, the diverse national legal systems and cultures that yield a broad range of possible legislative, policy, or procedural actions that may constitute satisfactory compliance.

Taking a case to the ECtHR

Where states fail – or are alleged to have failed – to meet their treaty obligations, the ECtHR offers individuals an additional level of legal recourse. Any state party to the ECHR or individual claiming that a Contracting State has committed a violation of the Convention against them may lodge directly with the Court an application alleging an abuse of one or more Convention rights.[77] Despite the historical reluctance of many of the Convention's founding states to accept individual applications, the right of individuals to petition the Court now represents one of the defining features of the European human rights system. Acceptance of individual petition has been compulsory for all Contracting States since the Court was made

---

and Juan Pablo Raymond (eds), *European Court of Human Rights: Remedies and Execution of Judgments* (London: British Institute of International and Comparative Law), p 4.

[76] Başak Çalı and Anne Koch (2014) 'Foxes Guarding the Foxes? The Peer Review of Human Rights Judgments by the Committee of Ministers of the Council of Europe', *Human Rights Law Review*, 14(2): 308; Donald and Leach, *Parliaments and the European Court of Human Rights*, p 25; *Scozzari and Guinta v Italy*, App nos. 39221/98 and 41963/98 (ECtHR, 13 July 2000), para 249.

[77] Article 34, ECHR.

permanent in 1998, and the Court now overwhelmingly deals with individual and nonstate group applications.

Claimants hoping to have their applications heard must meet the Court's stringent admissibility criteria, including having exhausted all available domestic remedies, submitting the application within four months of the highest domestic legal institution reaching a final decision, and not presenting a case that has already been heard by any other international tribunal.[78] The Court has the authority to waive the exhaustion of domestic remedies criterion in extenuating circumstances, particularly if taking a human rights claim to domestic courts poses a risk to the victims or their counsel, or if the domestic system suffers from severe delays.[79]

Cases that meet the admissibility threshold are assessed on their substance or 'merit' by one of three types of judicial bench. Cases related to already well-established case law are reviewed by three-judge Committees. Cases concerning novel aspects of Convention law, applications over which the Committees could not reach a unanimous decision, and all interstate cases are referred to a seven-judge Chamber, where decisions are made by a majority vote and rendered final three months after being announced.[80] During this period, the judgments and any dissenting judges' opinions are made public, and any parties to the case may appeal and refer the case to the final bench, the Grand Chamber. If the Grand Chamber hears the case, its judgment then becomes the ultimate decision on the case.

Supervision by the Committee of Ministers

The actual process of compliance – how respondent states implement individual and general measures following a judgement – is supervised by the Committee of Ministers of the Council of Europe. The Committee, which consists of the foreign ministers of the Council's member states and their deputies, or permanent ambassadors, is the primary decision-making body of the Council of Europe, responsible for drafting treaties and policies, and directing the Council's agenda. Supervising the execution of judgments is one of the core duties of the Committee, and is carried out in quarterly meetings in which the ministers or their deputies evaluate the progress of cases under their supervision. The Committee is also assisted by the Department for the Execution of Judgments of the ECHR, which provides administrative support to the Committee, and

[78] Article 35, ECHR.

[79] European Court of Human Rights (2014) *Practical Guide on Admissibility Criteria*, Strasbourg: ECtHR, p 23.

[80] Articles 29, 31, 44, ECHR.

technical expertise to member states to ensure they comply with ECtHR judgments effectively.[81]

With the assistance and guidance of the Department, states are required to submit action plans and reports to the Committee, outlining the measures they intend to take or have taken in order to meet their obligations following an adverse ruling from the ECtHR. These reports are 'key tools in the dialogue between the Committee of Ministers and the States Parties',[82] as they provide a clear, publicly available record of the steps states take to respond to judgments, as well as (sometimes) justifications for why states believe their measures constitute satisfactory compliance and the case should be closed. They enable the Committee to keep track of states' progress and to point out where improvements need to be made, while allowing states to take the primary responsibility for determining how they want to respond to the judgment.[83] To this end, the Committee of Ministers has described action plans as 'the practical expression of the principle of subsidiarity'.[84]

Since 2010, the Committee has also used a 'twin-track' approach to supervision, monitoring cases under either the standard or enhanced supervision procedure.[85] Cases which require urgent or sensitive individual measures, pilot judgments, interstate cases, cases concerning severe structural or political problems, and cases in which the respondent state has failed to submit an action plan to the Committee within six months of the final judgment are all automatically allocated to the enhanced procedure, where they are scrutinized more closely by the Committee and offered greater support from the Department until they demonstrate sufficient progress to be restored to the standard procedure or to be closed. Almost all instances of obstinacy or resistance towards compliance by states are supervised under this category.

---

81 Council of Europe (no date b) 'Presentation of the Department', Department for the Execution of Judgments of the European Court of Human Rights, Strasbourg. Available at: https://www.coe.int/en/web/execution/presentation-of-the-department (accessed 29 March 2024); Committee of Ministers (2017c) *Supervision of the Execution of Judgments and Decisions of the European Court of Human Rights 2016*, 10th Annual Report of the Committee of Ministers, Strasbourg: Committee of Ministers, p 286.

82 Committee of Ministers, Brussels Declaration, p 6.

83 Committee of Ministers (2015b) *Supervision of the Execution of Judgments and Decisions of the European Court of Human Rights 2014*, 8th Annual Report of the Committee of Ministers, Strasbourg: Committee of Ministers, p 203.

84 Committee of Ministers, *Supervision*, 8th Annual Report, p 203.

85 Committee of Ministers (2010) 'Supervision of the Execution of Judgments and Decisions of the European Court of Human Rights: Implementation of the Interlaken Action Plan – Modalities for a Twin-Track Supervision System', CM/Inf/DH(2010)37, 6 September. Available at: https://rm.coe.int/16804a327f (accessed 29 December 2017).

The Committee of Ministers depends on noncoercive and participatory social and political measures, including peer-to-peer diplomatic negotiations with the respondent state and public questioning or shaming in sessions of the Committee or the Parliamentary Assembly.[86] The limited hard mechanisms available to enforce the Convention and ECtHR rulings from above mean that, like the Court, the Committee often compromises on what we might call 'ideal' compliance standards to accept what it understands to be politically achievable.[87] Ultimately, principles such as subsidiarity and the notion that the Convention rights reflect the existing human rights structures of its (original) members mean that the system is primarily structured around the self-enforcement and consent of Contracting States. Although most members of the European human rights system are willing to uphold most of their obligations, they retain considerable leeway to determine how and when to comply. This arrangement reflects early conceptions of the Convention's role as a minimal safety net, as well as the compromises between national autonomy and international oversight struck throughout the system's history. Moreover, it means that compliance with the ECtHR is a fluid, two-way process between the European supervisory institutions and national authorities, in which the meanings of rights and the measures used to uphold them are often heavily contingent on the particular normative understandings and political preferences of national governments, legislatures, judiciaries, and civil society actors, albeit in conversation with the Court and Committee of Ministers. Intrastate dynamics, including local political and cultural understandings of the rights being complied with, are an essential component of the compliance process, as they often hold the key to understanding how state actors are likely to interpret and react to the obligations handed down by Strasbourg.

Conclusion

The European human rights system is the product of compromise. From its relatively constrained beginnings as an instrument of weak international supervision for otherwise capable states, to its current status as a central

[86] The Council of Europe can also threaten noncompliant states with expulsion, a measure it used for the first time in 2022 when Russia invaded Ukraine – not for noncompliance with the ECHR per se (though that is indeed an ongoing problem with cases against Russia) but for fundamentally violating its obligations to uphold the rule of law and guarantee human rights under Article 3 of the Statute of the Council of Europe. Committee of Ministers (2022b) Resolution CM/Res(2022)2 on the Cessation of the Membership of the Russian Federation to the Council of Europe, 16 March, 1428 meeting of the Ministers' Deputies.

[87] Dembour, *Who Believes in Human Rights?*, p 9.

component of the European constitutional landscape, the ECtHR and ECHR have been vectors for friction, contestation, and compromise over rights and norms that need protecting, and which actors are responsible for protecting them. These historical and ongoing compromises make up many of the system's legitimacy fault lines – the pressure points where ambiguity or disagreement over the best course of action (for the Court, for states, for the people whose rights are at stake) are most likely to erupt. In a system that bakes both pan-Europeanism and 'genius of diversity' into its foundational narratives, the particular trajectories the Court may take and their outcomes for human rights may be uncertain, but compromises and conflicts are inevitable. As Marie-Bénédicte Dembour puts it, 'the prima facie objective of establishing common standards while acknowledging the need to respect social diversity, means that the Court cannot but pursue a controversial path'.[88]

Two struggles in particular appear throughout the Strasbourg system's history and have significant ramifications for understanding compliance with it. The first is the evolution of the Court from its originally envisaged role as a simple oversight body with relatively weak powers of review, to an increasingly authoritative role as a quasi-constitutional court for European human rights. The originalist–activist dichotomy produced by Strasbourg's evolution is increasingly relevant to understanding the politics of compliance with ECtHR judgments, as states attempting to limit their obligations draw on arguments that the Convention was initially intended to have only a limited role in reviewing national human rights. More importantly, the Court's dynamic approach to interpretation and the creation of new applications of the Convention rights means that there is always potential for states that adopt the Convention to be confronted with new, unexpected international obligations. This evolution is significant for understanding compliance with the ECtHR, because it moves the analytical focus away from states' *ex ante* support for human rights norms that converge with existing domestic norms, towards what are often viewed as far more onerous and unexpected obligations. Contestation between states and Strasbourg over what the legitimate and acceptable meanings and uses of the Convention rights are, is therefore a central component of investigating compliance.

Second is the tension between states and the Court over who has the ultimate authority to determine the meaning and applicability of the Convention rights. As the dynamics surrounding principles such as subsidiarity and evolutive interpretation demonstrate, the particular human rights norms upheld by the Strasbourg system are fluid and often heavily contested. This contestation, and the flexibility states have to implement the

[88] Dembour, *Who Believes in Human Rights?*, p 9.

Convention and ECtHR judgments in accordance with national frameworks and traditions, creates a wide discretionary space between ideal-type compliance (efficient, effective, without resistance) and total noncompliance, in which what constitutes satisfactory or reasonable compliance can mean different things to different actors. This fluidity does not mean that compliance cannot be accurately defined or measured, but it does mean that understanding the cultural, political, and historical influences that inform contestation is essential for understanding state actors' particular decisions in response to particular obligations.

Although the history of the ECtHR demonstrates its increasing authority on matters of human rights since its inception, the interpretative and supervisory mechanisms that have been built into the Strasbourg system ultimately still grant national authorities considerable flexibility and autonomy to determine how best to protect Convention rights and comply with ECtHR judgments themselves. In this way, the notion that there can be commonly accepted principles and norms across Europe, but that the interpretation and acceptance of those norms is an inherently localized process, is ingrained in the European human rights system. Judge Ryssdal acknowledged this in 1995, noting that the Convention is 'not intended to destroy the richness of the cultural and other variety found in Europe by imposing rigid, uniform solutions', but rather recognizes 'the right of free societies, within limits, to choose for themselves the human rights policies that best suit them'.[89] Viewed through the prism of historical context and the framework for analysing the cultural politics of human rights outlined in Chapter 2 – both stressing the diversity of different actors' approaches to, and interpretations of, their compliance obligations – the dynamics between the ECtHR and its Contracting States, and thus the variations in forms of compliance across and within states, become clearer.

[89] Rolv Ryssdal (1996a) 'The Coming of Age of the European Convention on Human Rights', *European Human Rights Law Review*, 1: 25–6.

4

The United Kingdom: The Superior British Approach to Rights

In June 2015, British Prime Minister David Cameron gave a speech to mark the 800th anniversary of the signing of Magna Carta.[1] The values of 'liberty, justice, democracy, the rule of law', Cameron declared, are 'sewn into the fabric of our nation', and Britons should be all the more proud for 'the fact that they took shape right here, on the banks of the Thames'.[2] But he also warned of a modern threat to this legacy, suggesting that 'the good name of "human rights" has sometimes become distorted and devalued'. In doing so, Cameron articulated one of the core narratives underpinning the environment of increasingly mainstream Euro- and Strasbourg-scepticism that has come to shape the UK's interactions with the European Court of Human Rights (ECtHR): that the UK's approach to human rights – centuries old and steeped in local traditions and notions of exceptionalism – is inherently different from, if not outright superior to, those on the continent.

This narrative of exceptionalism holds powerful sway in the UK's cultural environment, and contributes to a political relationship with the ECtHR that ranges from 'strained'[3] or 'begrudging'[4] to openly hostile, as the UK

1 Parts of this chapter have been previously published in Zoë Jay (2017) 'Keeping Rights at Home: British Conceptions of Rights and Compliance with the European Court of Human Rights', *British Journal of Politics and International Relations*, 19(4): 842-860. Reprinted here with permission from Sage publishers.

2 David Cameron (2015) Magna Carta 800th anniversary: Prime Minister's speech, Runnymede, Surrey, 15 June. Available at: https://www.gov.uk/government/speeches/magna-carta-800th-anniversary-pms-speech (accessed 29 May 2021).

3 Katja S. Ziegler, Elizabeth Wicks, and Loveday Hodson (eds) (2015) *The UK and European Human Rights: A Strained Relationship?* (Portland: Hart Publishing), p 3.

4 Courtney Hillebrecht (2014) *Domestic Politics and International Human Rights Tribunals: The Problem of Compliance* (New York: Cambridge University Press), p 99.

grapples with competing ideas and expectations about national and European roles in the legal protection of rights. Yet, for all its fraught history with the ECtHR and with Europe, the UK continues to comply swiftly and effectively with almost all of its commitments to the Strasbourg human rights system. Despite public discourses fiercely criticizing the ECtHR for overreaching its mandate and undermining domestic legal processes, British lawyers were some of the primary architects of the European Convention on Human Rights (ECHR), and the UK has been regarded as one of the ECtHR's best role models for demonstrating how to comply with international legal obligations and protect human rights.

This chapter examines the cultural politics that shape and contest these notions of rights in the UK, and their effects on British actors' perceptions of the legitimacy of the Strasbourg system and their decisions to comply with ECtHR rulings. I argue that British discourses surrounding human rights reveal a perception that the British rights culture is distinct from the European system. This perception champions the British institutions of parliamentary sovereignty, the common law, and so-called common-sense values as the best way to uphold rights, and is built on cultural politics that (apocryphally) trace the 'British approach' to rights protection to the 1689 Bill of Rights and Magna Carta. Adherents to this view – most commonly but certainly not exclusively members of the Conservative Party and Eurosceptic press – also paint the ECtHR as 'foreign', run by judges that cannot comprehend the specific human rights needs of British society because they do not appreciate British culture. In this sense, the UK's relationship with the ECtHR is tainted by a notion that human rights are better protected at home than in Strasbourg. The cultural politics at play here incorporate a variety of principles and ideas that are at times contradictory and highly politicized. Nonetheless, the core theme that British legal institutions and traditions are unique in Europe ties together a tangible, hegemonic narrative about the British approach to rights and law that informs the UK's assessments of ECtHR judgments and European human rights norms.

The chapter demonstrates the powerful influence of British human rights cultural politics over the UK's decisions to comply with ECtHR judgments, by determining local notions of what is or is not a legitimate judgment or human rights norm. British governments and courts use ideas of a hegemonic, uniquely British rights culture and longstanding traditions to interpret and accept or reject ECtHR rulings – a process that is evident in the heated public debates and evaluations of whether the ECtHR has properly understood the nature of domestic rights issues triggered by controversial judgments. Thus the chapter explains why, and in what circumstances, UK governments and courts are willing to comply with the ECtHR. It shows that UK compliance actors are most likely to perceive ECtHR judgments as legitimate when they closely reflect British conceptions of rights and law, while noncompliance, although rare, arises when ECtHR judgments (appear to) fundamentally challenge these conceptions.

The ECHR in the British constitutional order

The UK was a founding member of the Council of Europe and played a critical role in the drafting of the European Convention on Human Rights. It signed the ECHR on 4 November 1950 and was the first state to ratify the Convention on 8 March 1951. However, it was the last of the original member states to incorporate the ECHR into domestic law, finally doing so by passing the Human Rights Act (HRA) in 1998. The HRA gives 'further effect to the rights and freedoms guaranteed under the European Convention on Human Rights', allowing British judges to interpret and apply the rights in domestic law.[5] Section 2 of the HRA also requires that UK courts 'take into account' the judgments and case law of the ECtHR.[6] This provides a mechanism by which British judges can consider, though they are not strictly bound by, the ECtHR's rulings and interpretations in British cases, and extends to the entire jurisprudence of the ECtHR, not just those cases brought against the UK. Shielded from the doctrine of implied repeal by applying to both past and future legislation, the HRA is the closest piece of legislation the UK has to a formal, permanent bill of rights, granting the ECHR a semi-entrenched position in domestic law and establishing a positive obligation on public authorities to act in a manner compatible with the ECHR.[7]

Yet, in other respects, the HRA meticulously protects the constitutional status quo. Section 19 of the HRA empowers Parliament to pass legislation that is incompatible with the Convention, provided the responsible minister publishes a statement prior to the second reading of the Bill that the government is aware of the incompatibility and 'nevertheless wishes the House to proceed with the Bill'.[8] This provision helps to preserve Parliament's status as the sovereign law-making institution, a role it has fulfilled since the 1689 Bill of Rights reaffirmed the 'ancient rights and liberties' that first placed limitations on the English monarchy.[9] The provision also serves as an important safeguard against surreptitious derogations from the UK's Convention obligations by requiring the government to demonstrate its awareness of the consequences of its actions for human rights. In other

5 Human Rights Act 1998.
6 Human Rights Act 1998, s2(1).
7 Human Rights Act 1998, s6.
8 Human Rights Act 1998, s19(b).
9 Bill of Rights 1689 (England), 1 William and Mary Sess 2, chapter 2.

words, this clause guarantees what one architect of the HRA, Lord Irvine, describes as 'an informed consent on the part of Parliament' by ensuring that 'it will not legislate incompatibly with the Convention, without being absolutely clear that it is doing so'.[10]

UK courts are likewise required to interpret all legislation in a manner compatible with the Convention 'so far as it is possible to do'.[11] Where it is not possible, the courts may make a 'declaration of incompatibility', which serves as a (nonbinding) notification to Parliament that a law is incongruent with one or more Convention rights.[12] This mechanism granted the judiciary new powers to declare statutory law incompatible with the Convention (if not outright 'unconstitutional') and to invite Parliament to review the legislation, while leaving Parliamentary sovereignty intact by keeping the responsibility to decide whether and how to overturn or amend the legislation within Parliament. Thus, the ECHR's status in UK law – through the HRA – represents a delicate compromise between opening the legal system to more direct enforcement of precise, written rights and international law, and maintaining the existing constitutional hierarchy with Parliament at the top.

The UK human rights cultural context: a 'British approach' to rights

Political constitutionalism and the distinctiveness of British institutions

The institutions, traditions, and narratives that constitute the UK's human rights cultural context contribute to a powerful overarching sense that there is a uniquely British approach to protecting rights. This belief operates on three levels. First, there are a number of institutional differences between the UK and Strasbourg legal systems. The UK's unwritten constitutional customs, implied rights, parliamentary sovereignty, and the common law all contrast sharply with the specific, codified rights of the ECHR, and the relatively strong powers of judicial review and civil law-style practices of the Strasbourg court and continental national judiciaries. The ECtHR also differs structurally from the British judiciary in its dynamic approach to legal interpretation, developed to ensure that the Convention is a 'living instrument' that is applied flexibly over time as new rights and circumstances arise.[13] The common law system's focus on the precise letter of the law of

10 Lord Irvine (2003) 'The Impact of the Human Rights Act; Parliament, the Courts and the Executive', *Public Law*, Summer: 311.

11 Human Rights Act 1998, s3.

12 Human Rights Act 1998, s4.

13 *Tyrer v United Kingdom*, App no. 5856/72 (ECtHR, 25 April 1975), para 31.

statutory legislation and pragmatic, grounded case interpretation contrasts with the ECtHR's broad interpretation of the 'spirit' of legal texts, once described by a member of the British delegation to the ECtHR during the *Golder v United Kingdom* case as 'a European way of thinking' that 'construe[s] texts in the "continental", not the common law manner'.[14]

What matters here is not that British institutions are distinct from European institutions per se, but that they are centred around a tradition of political, rather than legal, constitutionalism.[15] British institutions function differently because they reflect a different set of principles about how politics, law, and rights should interact. This distinction exists both in the actual nature of British institutions, and in the way they are perceived by Britons, perpetuating a cycle of ideas about how British constitutional principles have evolved and are applied. First among these principles is the doctrine of parliamentary sovereignty: the idea that Parliament holds 'the right to make or unmake any law whatever'[16] and that no other institution can overrule Parliament. Likewise, the common law is grounded in the notion that law should be flexible and responsive to evolving social needs, but – unlike the legal constitutionalist systems of Europe, with entrenched rights and strong judicial review – ultimately should be applied on a pragmatic case-by-case basis, and tempered by the sovereign, democratically representative Parliament.[17]

The significance of parliamentary sovereignty and a deferential judiciary corresponds to a conception of rights as political constructs. The meanings, applicability, and limits of rights are inherently contestable, so it is essential that their affirmation in law occurs in the democratic Parliament, rather than the less accountable judiciary.[18] Thus, for British political constitutionalists, the idea of rights being determined primarily by courts rather than Parliament

---

[14] William Dale (1976) 'Human Rights in the United Kingdom: International Standards', *International and Comparative Law Quarterly*, 25(2): 302.

[15] Richard Bellamy (2007) *Political Constitutionalism: A Republican Defence of the Constitutionality of Democracy* (New York: Cambridge University Press); John A.G. Griffith (1979) 'The Political Constitution', *Modern Law Review*, 42(1): 1–21; Albert V. Dicey (1915) *Introduction to the Study of the Law of the Constitution* (8th edn, London: Macmillan); Graham Gee and Grégoire Webber (2013) 'Rationalism in Public Law', *Modern Law Review*, 76(4): 708–34.

[16] Dicey, *Introduction to the Study of the Law of the Constitution*, p 38.

[17] Lord Neuberger (2016) 'Has the Identity of the English Common Law Been Eroded by EU Laws and the European Convention on Human Rights?', speech at the National University of Singapore, 18 August, p 3. Available at: https://www.supremecourt.uk/docs/speech-160818-01.pdf (accessed 3 July 2017); Ian Leigh and Roger Masterman (2008) *Making Rights Real: The Human Rights Act in its First Decade* (Portland, OR: Hart Publishing), p 8.

[18] Griffith, 'The Political Constitution', p 18; Alison Young (2005) 'A Peculiarly British Protection of Human Rights?', *Modern Law Review*, 68(5): 859.

is, in Lord Neuberger's words, 'little short of offensive to [British] notions of constitutional propriety'.[19] This dynamic is also apparent in the fact that, prior to the creation of a separate Supreme Court in 2009, the highest British court – the Lords of Appeal in Ordinary – sat within the House of Lords. Whereas continental legal systems tend to have more distinct separations of powers, the judiciary and executive in the UK have traditionally been fused together within the Parliament. Consequently, the British Parliament has historically represented a particularly strong source of power, uniquely equipped to oversee the constitutional rights of the British people relative to the executive and judiciary. This structure instils a scepticism towards courts as arbiters of rights, especially courts perceived as having strong powers of review, a perception that is evident in repeated criticisms by members of parliament that the ECtHR overreaches its mandate, and in calls to 'restore' parliamentary sovereignty by limiting the powers of the ECtHR.

The emphasis on rights being provided on an 'as needed' basis by Parliament and the common law further reflects what is arguably a distinctly British tradition of negative liberty, whereby British citizens intrinsically possess rights and freedoms, unless explicit limitations are imposed through statute or common law. Thus, as Lord Brown-Wilkinson asserts:

> Basic constitutional rights in this country such as freedom of the person and freedom of speech are not based upon any express provision conferring such a right but on freedom of an individual to do what he will save to the extent that he is prevented from doing so by the law. … These fundamental freedoms therefore are not positive rights but an immunity from interference by others.[20]

This conception of rights as an inherent possession of British citizens, or – where they must be specified – as determined by the representative Parliament and flexible, pragmatic common law, is an important distinction that helps to explain resistance to the explicit enumeration of rights through entrenched constitutional law, or in the case of the ECHR through international treaty law. Thus British institutions reflect – and reproduce – a cultural context that frames rights as political, rather than legal, constructs, emphasizing Parliament as the primary creator of rights, and privileging a flexible, adaptable approach to their evolution over the (seemingly) more static entrenchment of rights in formal constitutions.

---

[19] Lord Neuberger (2014) 'The British and Europe', Cambridge Freshfields Annual Lecture, Cambridge, 12 February. Available at: https://www.supremecourt.uk/docs/speech-140212.pdf (accessed 3 July 2017).

[20] *Wheeler v Leicester CC* [1985] AC 1054, 1065.

The rights mythology

On the second level, a mythology has been built around the British legal system that frames the British approach to human rights as unique in Europe. This is an especially powerful component of contemporary memory and national identity politics in the UK because it paints the British rights tradition as ancient, intrinsically guaranteed to British citizens, and, most importantly, the source of modern principles of parliamentary democracy and the rule of law. The notion that the UK is a 'rights entrepreneur', exporting British legal innovations, rather than importing ideas from elsewhere, underpins how the UK believes rights should be protected through law, and thus how it interprets international legal norms.

Magna Carta especially has garnered a mythical status in the UK as the foundation of a now 800-year-old tradition of protecting rights and freedoms through law. The actual legal protection of rights by Magna Carta is contested; many of its original provisions have been repealed and bear little resemblance to modern human rights.[21] Nonetheless, historical events and constitutional documents such as the 1688 Glorious Revolution and Bill of Rights, and the development of principles such as the writ of habeus corpus contribute to a narrative of continuous rights protection, suggesting that the UK 'has always been a beacon for liberty and democracy'.[22] To this end, the belief that Magna Carta established the first rights of individuals against their sovereign is an important part of British – especially English – identity and public narrative, and is crucial for understanding how longstanding many Britons believe their legal and human rights traditions are.

Political discourses demanding a need to 'restore common sense'[23] to human rights in the UK further contribute to the British rights mythos. Politicians' references to common sense when discussing human rights suggest that the way rights were protected in the UK before the ECHR – through gradual development in common law and Parliament, and with a focus on individual, negative liberties – was 'right' or 'sensible', while casting the European alternative as ridiculous. Former Prime Minister David Cameron used the phrase regularly to imply that there are limits to how far rights extend, especially for criminals and terrorists, who are perceived as having

[21] Lord Dyson (2015) 'Delay Too Often Defeats Justice', speech at The Law Society, London, 22 April; Colin Murray (2018) 'Magna Carta's Tainted Legacy: Historic Justifications for a British Bill of Rights and the Case Against the Human Rights Act', in Frederick Cowell (ed), *Critically Examining the Case Against the 1998 Human Rights Act* (Abingdon: Routledge), pp 36–8.

[22] Lord Faulks, Hansard (2016) HL Deb, 24 May 2016, vol 733, col 281.

[23] Conservative Party (2015) *The Conservative Party Manifesto* (London: Conservative Party), p 73.

violated the rights of others.[24] But suggestions that there are common-sense ways of handling human rights appear across the political spectrum: former Labour Home Secretary and one of the architects of the Human Rights Act, Jack Straw, praised the ECtHR for 'an outbreak of common sense' when it denied compensation to applicants in prisoner voting cases, implying that such sense was usually lacking in the Court's rulings.[25] Common sense also has a deeper meaning in England, as a philosophical tradition dating back to the Victorian and Enlightenment eras that is wary of the abstract theories and ideologies advocated by continental and Scottish intellectuals, preferring instead the gradual development of ideas and institutions through historical experience, as well as through plain language and pragmatic, applied reasoning.[26] This notion of common sense mirrors the nature of British political and legal institutions, which have evolved through convention and experience. It also implies the pragmatic application of 'plain facts' and reason to produce 'standard' or literal interpretations of the law – a practice that is evident in common law judges' reluctance to establish broad legal principles.[27] In this view, the ECtHR's broad interpretations of the Convention are seen as too generalized to be practical, entitling the ECtHR to engage in judicial activism that imposes on the independence of national authorities. The concept of common sense therefore serves both a rhetorical function and a broader, mythical function. It ties rights to a sense of duty or responsibility, as well as to the view that rights are political constructs subject to the values of the society in which they are created. But its use also harks back to a specific tradition and way of doing things that is inextricable from a sense that Britain is unique in Europe.

---

[24] David Cameron, Hansard (2013b) HC Deb, 16 Oct 2013, vol 568, col 736; Tom McTague (2014) 'Tory Plans to Shackle Human Rights Judges REJECTED by Europe, Leaving Britain's Membership of Court Hanging by a Thread', *Daily Mail,* 3 October. Available at: https://www.dailymail.co.uk/news/article-2779401/Tory-plans-shackle-European-human-rights-judges-REJECTED-Strasbourg-court-row-intensifies.html (accessed 8 February 2017); Tom Utley (2005) 'We Need Common Sense and Justice – not "Human Rights"', *Telegraph*, 4 March. Available at: http://www.telegraph.co.uk/comment/columnists/tomutley/3615318/We-need-common-sense-and-justice-not-human-rights.html (accessed 9 May 2016).

[25] Owen Bowcott (2015) 'Strasbourg Court has Backed Off over Rights Rulings, says Jack Straw', *Guardian*, 21 May. Available at: https://www.theguardian.com/law/2015/may/21/strasbourg-court-backed-off-human-rights-jack-straw (accessed 18 January 2024).

[26] Edmund Burke (1790) *Reflections on the Revolution in France* (London: Dent, Everyman's Library); Christoph Henke (2014) *Common Sense in Early 18th Century British Literature and Culture: Ethics, Aesthetics, and Politics, 1680–1750* (Berlin: De Gruyter); David Allan (2008) *Making British Culture: English Readers and the Scottish Enlightenment, 1740–1830* (New York: Routledge); Angus Hawkins (2015) *Victorian Political Culture: 'Habits of Heart and Mind'* (Oxford: Oxford University Press).

[27] Leigh and Masterman, *Making Rights Real*, p 12.

The ECHR as a British invention

Finally, the UK's prominent role as a founder of the Council of Europe and drafter of the ECHR contributes to perceptions of the Convention as a British invention. The ECHR was largely drafted by British representatives and thus closely reflects existing British rights and freedoms, as well as common law principles and practices.[28] Kenneth Younger, the Minister of State for the Foreign Office in 1950, best articulates this sentiment, noting in correspondence to the Cabinet that the final draft of the ECHR 'contains a definition of the rights and limitations thereto which follows almost word for word the actual texts proposed by the United Kingdom representatives (Articles 2–17), and which is thought to be consistent with our existing law in all but a small number of comparatively trivial cases'.[29] Despite this, the Attlee government initially opposed the creation of an international court to enforce the Convention, as well as the right of individuals to petition the court – especially before the Convention rights were finalized – lest the UK be subject to a 'blank cheque' of judicial review.[30] The government and British delegates to the Council of Europe envisioned the Convention as an international safeguard against totalitarianism, to be upheld by states themselves, and firmly resisted proposals for the Convention to become the 'European bill of rights' with international judicial oversight, as advocated by France and other continental states.[31] The UK nonetheless became the first state to ratify the Convention in 1951 and accepted the interstate (but not individual) jurisdiction of the Court in 1959 as it became clear that the other European states involved in drafting the Convention would be signing it – to avoid being 'one of an embarrassingly small minority in opposing it'.[32]

---

[28] Jesse Norman and Peter Oborne (2009) *Churchill's Legacy: The Conservative Case for the Human Rights Act* (London: Liberty).

[29] In Geoffrey Marston (1993) 'The United Kingdom's Part in the Preparation of the European Convention on Human Rights, 1950' *International and Comparative Law Quarterly*, 42(4): 811.

[30] Foreign Office 371/78936 [UNE 3567/17311/96/1949], cited in Marston, 'The United Kingdom's Part in the Preparation of the European Convention on Human Rights', p 806.

[31] Ed Bates (2010) *The Evolution of the European Convention on Human Rights: From its Inception to the Creation of a Permanent Court of Human Rights* (New York: Oxford University Press), pp 44–107; A. W. B. Simpson (2004) *Human Rights and the End of Empire: Britain and the Genesis of the European Convention* (Oxford: Oxford University Press); Elizabeth Wicks (2000) 'The United Kingdom Government's Perceptions of the European Convention on Human Rights at the Time of Entry', *Public Law*, Autumn: 442–4.

[32] Foreign Office, in Marston, 'The United Kingdom's Part in the Preparation of the European Convention on Human Rights', p 812.

Nonetheless, a sense of distrust of an international court with an expansive jurisdiction and strong review powers has persisted throughout the UK's membership in the ECHR system. Selective renewal of the Convention's optional clauses and the Court's jurisdiction prior to 1998 served as a key opportunity for the UK to remind the ECtHR that the UK itself retained control over which laws would take effect within its jurisdiction.[33] Likewise, attempts by the Heath (Conservative), Wilson, and Callaghan (Labour) governments in the 1970s, in cases such as *Golder v United Kingdom* and *The Sunday Times v United Kingdom*, to limit the scope of the ECtHR and retain national control over human rights issues largely backfired. The Court's rulings in these cases expanded its interpretational capabilities and established much tighter control over when respondent states could apply the margin of appreciation.[34] Thus, although these are landmark cases in the evolution of the ECtHR, they also contributed to notions within the UK that human rights were better protected at home than in Strasbourg.

More recently, the view that ECHR rights originated, and are better protected, in the UK manifested in the decision to incorporate the ECHR into domestic law in the late 1990s. Despite being one of the first states to sign and ratify the Convention in 1950–51, the UK was the last of the original signatories to integrate the Convention into domestic law. The shift in favour of incorporation occurred as judges and legal scholars became increasingly concerned during the 1980s and 1990s that the common law was failing to adequately protect human rights and the ECtHR was finding the UK in violation of the Convention in a growing number of cases. The Thatcher and Major governments remained committed to the position that the common law was sufficient, and criticized Labour's calls for an entrenched bill of rights or incorporation of the ECHR on the grounds that it 'would risk transferring power away from parliament to legal courts – undermining the democratic supremacy of parliament as representatives of the people' – and consequently would not be 'appropriate to the UK'.[35]

Yet when the Blair government came to power in 1997 on the promise of grand constitutional reforms, incorporation of the ECHR in 1998 through the Human Rights Act was advocated as an opportunity to 'bring rights home' and grant Britons greater control over how the Convention affects

---

33 Bates, *The Evolution of the European Convention on Human Rights*, p 316.

34 *Golder v United Kingdom*, App no. 4451/70 (ECtHR, 21 February 1975); *The Sunday Times v United Kingdom*, App no. 6538/74 (ECtHR, 26 April 1979).

35 Conservative Party (1997) *Conservative Party Manifesto 1997* (London: Conservative Party). Available at: http://www.conservativemanifesto.com/1997/1997-conservative-manifesto.shtml (accessed 31 July 2016).

British law.[36] Labour members of parliament Jack Straw and Paul Boateng argued that incorporation would 'repatriate British rights to British courts' by allowing British citizens to access the rights they have possessed under the ECHR since 1950 within the domestic legal system, and by enabling judges to develop 'a body of case law on the Convention which is properly sensitive to British legal and constitutional traditions'.[37] In other words, the HRA would give Britons access to rights that were essentially 'British', rather than 'European'.

The Blair government released a White Paper in 1997 entitled *Rights Brought Home: The Human Rights Bill* to advocate for the incorporation of the ECHR into domestic law. The paper argued that incorporating the ECHR would open up a dialogue between British courts and the ECtHR, noting that although 'United Kingdom judges have a very high reputation internationally … the fact that they do not deal in the same concepts as the European Court of Human Rights limits the extent to which their judgments can be drawn upon and followed'.[38] Incorporation would therefore grant British judges greater scrutiny and interpretive power over the application of Convention rights in the UK, and in turn enable British judges 'to make a distinctively British contribution to the development of the jurisprudence of human rights in Europe' through the creation of British human rights case law and dialogue with the ECtHR.[39] Giving the ECHR direct effect in UK law would both enable British governments and courts to retain sovereignty over human rights issues, and to more effectively influence how, and in what circumstances, Convention rights would evolve and be applied in the UK and Europe. Incorporation therefore marks an important point in the UK–Strasbourg relationship, as it demonstrates that, even among advocates of the ECHR, there is a sense that 'British' rights and law are intrinsically superior to 'European' rights, and that incorporation could be used to strengthen the influence of British judges relative to that of Strasbourg.

Combined, the above elements – distinct institutions and constitutional traditions, the ancient rights and liberties narrative, and sense of ownership over the ECHR – imply that the rights guaranteed under British law are more extensive and appropriately applied than those provided for by the ECHR, producing a sense that Britain does not need European

---

[36] Jack Straw and Paul Boateng (1997) 'Bringing Rights Home: Labour's Plans to Incorporate the European Convention on Human Rights into UK Law', *European Human Rights Law Review*, 1: 71.

[37] Straw and Boateng, 'Bringing Rights Home', p 72.

[38] Home Office (1997) *Rights Brought Home: The Human Rights Bill* (London: The Stationery Office), p 8.

[39] Home Office, *Rights Brought Home*, p 7.

rights protections, as the British rights culture is what informed the European system in the first place. As former Prime Minister John Major ostentatiously put it: 'we have no need of a Bill of Rights because we have freedom'.[40] The perception that the UK has a unique, coherent rights culture has also generated assumptions that only British lawmakers can truly understand British law. Lord Irvine argues that Britons 'should trust our own judges to reach a "better" answer' than Strasbourg, because 'it is our own Judges who are embedded in our culture and society and so are best placed to strike the types of balance between the often competing rights and interests which adjudication under the HRA requires'.[41] Such views permeate both Labour and Conservative governments', as well as the judiciary's, interactions with the ECtHR, and have a significant impact on how compliance actors in the UK perceive and decide to comply with ECtHR judgments by contributing to beliefs that 'British rights' are more legitimate than 'European rights'. Further, they create a peculiar dynamic wherein many politicians and judges claim great ownership over the Convention and are eager to promote norms that reflect their own interpretations of the meanings of rights and law, but are deeply reluctant to have new interpretations of those same norms imposed on the UK from outside. This paradox is apparent in both Britain's judicial and political relationships with Strasbourg, highlighting the strength of the 'British approach' narrative's influence on local cultural politics and on how British actors perceive and interact with Strasbourg.

Human rights in the devolved nations

The notion of a British approach to human rights advocated in state-level political discourses is complicated by the distinct cultures and legal systems of the separate nations within the United Kingdom, particularly since devolution was implemented across the UK at the turn of the millennium. Scotland and Northern Ireland in particular have very different experiences with the ECHR rights and HRA within their devolved jurisdictions. The Scottish, Northern Irish, and Welsh governments and parliaments are required to comply with the Convention rights, which are expressly included in their respective devolution agreements.[42] The devolved legislatures do not possess the privilege of parliamentary sovereignty or the power to make declarations

40 John Major (1996) Speech on British Constitution, Centre for Policy Studies, London, 26 June.

41 Lord Irvine (2011) 'A British Interpretation of Convention Rights?', University College London Judicial Institute Lecture, London, 14 December.

42 Northern Ireland Act 1998 s6(2)(c) and 24(1)(a); Scotland Act 1998 s29(2)(d) and 57(2); Government of Wales Act 2006 s81(1) and 94(6)(c).

of incompatibility, meaning that they cannot legislate or enact policy contrary to the HRA. Moreover, the Scottish and Northern Irish courts have the power to strike down noncompliant laws produced by the devolved authorities. The Convention rights are therefore permanently entrenched in the devolved legal systems, and function much more like a traditional constitutional restraint on the devolved parliaments and governments. This has produced a vastly different approach to judicial scrutiny of human rights legislation in the devolved nations to that undertaken in English and national courts – one based more on principles of legal constitutionalism and the supremacy of courts than the English tradition in which Parliament has the last word.[43]

The dynamics that stem from the English traditions of political constitutionalism and the absolute sovereignty of Parliament are not present in Scotland, where the legal system more closely resembles European-style entrenched rights and strong judicial review. The Northern Ireland legal system may have more in common with the English (and Irish) common law traditions, but the HRA is entrenched through the Northern Ireland Act 1998 as well as the 1998 Belfast (Good Friday) Agreement.[44] Rather than generating perceptions of human rights frameworks undercutting prior traditions, then, the HRA and ECHR are crucial for maintaining the delicate peace process in Northern Ireland. Likewise, many of the mythologies that contribute to the modern 'British' rights culture are bound up in notions of English nationalism and identity, and do not hold the same sway in Scottish and Irish history; Magna Carta and the 1689 Bill of Rights are English texts, drafted to place limitations on English monarchs long before the Acts of Union brought the Kingdom of Scotland into the United Kingdom in 1707, and whose principles conflict with the denial of rights and independence to Ireland for centuries under English rule.[45]

To this end, the 'British' approach to human rights resonates much more closely with 'Englishness' and English national identity. Public and political perceptions of the European human rights system and the HRA, as well as of the respective roles of political and judicial institutions in protecting rights, reflect different and additional histories and experiences with rights in the devolved nations. Multiple political and academic inquiries into human rights in the UK have identified much stronger levels of support

---

43 Aidan O'Neill (2006) '"Stands Scotland Where it Did?": Devolution, Human Rights and the Scottish Constitution Seven Years On', *Northern Ireland Legal Quarterly*, 57(1): 106.

44 European Union Committee (2016) *The UK, the EU and a British Bill of Rights: 12th Report of Session 2015–16*, HL Paper 139 (London: House of Lords), pp 44–7; Belfast Agreement 1998.

45 Conor Gearty (2016) *On Fantasy Island: Britain, Europe, and Human Rights* (Oxford: Oxford University Press), p 201.

for the HRA and ECtHR in Scotland, Wales, and Northern Ireland than in England, while the plans of successive Conservative governments since Cameron's premiership to repeal or replace the HRA across the UK have been met with firm resistance from the leaders of the devolved governments, particularly from the Scottish National Party.[46] These differences illustrate the patchwork nature of the cultural politics of rights in the UK, highlighting the influence different historical experiences and legal structures can have over perceptions of the legitimacy of particular human rights structures and meanings within the UK. Nonetheless, politicians in Westminster regularly speak in terms of a universal 'British' rights culture, articulating homogenized conceptions of British national identity and values to inform and justify their interactions with Strasbourg and their compliance with its obligations.

Cultural politics in action: the UK's relationship with Strasbourg

The judicial relationship

The relationship between the UK's domestic courts – particularly the Supreme Court, or House of Lords prior to 2009 – and the ECtHR is a key source of the UK's sense of a distinctly British approach to the interpretation and application of human rights. Prior to the incorporation of the ECHR into domestic law, British judges were not compelled to apply the Convention or case law from the ECtHR in their proceedings. The influence of the Convention on UK human rights protections was largely indirect, stemming from the government's responses to ECtHR cases.[47] Where the Convention was applied directly by British judges, the applications were often limited, and only used to clarify ambiguous legislation. In *R v Secretary of State for the Home Department, Ex parte Brind*, for example, the House of Lords acknowledged that where a provision in domestic legislation has a meaning that may either conform to or conflict

[46] Commission on a Bill of Rights (2012) *A UK Bill of Rights?: The Choice Before Us*, vol. 1 (London: Ministry of Justice), pp 15 and 18; European Union Committee, *The UK, the EU and a British Bill of Rights*, pp 40–8; Jane Gordon (2010) 'A Developing Human Rights Culture in the UK? Case Studies of Policing' *European Human Rights Law Review*, 6: 612–13; Jon Stone (2015) 'Scottish Government will Block Human Rights Act Repeal for the Whole UK, says Nicola Sturgeon', *Independent*, 23 September. Available at: http://www.independent.co.uk/news/uk/politics/scottish-government-will-block-human-rights-act-repeal-for-the-whole-uk-says-nicola-sturgeon-10514015.html (accessed 11 August 2017).

[47] Samantha Besson (2008) 'The Reception Process in Ireland and the United Kingdom', in Helen Keller and Alec Stone Sweet (eds), *A Europe of Rights: The Impact of the ECHR on National Legal Systems* (New York: Oxford University Press), p 33.

with the ECHR, the courts will presume that Parliament intended the legislation to conform with the UK's international treaty obligations, establishing a built-in understanding that the UK and its courts anticipate compliance with international law as a general principle.[48] Nonetheless, the Lords argued that this general principle did not apply to *Brind*, asserting that the ECHR right to freedom of expression did not need to be considered in that case, as the applicants claimed, as it was not then part of English law and its application would have been beyond the scope of the English courts' obligation to consider the ECHR.[49] Indeed, English judges rarely applied the Convention directly in the pre-HRA era. As research by Francesca Klug and (then barrister, currently Prime Minister) Keir Starmer reveals, of the 316 cases in which the ECHR was cited in English courts between 1975 and 1996, the Convention influenced the interpretation of legislation in just 11 cases, highlighting the minimal and narrow application of Convention rights in domestic law prior to incorporation.[50]

Interactions between UK courts and the ECtHR have increased substantially since incorporation, especially due to the requirement under section 2 of the HRA that courts 'take into account' the case law of the ECtHR.[51] This extends to the entire jurisprudence of the ECtHR, not just cases brought against the UK. However, it does not oblige domestic courts to follow judgments of the ECtHR. Rather, courts are required to consider relevant judgments in the same way that they consider pertinent domestic case law under the common law rules of statutory interpretation. As Lord Irvine asserts, '"take account of" is not the same as … "be bound by"', emphasizing Parliament's deliberate choice to maintain the independence of British courts.[52] Judges do sometimes divert from Strasbourg jurisprudence to apply alternative interpretations that more appropriately reflect British legal principles, particularly when Strasbourg has only limited relevant case law on an issue.[53] For the most part, however, judges generally accept the notion that although ECtHR case law is 'not strictly binding', UK courts should nevertheless, 'in the absence of some special circumstances, follow clear and constant jurisprudence of the Strasbourg court'.[54] This indicates that, despite provisions for retaining parliamentary sovereignty and national control over human rights decisions, UK courts have generally expressed

48 *R v Secretary of State for the Home Department, Ex parte Brind* [1991] 1 AC 696 (HL).

49 *R v Secretary of State for the Home Department, Ex parte Brind* [1991] 1 AC 696 (HL).

50 Francesca Klug and Keir Starmer (1997) 'Incorporation Through the Back Door?' *Public Law*, Summer: 223–33.

51 Human Rights Act 1998, s2.

52 Irvine, 'A British Interpretation of Convention Rights?', p 3.

53 *R (Quila) v Secretary of State for the Home Department* [2011] UKSC 45.

54 *R (Ullah) v Secretary of State for the Home Department* [2004] UKHL 26, para 20.

a desire to produce domestic law consistent with the ECHR, or at least to engage in dialogue and compromise with the ECtHR.

Recently, however, debate has emerged about whether the judiciary should 'mirror' Strasbourg judgments, or more readily diverge from Strasbourg to take its own approaches, even if this means providing a different or lesser standard of protection.[55] In *R v Horncastle*, Lord Phillips notes that where British courts are concerned that Strasbourg has not appropriately understood or accommodated domestic processes, they can 'decline to follow the Strasbourg decision'.[56] This in turn allows Strasbourg to review its interpretation in light of clarifications and justifications provided by the British courts, 'so that there takes place what may prove to be a valuable dialogue between this court and the Strasbourg Court'.[57] Lord Neuberger makes the point even more emphatically, arguing in *Manchester CC v Pinnock* that not only are British courts 'not bound to respect every decision of the [ECtHR]' but doing so 'would destroy the ability of the court to engage in the constructive dialogue with the European court which is of value to the development of Convention law'.[58]

These cases reflect a growing demand in the UK for courts to re-establish their own authority and legitimacy away from the ECtHR. For the lawyers and judges who engage regularly with Strasbourg, this is a practical step to improve British courts' ability to make useful and original contributions to the development of ECHR case law. As Lord Irvine notes, '[a] Court which subordinates itself to follow another's rulings cannot enter into a dialogue with its superior in any meaningful sense'.[59] Mimicking or predicting the exact decisions of the ECtHR all the time denies British judges the opportunity to draw on their unique experiences with law and human rights protection, which was largely the point of implementing the HRA in the first place. Yet, in the context of increasingly Strasbourg- and HRA-sceptic political and public discourses, this demand indicates that too close a relationship between UK courts and Strasbourg – even a healthy, dialogue-based relationship – undermines domestic courts' perceived independence and legitimacy. In cases where UK courts assert a margin of appreciation over an issue, or argue that the ECtHR's decision is incorrect, Merris Amos notes that the courts are perceived as having greater legitimacy than cases in which they do not, because they are defending British legal traditions from

55 Richard Clayton (2015) 'Should the English Courts under the HRA Mirror Strasbourg Case Law?', in Katja S. Ziegler, Elizabeth Wicks, and Loveday Hodson (eds) *The UK and European Human Rights: A Strained Relationship?* (Portland: Hart), pp 95–113.

56 *R v Horncastle* [2009] UKSC 14 [2010] 2 AC 373 [11].

57 *R v Horncastle* [2009] UKSC 14 [2010] 2 AC 373 [11].

58 *Manchester CC v Pinnock* [2011] UKSC 6 [48].

59 Irvine, 'A British Interpretation of Convention Rights?', p 9.

the ECtHR.[60] The shift away from the 'mirror principle' is a key illustration of British distrust of powerful judiciaries and the belief that British courts are better equipped to handle rights cases than the ECtHR, because it is the British and English courts that understand British traditions such as pragmatic legal interpretation and deference to Parliament.

The political relationship

The UK's fractious political relationship with Strasbourg reflects a number of tensions between balancing the state's international legal obligations and human rights values with democratic governance and the public interest, as well as broader concerns about the symbolism of ceding authority to a 'foreign' institution. Many of these tensions have their origin in the determination of the government and Foreign Office in the 1950s that, as an unincorporated international treaty, the ECHR should have little influence in Britain, save where the government expressly welcomed it.[61] Yet, as the Court's jurisdiction gradually expanded, the UK became embroiled in significantly more cases than it anticipated, setting off a historical resentment towards Strasbourg's apparently excessive intervention in British affairs.

This resentment has intensified over time. Since the introduction of the HRA, many in the UK have vehemently opposed decisions made by the ECtHR – especially those pertaining to national security or which (appear to) expand the power and influence of the ECtHR. The media – most frequently and sensationally, but not exclusively, Eurosceptic tabloids – often insinuate that British institutions, especially Parliament, and traditional British civil liberties and 'common sense' are under siege from human rights laws that allow criminals and terrorists to make spurious rights claims to avoid punishment.[62] MPs draw on these narratives to reinforce the supremacy of Parliament and to attempt to justify noncompliance. Former Home Secretary

[60] Merris Amos (2012) 'The Dialogue between United Kingdom Courts and The European Court of Human Rights', *International and Comparative Law Quarterly*, 61(3): 576.

[61] Bates, *The Evolution of the European Convention on Human Rights*, pp 114–18; Ed Bates (2012) 'British Sovereignty and the European Court of Human Rights', *Law Quarterly Review*, 128(July): 385; Marston, 'The United Kingdom's Part in the Preparation of the European Convention on Human Rights', pp 822–3. Later, the fact that the ECtHR had only reviewed a handful of cases in its initial years, and thus appeared to have minimal influence, played an important hand in the British government being convinced to accept the Court's jurisdiction in 1966. Lord Lester (1998) 'UK Acceptance of the Strasbourg Jurisdiction: What Really Went on in Whitehall in 1965', *Public Law*, Summer: 237–53.

[62] David Mead (2015) '"You Couldn't Make It Up": Some Narratives of the Media's Coverage of Human Rights', in Katja S. Ziegler, Elizabeth Wicks, and Loveday Hodson (eds), *The UK and European Human Rights: A Strained Relationship?* (Portland: Hart), pp 467–70.

Theresa May's claim that the ECtHR's 'crazy interpretation of our human rights laws' prevented the UK from deporting a terror suspect to Jordan is a key example.[63] Likewise, following the infamous prisoner voting case, *Hirst v United Kingdom (no. 2)*, headlines in tabloids like *The Sun* such as 'Prison Paedos "Will Get Vote"' and then-Prime Minister Cameron's assertion that 'if Parliament decides that prisoners should not get the vote then I think they damn well shouldn't' helped to create the impression that Strasbourg imposes its rulings on Britain at will, without considering the practical implications for Britons or understanding British law.[64] These claims are so widespread and recognizable that the actor Patrick Stewart lampooned the idea that the ECtHR threatens 'the very essence of our Britishness' in the Monty Python-inspired sketch, 'What has the ECHR Ever Done for Us?', referring to rights to a fair trial, freedom from slavery, and freedom from torture among others to remind the British public of the value of the Convention.[65] Nonetheless, even with pushback from supporters of the ECHR, critics' claims of exceptionalism play on both perceived and real differences between British and European law, serving not only to delegitimize the ECtHR's rulings, but also to legitimize defiance or minimization of the UK's international legal obligations as a necessary bulwark against European interference in longstanding national practices and traditions.

Resentment towards Strasbourg is further complicated by the fact that the ECtHR is often discussed and reported on inaccurately. The tabloid press, in particular, regularly conflates concerns about the Convention system with concerns about other European issues and the EU.[66] This conflation ties the Strasbourg Court to the perceived democratic illegitimacy of the EU and to the more extensive scope of EU regulations, creating the impression that Strasbourg rulings are much more frequent and are enforced with much greater institutional power than they actually are. The UK's withdrawal from the EU has only exacerbated this confusion, sparking debate about

---

63 Alan Travis (2013) 'Theresa May Criticises Human Rights Convention after Abu Qatada Affair', *Guardian*, 9 July. Available at: http://www.theguardian.com/world/2013/jul/08/theresa-may-human-rights-abu-qatada (accessed 9 May 2016).

64 Craig Woodhouse (2012) 'Prison Paedos "Will Get Vote"', *Sun*, 23 December, p 2; *Guardian* (2013) 'Prisoners "Damn Well Shouldn't" be Given Right to Vote, says David Cameron', *Guardian*, 14 December. Available at: http://www.theguardian.com/politics/2013/dec/13/prisoners-right-to-vote-david-cameron (accessed 9 May 2016).

65 *Guardian* (2016) 'Patrick Stewart: What has the ECHR Ever Done for Us? – Video', *Guardian*, 25 April. Available at: https://www.theguardian.com/culture/video/2016/apr/25/patrick-stewart-sketch-what-has-the-echr-ever-done-for-us-video (accessed 23 January 2024).

66 Zoë Jay (2022) 'A Tale of Two Europes: How Conflating the European Court of Human Rights with the European Union Exacerbates Euroscepticism', *British Journal of Politics and International Relations*, 24(4): 563–81.

how Brexit will affect human rights and whether Britain should renegotiate its position with Strasbourg as well.[67] This in turn fuels public opposition to intervention in British political issues by an international court, and is a key factor in understanding why politicians often claim to be aggrieved by Strasbourg rulings.

Tensions in the relationship between UK political actors and the ECtHR have worsened drastically since the mid-2010s. Alongside the infamous proposal in 2015 to offer a referendum on British membership in the EU, the Cameron government pushed a parallel plan to 'scrap Labour's Human Rights Act and introduce a British Bill of Rights which will restore common sense to the application of human rights in the UK'.[68] The plan built on the argument that the HRA requirement for British judges to 'take into account' ECtHR decisions has resulted in UK courts going to 'artificial lengths to change the meaning of legislation so that it complies with [the ECtHR's] interpretation of the Convention rights', and therefore undermines British judges' capacity to come to their own interpretations based on 'British' – rather than 'European' – definitions of rights and law.[69] The original plan also reflects the paradox of claiming ownership over the text of the ECHR yet resenting non-British interpretations of it; the policy document emphasizes the party's commitment to 'remain faithful to the basic principles of human rights' in the original ECHR, while reversing Strasbourg's and the HRA's so-called 'mission creep that has meant human rights laws being used for more and more purposes'.[70]

Since leaving the EU in 2020, Conservatives and the Eurosceptic press have returned to zealously targeting the HRA and ECHR for thwarting various harebrained government schemes, from blocking life sentences without judicial review, to former Prime Minister Rishi Sunak's (unsuccessful)

[67] Will Worley (2016) 'Theresa May "Will Campaign to Leave the European Convention on Human Rights in 2020 Election"', *Independent*, 29 December. Available at: http://www.independent.co.uk/news/uk/politics/theresa-may-campaign-leave-european-convention-on-human-rights-2020-general-election-brexit-a7499951.html (accessed 20 January 2017); Anushka Asthana and Rowena Mason (2016) 'UK Must Leave European Convention on Human Rights, says Theresa May', *Guardian*, 26 April. Available at: https://www.theguardian.com/politics/2016/apr/25/uk-must-leave-european-convention- on-human-rights-theresa-may-eu-referendum (accessed 20 January 2017); Patrick Christys (2017) 'British Bill of Rights Shelved as Country "Can't Handle" Even More Constitutional Change', *Express*, 25 February. Available at: http://www.express.co.uk/news/uk/771924/EU-Human-Rights-Act-Brexit-Artic-Britain-Theresa-May-Liz-Truss-politics-Brexit-Article-50 (accessed 26 February 2017).

[68] Conservative Party, *Conservative Party Manifesto 2015*, p 73.

[69] Conservative Party (2014) *Protecting Human Rights in the UK: The Conservatives' Proposal for Changing Britain's Human Rights Laws* (London: Conservative Party), p 4.

[70] Conservative Party, *Conservative Party Manifesto 2015*, p 73.

attempts to deport so-called 'illegal migrants' to Rwanda. Unable to present a version of the Rwanda scheme that would be compatible with the ECHR (not to mention any of the UK's other international legal obligations), Sunak vowed to 'disapply' the Convention, labelling the ECtHR a 'foreign' rather than international court to cast it as an illegitimate voice in the UK's ongoing debates about migration.[71] The House of Lords and Supreme Court have quashed this and other attempts by Conservative governments to skirt their international legal obligations, but the rhetorical damage is done. The evolution from Cameron's proposal to replace the HRA with a homegrown British bill of rights and to reform the Strasbourg system, to more forceful demands from May and Sunak to withdraw from or ignore the ECHR with nothing to replace it, shows how the same cultural tools can be used to shift and erode local perceptions of legitimacy over time. In a cultural context rife with narratives that European institutions are insensitive to local British sensibilities, the language of British common sense and European mission creep paints pictures of increasingly incompatible views of human rights. The idea that a 'British bill of rights' enumerating largely the same rights as the ECHR could replace the HRA but hold a higher degree of legitimacy and public acceptance by virtue of being 'British', illustrates the importance of homegrown conceptions of rights in UK human rights discourses;[72] but as Strasbourg-sceptic politicians continue to push the idea that the 'foreign' ECtHR interferes with the will of the British government and Parliament to skirt human rights obligations, even locally constructed human rights begin to appear illegitimate.

Why don't rights norms stick?: the clash of British and European rights

The inability of the HRA, and by extension the ECHR, to embed itself effectively in the UK is a key source of trouble in the UK's relationship with Strasbourg. Part of the problem is explained by the level of support provided by government institutions after the HRA came into effect. The HRA was intended by its proponents to fundamentally transform British

[71] *R (AAA and others) v Secretary of State for the Home Department* [2023] UKSC 42; Jennifer Scott (2024) 'Rwanda Bill: Rishi Sunak "Crystal Clear" He will Ignore International Law to Ensure Asylum Seekers are Deported', SkyNews, 18 January. Available at: https://news.sky.com/story/rishi-sunak-crystal-clear-he-will-ignore-international-law-to-get-asylum-seekers-sent-to-rwanda-13050781 (accessed 23 January 2024); Aletha Adu and Kiran Stacey (2023) 'Rishi Sunak "Won't Allow Foreign Court to Block" Rwanda Plan', *Guardian*, 1 December. Available at: https://www.theguardian.com/uk-news/2023/dec/01/rishi-sunak-wont-allow-foreign-court-to-block-rwanda-plan (accessed 23 January 2024).

[72] Commission on a Bill of Rights, *A UK Bill of Rights?*

society through the development of a human rights culture. This aspiration to 'inaugurate a gradual [cultural] transformation' via the HRA is described by former Lord Chancellor, Lord Irvine:

> What I mean and I am sure what others mean when they talk of a culture of respect for human rights is to create a society in which our public institutions are habitually, automatically responsive to human rights considerations in relation to every procedure they follow, in relation to every practice they follow, in relation to every decision they take, in relation to every piece of legislation they sponsor.[73]

But this 'new culture' largely failed to emerge, at least beyond the academic and legal circles that engage with the HRA and ECHR in their work.[74] While Labour MPs almost immediately began to criticize their own creation as it constrained the Blair government's ability to appear tough on national security and antiterrorism in the 9/11 era, liberal human rights NGOs (nongovernmental organizations) worried that the HRA did not go far enough to effectively enforce 'internationally recognised human rights and traditional British liberties'.[75] For the public at large, criticisms from all sides facilitated an environment in which the HRA became mired in misconceptions – often articulated by government ministers and repeated by the media – that have grown to portray the HRA as flawed legislation that is often blamed for unpopular decisions and for granting too much power to unelected judges, 'foreign' European institutions, and 'undeserving' claimants.[76] Jane Gordon attributes this to an 'institutional failure' to establish any mechanisms to support implementation of the HRA and to offer guidance to public authorities and government institutions on how to facilitate a human rights culture.[77] The Labour government noted that 'with hindsight it is fair to say we took a lot of what we saw as the obvious benefits of the Human Rights Act for granted and … we didn't spend enough effort on promoting it'.[78]

---

73 Joint Committee on Human Rights (2001) 'Minutes of Evidence', 19 March, p 38. Available at: http://www.publications.parliament.uk/pa/jt200001/jtselect/jtrights/66/1031906.htm (accessed 18 April 2016).

74 Lord Lester, 'A Personal Explanatory Note', in Commission on a Bill of Rights, *A UK Bill of Rights?*, pp 232–3.

75 Francesca Klug (2010) 'Human rights don't Belong to Political Parties', *Guardian*, 2 February. Available at: https://www.theguardian.com/commentisfree/libertycentral/2010/feb/02/human-rights-political-parties (accessed 19 January 2024).

76 Gordon, 'A Developing Human Rights Culture in the UK?'; Lieve Gies (2015) *Mediating Human Rights: Media, Culture and Human Rights Law* (Abingdon: Routledge), pp 10–11.

77 Gordon, 'A Developing Human Rights Culture in the UK?', p 612.

78 Gordon, 'A Developing Human Rights Culture in the UK?', p 613.

Similarly, the parliamentary Joint Committee on Human Rights asserts that 'the Government has done nowhere near enough over the past decade to use the Human Rights Act as a tool to improve the delivery of public services', arguing further that 'this failure has contributed to the poor public image of the Act and "human rights" in general', allowing negative, often inaccurate, perceptions of the ECtHR and ECHR to flourish unchecked.[79]

The clash between the HRA and the extant rights environment also has a deeper explanation. The assumption that the HRA would herald a cultural transformation builds on the argument made by proponents of more formal, entrenched rights that pre-HRA common law was struggling to adequately protect human rights in the UK, but jars with the longstanding sense that rights are an intrinsic element of British political and legal identity by implying that a previous culture was lacking, or nonexistent. Moreover, even with the support of the 'bringing rights home' narrative's claim that the HRA would bolster British rights, the fact that these rights came home via Europe means they are still seen as foreign.

This points to the fundamental problem in the UK's relationship with Strasbourg: the legislation intended to legitimate the ECHR by incorporating it into domestic law is not seen by many in the UK as a legitimate instrument of human rights protection, because it is not endogenous to the existing cultural environment and constitutional order.[80] By drawing a distinction between a (more legitimate) domestic human rights culture and a (less legitimate) foreign or international human rights culture, the dominant rights narratives in the UK continue to frame British rights and European rights as distinct and irreconcilable. The perception that the UK was the lead creator of the ECHR infuses the Convention with legitimacy as an international treaty intended to help continental European states and fight communists, but this is not enough to generate internal legitimacy for products that stem from the Convention, including the HRA, if those products are turned back on the UK. Without internal acceptance of the domestic legislation that ties the ECHR to British law, the Convention, Court, and HRA are likely to continue to be viewed as foreign institutions that do not adequately reflect the British rights culture, and therefore foster reluctance to comply.

[79] Joint Committee on Human Rights (2008) *The Work of the Committee in 2007 and the State of Human Rights in the UK: Sixth Report of Session 2007–08* (London: The Stationery Office), p 7.

[80] Merris Amos (2013) 'Transplanting Human Rights Norms: The Case of the United Kingdom's Human Rights Act', *Human Rights Quarterly*, 35(2): 386–407.

The effects of British cultural politics of rights on compliance

Despite political tensions, the UK has maintained, for the most part, one of the highest compliance rates in the Strasbourg system. The number of cases with which the UK has been required to comply since the UK accepted the Court's jurisdiction in 1966 is low: of the 23,197 cases concerning the UK allocated to a judicial formation between 1959 and 2021, the Court has delivered a judgment on 563, and found a violation of the Convention in only 327.[81] In other words, the UK has only 'lost' approximately 1.4 per cent of the cases brought against it since the ECHR was incorporated into domestic law. That the Committee of Ministers is often able to adopt final resolutions on the UK's satisfactory compliance with judgments within two to three years of the ECtHR's final judgment demonstrates that governments are generally willing and able to respond to judgments swiftly.[82] It also helps to explain the UK's relatively low repeat-case numbers, as cases tend to be complied with before repetitive violations can accumulate.

In January 2024, the UK had only 12 cases pending satisfactory compliance before the Committee of Ministers.[83] Of the first 11 cases, eight were classified as leading cases, and four were classified as repetitive cases (one case received both classifications so is counted twice here). The twelfth case was a friendly settlement. Six of these cases are under enhanced supervision. The low number of cases can be explained in part by the closure of the *Hirst v United Kingdom* group of cases on prisoner voting, which were finally resolved in 2017 after 12 years of supervision.[84] Three of the remaining enhanced supervision cases – *McKerr v United Kingdom* and two related repetitive cases – concern the UK's failure to adequately investigate deaths in Northern Ireland in the 1980s, and have been pending for over 20 years.[85]

[81] The period 1959–2021 is the most recent from which the European Court of Human Rights Public Relations Unit has calculated the Court's case figures. European Court of Human Rights (2022) 'Overview: 1959–2021' (Strasbourg: ECtHR). Available at: https://www.echr.coe.int/documents/d/echr/Overview_19592021_ENG (accessed 10 January 2024).

[82] Başak Çalı and Alice Wyss (2009) *Why do Democracies Comply with Human Rights Judgments?: A Comparative Analysis of the UK, Ireland and Germany*, SSRN Working Paper, 26 August, p 11.

[83] Council of Europe (no date a) HUDOC-EXEC Case Database, Department for the Execution of Judgments of the ECHR, Strasbourg. Available at: https://hudoc.exec.coe.int (accessed 10 January 2024).

[84] *Hirst v United Kingdom (no. 2)*, App no. 74025/01 (ECtHR, 6 October 2005).

[85] *McKerr v United Kingdom*, App no. 28883/95 (ECtHR, 4 August 2001); *Kelly v United Kingdom*, App no, 30054/96 (ECtHR, 4 August 2001); *Finucane v United Kingdom*, App no. 29178/95 (ECtHR, 1 October 2003).

In both the now resolved *Hirst* cases and still pending *McKerr* cases, the collection of repetitive cases and long-term enhanced supervision reflect the UK's obstinacy over a few key politically sensitive issues.

The Council of Europe's Department for the Execution of Judgments has previously relied on the UK and similar 'good' compliers to lead by example 'to push reluctant member states' to implement Strasbourg judgments.[86] The UK's strong compliance record in the face of political tensions highlights the value government ministers place on being seen to adhere to the rule of law, because, as former Attorney-General Dominic Grieve asserts, 'it is only by setting an example at home that the UK is able to exert influence in the international arena and retain the moral authority to intervene and to enforce international law'.[87] But this robust track record makes the UK's resistance in a handful of cases all the more puzzling. Why does the UK's commitment to human rights and the rule of law extend to most, but not all, of its cases before the ECtHR, and what is it about the few difficult cases that means they fall outside the limits of what the UK is willing to comply with? As the following cases show, the political circumstances surrounding each compliance decision vary, but all depend on domestically constructed arguments about the legitimacy of local cultural understandings of human rights to push the government towards compliance.

Rule Britannia: compliance as commitment to British rule of law

One of the clearest examples of the UK's willingness to comply with difficult cases is *A. and Others v United Kingdom* in 2009.[88] The applicants had been detained preventatively as suspected terrorists by the UK authorities pursuant to the Anti-Terrorism, Crime and Security Act 2001 and a derogation from Article 5 of the ECHR (the right to liberty and security) made by the UK following the 9/11 attack in 2001. The ECtHR Grand Chamber found that the UK had unlawfully detained the suspects, and ordered the UK to pay reparations. The Home Secretary, Jacqui Smith, asserted that the government was 'very disappointed' with the ruling, although the compensation was paid quickly and the notice of derogation from Article 15 of the ECHR was withdrawn.[89]

---

86 Alice Donald, Jane Gordon, and Philip Leach (2012) *The UK and the European Court of Human Rights* (Manchester: Equality and Human Rights Commission), p 144.

87 Dominic Grieve (2011) 'European Convention on Human Rights – Current Challenges', speech at Lincoln's Inn, London, 24 October.

88 *A. and Others v United Kingdom*, App no. 3455/05 (ECtHR, 19 February 2009).

89 Jenny Percival (2009) 'Abu Qatada gets £2,500 Compensation for Breach of Human Rights', *Guardian*, 20 February. Available at: https://www.theguardian.com/world/2009/feb/19/abu-qatada-compensation-european-court (accessed 20 January 2017).

The case followed an earlier House of Lords declaration from 2004, in *A. v Secretary of State for the Home Department* (commonly known as the *Belmarsh* case), that the Article 5 derogation was incompatible with the ECHR because it discriminated between nationals and non-nationals by only permitting preventative detention of the latter.[90] Although the government eventually amended its terrorism legislation to make the detention and deportation provisions more consistent with the ECHR, and rescinded the derogation from Article 5, the Lords' ruling initially triggered a warning from the Home Secretary, Charles Clarke, that the government was 'clearly minded to renew' the legislation, rather than amend or repeal it.[91] More importantly, when the case reached the ECtHR, the government attempted to overturn the *Belmarsh* decision, arguing that the Lords' ruling was questionable. Ultimately, Strasbourg corroborated the Lords' decision, noting that in 'the unusual circumstances' of a government appealing the conclusions of its own highest court, the ECtHR 'considers that it would be justified in reaching a contrary conclusion only if satisfied that the national court had ... reached a conclusion which was manifestly unreasonable'.[92]

Strasbourg evidently did not believe the *Belmarsh* decision was 'manifestly unreasonable', and the UK's claim was subsequently dismissed. To this end, the Lords' decision in *Belmarsh* softened the blow from Strasbourg's *A. and Others* decision by establishing the need for equal treatment of national and non-national suspects in British case law, and thus granting the Lords' and Strasbourg's decisions more legitimacy in the view of the government, because they reached the same conclusion. This helps to explain the government's willingness to comply despite its initial pushback and strong public support for stricter antiterror laws. Strasbourg's ruling was bolstered by British law and vice versa, meaning the government had no legal avenue through which to pursue noncompliance and so ultimately felt compelled to respect the decisions. In this sense, the *A. and Others* case's legitimacy stems from the fact that all possible legal avenues were exhausted, as well as the fact that the House of Lords reached its conclusion about the case before Strasbourg, rather than from persuasive legal reasoning or institutional legitimacy of the ECtHR. Thus, the legitimizing process was endogenously motivated; the government's own perceptions about the importance of the principle of the rule of law represented a stronger normative push

90 *A. v Secretary of State for the Home Department* (2004) UKHL 56.

91 Clare Dyer, Michael White, and Alan Travis (2004) 'Judges' Verdict on Terror Laws Provokes Constitutional Crisis', *Guardian*, 18 December. Available at: https://www.theguardian.com/uk/2004/dec/17/terrorism.humanrights3 (accessed 20 January 2017).

92 *A. and Others v United Kingdom*, para 174.

than external forces. This is crucial for understanding how conceptions of rights and law inform compliance, as it demonstrates that compliance is not necessarily a top-down process of norm diffusion and international socialization, or the result of domestic institutions pressuring governments to act. The case was only ever monitored under the standard supervision procedure, so the Committee of Ministers exerted little influence over domestic discussions of the case, while public support for strong antiterror measures could have provided justification for greater resistance or a more minimalist approach (such as paying compensation to the claimants but retaining the Article 5 derogation).[93] Instead, the UK complied because the government found a way to contextualize the need to comply and the legitimacy of the government's actions in light of local, rather than European, legal proceedings (and couldn't find a way to legitimately contextualize possible noncompliance).

The *Othman (Abu Qatada) v United Kingdom* case illustrates a similar commitment to a locally constructed understanding of the rule of law in the face of a politically sensitive judgment.[94] The *Abu Qatada* case is related to *A. and Others* – extremist Islamic cleric and terror suspect, Abu Qatada, was one of the applicants awarded compensation for being indefinitely detained – but concerns the government's efforts to deport Qatada to Jordan, where he was likely to be tried in criminal proceedings on evidence obtained through the torture of third parties. The ECtHR ruled that while the UK was generally within its rights to deport any non-nationals considered to be threats to national security, the deportation would in this case constitute a violation of the Article 6 ECHR right to a fair trial as long as the possibility that Jordanian authorities would use evidence obtained through torture remained.[95] Although the Cameron government had reached an agreement with the King of Jordan that the evidence would not be used against Qatada, the ECtHR expressed concerns that these assurances were not reliable given Jordan's human rights record.[96] In making its ruling, the ECtHR disagreed over the violation of Article 6 with the House of Lords – which had unanimously affirmed in February 2009 that the government's assurances from Jordan were sufficient to allow deportation – although it

93 Committee of Ministers (2013c) Resolution CM/ResDH(2013)114, *A and others against the United Kingdom*, adopted by the Committee of Ministers on 6 June 2013 at the 1172nd meeting of the Ministers' Deputies; Committee of Ministers (2013b) Action Report – Communication from the United Kingdom Concerning the Case of *Othman (Abu Qatada) against the United Kingdom*, DH-DD(2013)315, 20 March.

94 *Othman (Abu Qatada) v United Kingdom*, App no. 8139/09 (ECtHR, 17 January 2012).

95 *Othman (Abu Qatada) v United Kingdom*, para 287.

96 *Othman (Abu Qatada) v United Kingdom*, paras 186–203.

concurred with the conclusions of the earlier judgment made by the (lower) Court of Appeal.[97]

The ruling was fiercely criticized for preventing the UK from being able to take control of its own national security, triggering calls for the UK to push for reform of the Strasbourg system, or even to temporarily derogate from the Convention in order to deport Qatada without being found in breach of Article 6 by the ECtHR.[98] Home Secretary May emphasized the steep costs of compliance for the UK, arguing that if the ECtHR had not 'moved the goalposts' by reading the Convention so broadly, the UK could have deported Qatada over a decade earlier, and saved £1.7 million in legal fees.[99]

Yet the government ultimately took great care to frame Qatada's deportation as being in accordance with the ECtHR's judgment, securing more substantive assurances from Jordan to ensure that evidence obtained through torture would not be used in his trial.[100] In the same speech to Parliament following Qatada's deportation in which she had criticized the Strasbourg decision, May also stressed the government's commitment to respecting the rule of law in the face of challenging cases:

> I want to make it clear that the Government have succeeded in deporting Qatada by respecting the rule of law at each and every stage of the process. We did not ignore court judgments we did not like. We did not act outside the law. We did what was right. And for a civilised nation, that is something of which we should be immensely proud.[101]

As with *A. and Others*, the government reached for an option and justificatory language that (they thought) would resonate locally. Neither May nor other members of the government made reference to a need to uphold the ECHR itself. Instead, May tapped into the idea of the UK sensibly modelling the good behaviour of a centuries-old empire, framing it as a 'civilised nation' that did 'what was right'. Of course, complying with the ruling was made easier to stomach when the government found a way to comply while deporting Qatada anyway – Human Rights Watch and Amnesty International

---

[97] *Othman (Abu Qatada) v United Kingdom*, para 263; *Othman (Jordan) v Secretary of State for the Home Department* [2008] EWCA Civ 290, paras 45–9.

[98] David Cameron (2012) Speech on the European Court of Human Rights, delivered to the Parliamentary Assembly of the Council of Europe, Strasbourg, 25 January; BBC (2012) '"Unacceptable" UK can't Deport Abu Qatada – Theresa May', BBC News, 7 February. Available at: http://www.bbc.com/news/uk-politics-16923527 (accessed 9 August 2017).

[99] Hansard (2013a) HC Deb, 8 July 2013, vol 566, col 23–4.

[100] Committee of Ministers, Action Report – DH-DD(2013)315.

[101] Hansard, HC Deb, 8 July 2013, vol 566, col 23–4.

condemned both the government's memorandum of understanding with Lebanon and the ECtHR Chamber's acceptance of the argument of the UK's representative before the Court that it would not violate ECHR Article 3.[102] But unlike in *A. and Others*, where the Law Lords agreed with Strasbourg and the government felt bound by its own legal system, in *Qatada* the government had the support of the House of Lords and could have relied on this support to justify action contrary to the ECtHR ruling. Moreover, the case played out contemporaneously with the *Hirst* prisoner voting case, in which Prime Minister Cameron emphatically 'defied' Strasbourg's ruling in order to uphold the decision of Parliament; political will for supporting the decisions of domestic institutions is likely to have been strong enough to support noncompliance on the *Qatada* case as well. Crucially, though, the commitment was to a domestic, British-made version of the rule of law. May's accusation that the ECtHR 'moved the goalposts' undermined any compliance pull the Court's own ruling might have possessed, by tying the case to the longstanding view among the Conservative elite that the ECtHR regularly exceeds its mandate to impose unreasonable obligations on Contracting States – a position the ECtHR arguably conceded to by accepting the memorandum.

That May emphasized the need to reform the ECtHR to restrict its apparent activism each time she discussed the deportation in Parliament further demonstrates that the government opposed the ECtHR's approach to interpreting the Convention.[103] This matters because it shows that neither the ECtHR as an institution nor the international or European rule of law as a norm possessed enough legitimacy in the British political environment to exert a pull towards compliance. The government's compliance is also not the product of a fundamental commitment to a static 'rule of law culture'. Instead, the *Qatada* compliance decision is best understood as the product of a cultural environment that contextualizes rule of law principles as a flexible political tool for upholding narratives of the British human rights tradition as exceptional. This tool was just as available to May as she sought to style the UK as a 'civilised nation' as it was available to Clarke when he responded more positively to the House of Lords' decision than Strasbourg's in *A. and Others*. While UK governments often vacillate on how to proceed with controversial cases, they eventually decide in favour of complying, pushing

[102] Amnesty International (2012) 'UK: Abu Qatada Still at Risk of Torture and Unfair Trial', public statement issued 9 May, AI Index EUR 45/010/2012; Adam Coogle (2014) 'Abu Qatada Case is No Victory for London', Human Rights Watch, 27 October. Available at: https://www.hrw.org/news/2014/10/27/abu-qatada-case-no-victory-london (accessed 23 January 2024).

[103] Hansard (2012a) HC Deb, 17 April 2012, vol 543, col 174; Hansard, HC Deb, 8 July 2013, vol 566, col 24.

themselves to implement Strasbourg judgments, not necessarily because they accept the ruling or believe the Court has acted appropriately, but in order to maintain domestically cultivated self-perceptions of the UK as a rights-protecting, rule-of-law-upholding 'civilised nation'.

Noncompliance and resistance: upholding obligations in our own way

In a human rights cultural context where most actors broadly accept in principle the importance of upholding international legal commitments – albeit sometimes reluctantly – rare instances of outright noncompliance appear particularly egregious. For 12 years, the United Kingdom refused to comply with one, now infamous, case: *Hirst v United Kingdom (no. 2)*.[104] The ECtHR first found the UK's blanket ban on prisoners voting to be in breach of the right to free elections under Article 3 Protocol 1 of the ECHR in 2005. Successive governments and parliaments failed to resolve the issue of prisoner voting in the subsequent decade. Parliament firmly rejected a proposal that would have brought the UK in line with the Convention in 2012, while Prime Minister Cameron went so far as to claim that the idea of allowing prisoners to vote made him 'physically ill'.[105]

The *Hirst* case triggered fierce criticism of the ECtHR from numerous British MPs. The ECtHR was accused of overreaching its mandate to interfere in domestic issues, and of undermining parliamentary sovereignty by subverting the decision-making authority of the democratically elected parliament to an ostensibly undemocratic international court. Then-backbench Conservative MP, David Davis, who instigated the motion in Parliament, argued that 'legislative decisions of this nature should be a matter for democratically elected lawmakers', while Labour's Jack Straw expressed concerns that the ECtHR was 'setting itself up as a supreme court for Europe, with an ever-widening remit'.[106] These criticisms fed into broader debates about the perceived legitimacy of the entire Strasbourg system, a dynamic which is best demonstrated by the fact that many of the MPs participating in the debate on the proposed Voting Eligibility (Prisoners) Draft Bill in 2012 emphasized constitutional and sovereignty-driven concerns about the Strasbourg court intruding in an issue that should be determined by the domestic parliament, rather than the substantive issue of prisoners' electoral disenfranchisement.[107] Claims from MPs that the case was 'an infringement

---

[104] *Hirst v United Kingdom (no 2)*, App no. 74025/01 (ECtHR, 6 October 2005).

[105] Hansard (2010) HC Deb, 3 Nov 2010, vol 517, col 921.

[106] Hansard (2011a) HC Deb, 10 Feb 2011, vol 523, col 493 and 502.

[107] Hansard (2012b) HC Deb, 22 Nov 2012, vol 553, col 745–62; Ed Bates (2014) 'Analysing the Prisoner Voting Saga and the British Challenge to Strasbourg', *Human Rights Law Review*, 14(3): 518–20.

of the UK Parliament's right to decide on matters which are fundamental to the British way of life' and that allowing criminals to vote would make 'a mockery of justice' highlight concerns that, rather than trusting the UK to protect human rights itself, the ECtHR interferes in domestic issues about which it knows little, ultimately to the detriment of the UK public.[108]

Parliament's and the Cameron government's refusal to comply with *Hirst* and its repetitive cases is firmly grounded in arguments that the British legal system, with its emphasis on politically determined limits on rights and on 'common-sense' balancing of the rights of individuals against the needs of society at large, is superior to the Strasbourg system when it comes to appreciating the specific legal needs of the UK. Successive Conservative governments, backed by Parliament, have criticized the Court's interpretations of Convention rights for taking an abstract, philosophical approach to the Convention without considering the practical implications of how their rulings will affect British society. Former Conservative Justice Secretary, Chris Grayling, argued in 2014 that the UK:

> cannot go on with a situation where crucial decisions about how this country is run and how we protect our citizens are taken by the ECHR and not by our parliament and our own courts. … [We] will make sure that we put Britain first and restore common sense to human rights in this country.[109]

But the same determination to maintain parliamentary sovereignty and to respect the British approach to rights that first generated the UK's noncompliance also explains the government's eventual solution. Recognizing that 'Parliament remains overwhelmingly unfavourable to relaxing the current ban', in 2017 the Secretary of State for Justice, David Lidington, quietly proposed a set of administrative changes that could be made without new legislation, including amending judicial procedures so people convicted with custodial sentences are informed of their disenfranchisement

[108] David Davis, in Tom Whitehead (2012) 'David Cameron Urged to Stand Up to Europe over Prisoner Vote Row', *Telegraph*, 22 May. Available at: http://www.telegraph.co.uk/news/politics/9283297/David-Cameron-urged-to-stand-up-to-Europe-over-prisoner-vote-row.html (accessed 3 July 2017); Dominic Grieve, in Alan Travis (2005) 'Worst Criminals will Not get Vote in Jail Despite European Court Ruling', *Guardian*, 7 October. Available at: https://www.theguardian.com/uk/2005/oct/07/constitution.ukcrime (accessed 3 July 2017).

[109] Owen Bowcott (2014) 'Conservatives Pledge Powers to Ignore European Court of Human Rights Rulings', *Guardian*, 3 October. Available at: http://www.theguardian.com/politics/2014/oct/03/conservatives-ignore-european-court-human-rights-rulings (accessed 14 May 2016).

before entering prison, and permitting prisoners serving home detention or temporary licence sentences to vote.[110] By adopting administrative, rather than legislative, reforms, Lidington was able to claim that the government was meeting its international commitments without directly contradicting Parliament. The government also relied on the narrative that British legal standards are superior to those in Europe to justify granting voting rights to noncustodial prisoners, arguing in communications to the Committee of Ministers that imprisonment standards are sufficiently high in the UK that restricting the liberties of anyone who is imprisoned is proportionate to the severity of the crimes committed.[111] In doing so, the government convinced Strasbourg that the UK no longer imposes a blanket ban,[112] while effectively maintaining its position that people in prisons should not possess the right to vote.

Given that the reforms enfranchised approximately 100 people in England and Wales,[113] it is hardly a satisfying outcome for the nearly 96,000 people whose suffrage rights are still denied across the UK prison system.[114] Different responses to the *Hirst* ruling in Scotland now mean that voting rights vary depending on the nation in which people are imprisoned.[115] It is also widely regarded among human rights advocates and legal scholars as an example of Strasbourg capitulating to the UK government's evasive compliance strategy, 'half-heartedly' accepting what was in effect an extremely narrow adjustment to the previous blanket ban in order to close the case as a means to preserve

---

[110] Committee of Ministers (2016b) Communication from the Authorities (05/02/2016) Concerning the Cases of *Hirst No. 2* and *Greens and M.T. against the United Kingdom* (74025/01, 600041/08), DH-DD(2016)188, 5 February; Committee of Ministers (2017b) Action Plan – Communication from the United Kingdom Concerning the Case of *Hirst (No. 2) v the United Kingdom*, DH-DD(2017)1229, 2 November, p 2.

[111] Committee of Ministers, Action Plan – DH-DD(2017)1229, p 2.

[112] Committee of Ministers (2018a) 1331 DH meeting, CM/Notes/1331/H46-35, Notes on the Agenda, *Hirst no. 2 group v United Kingdom* (74025/01), 4–6 December, p 2.

[113] BBC (2017b) 'Prisoner Voting Compromise Ends Dispute with European Court', BBC News, 7 December. Available at: https://www.bbc.com/news/uk-42271100 (accessed 23 March 2024).

[114] Georgina Sturge (2023) *Research Briefing: UK Prison Population Statistics* (London: House of Commons Library), 8 September. Available at: https://commonslibrary.parliament.uk/research-briefings/sn04334/ (accessed 23 March 2024).

[115] The Scottish parliament passed the Scottish Elections (Franchise and Representation) Act in 2020, which allows all prisoners serving terms of up to 12 months to vote in Scottish and local elections. The Welsh government pledged in 2021 to consider a parliamentary committee proposal to allow voting rights for all prisoners serving up to four-year terms, but has not as yet implemented such reforms. See Colin R.G. Murray (2021) 'Prisoner Voting and Devolution: New Dimensions to an Old Dispute', *Edinburgh Law Review*, 25(3): 292.

its own legitimacy.[116] In deliberations in Parliament at the very beginning of the saga, Dominic Raab dismissed a similar reform to the one ultimately implemented by Lidington, that would have granted the vote to prisoners with sentences of fewer than 6–12 months, on the grounds that:

> it is not a compromise because it is bound to be rejected by Strasbourg. The Court made that crystal clear in the Frodl case last year. … Such so-called compromise proposals are the worst of all worlds. We buckle and accept the erosion of our democracy and Strasbourg rejects the compromise anyway.[117]

By 2017, not only had Strasbourg accepted the Lidington Compromise but, as Colin Murray points out, where the ECtHR originally stressed that the human rights violation stemmed from the 'automatic and indiscriminate' restriction the blanket ban imposed, the Committee of Ministers' final resolution makes no reference to the fact that automatic restrictions remain in place for the vast majority of imprisoned people, citing only the 'wide margin of appreciation in this area' as the reason to accept the UK's proposal.[118] A comprehensive account of the compliance process for this case therefore needs to recognize just how far the bar for action that would constitute sufficient reform had been lowered for the UK.

---

[116] Kanstantsin Dzehtsiarou (2024) 'The United Kingdom and the European Convention on Human Rights: Together Until the End?', *European Convention on Human Rights Law Review*, 5(1): 5; BBC (2017a) 'Human Rights Lawyer: Prisoner Votes Plan is "Cynical"', BBC News, 30 October. Available at: https://www.bbc.com/news/uk-41803722 (accessed 23 March 2024); Rob Allen (2017) 'The Great Revolution in Prisoner Voting will Affect … a Few Dozen People', *Guardian*, 30 October. Available at: https://www.theguardian.com/commentisfree/2017/oct/30/prisoner-voting-government-proposal-european-court-human-rights (accessed 23 March 2024); Mugambi Jouet (2023) 'The Abolition and Retention of Life without Parole in Europe: A Comparative and Historical Perspective', *European Convention on Human Rights Law Review*, 4: 326.

[117] Hansard (2011b) HC Deb, 10 February 2011, col 583. The ECtHR actually makes no such reference to the idea that enfranchising people serving sentences of less than 12 months would be unacceptable in the *Frodl v Austria* case. It does note that Austrian legislation restricting prisoner voting rights is not incompatible with the ECHR per se because disenfranchisement is restricted 'to a more narrowly defined group of persons [than *Hirst*] since it applies only in the case of a prison sentence exceeding one year and only to convictions for offences committed with intent'. However, it stressed that the core rights issues at stake for prisoner voting rights cases are 'ruling out automatic and blanket restrictions' and the need for judges to provide clear and proportionate justifications for decisions on disenfranchisement in light of applicants' particular circumstances. *Frodl v Austria*, App no. 20201/04 (ECtHR, 4 October 2010), ss 33–4.

[118] Murray, 'Prisoner Voting and Devolution', p 299.

Nonetheless, the fact that the government was willing to make any compromise at all demonstrates that, throughout the process, the push towards defending what members of the Conservative government and of Parliament consider to be central tenets of a British rights culture was greater than the pull of a commitment to the Strasbourg system or pressure from other domestic institutions. Resistance towards the *Hirst* ruling was fiercest when the case appeared to threaten the authority of Parliament, and went beyond perceived common-sense limits to the balance between individual rights and public safety. Only when the government found a compromise that allowed it to keep these values intact in the eyes of MPs, the Conservative Party, and Eurosceptic tabloids was the UK able to break the impasse and have the case closed by the Committee of Ministers. As Lidington put it when presenting the reforms to Parliament: 'The United Kingdom has a proud constitutional tradition and it is clearly right that we uphold our obligations, but the British public expect us to do so in our own way, consistent with British values of rights and responsibilities.'[119]

Identity, legitimacy, and compliance: defending a British rights culture

The cases in this chapter highlight the substantial impact of British elites' conceptions of rights and law on compliance. The preference for politically determined rights and parliamentary sovereignty over judicial review, and public narratives that portray the British rights tradition as ancient, unique, and inherently sensible contribute to widespread beliefs that the ECtHR cannot appreciate the idiosyncrasies of the British rights culture. This perception, which serves as a lightning rod for Eurosceptic sentiments towards the ECtHR, is central to understanding how UK sovereignty and national identity inform British understandings of the role of international law and human rights norms, and in turn inform its approach to compliance. In particular, British MPs, government ministers, media outlets, and even some judges view participation in the international legal system as a means to affirm the UK's own normative preferences, rather than to receive external norms or be socialized into an external culture that limits or threatens the UK's existing values and identity – a point echoed by Çalı and Wyss' argument that British human rights 'are exported rather than imported concepts'.[120] As David Lidington declared during the final House of Commons debate on the *Hirst* reforms, 'We rightly talk about British values … and among those values are respect for the rule of law and a rules-based international

[119] Hansard (2017a) HC Deb, 2 November 2017, vol 630, col 1007.

[120] Çalı and Wyss, *Why do Democracies Comply with Human Rights Judgments?*, p 13.

order. It is certainly harder to urge respect for those principles on others if we are not clear about doing so ourselves.'[121]

In a speech to the British Council in 2004, then-Chancellor Gordon Brown argued that British identity is not based on 'traditional' identifiers such as race or religion, but on 'the values we share and … the way these values are expressed through our history and our institutions'.[122] A liberal conception of human rights as negative freedoms and as something the UK needs no help learning is a central component of this identity, as are the principles of parliamentary sovereignty, and understandings of the rule of law and human rights as having 'common-sense' limits. These values are evident in the UK's compliance record with the ECtHR; the UK regularly complies with ECtHR judgments, including judgments with which it substantively disagrees, because governments can generally draw on these concepts as rhetorical tools to frame and contextualize their decisions in ways that appear to uphold a rule-of-law-following identity. But the expectation that the UK will uphold its obligations 'in our own way'[123] also explains why, despite its strong compliance record, UK governments baulk at certain cases, and provides insight into the types of cases most likely to cause strains in the UK–Strasbourg relationship. Tensions are at their strongest when the ECtHR's interpretations of the Convention or specific rights norms vary so drastically from those with sufficient mainstream traction in UK cultural politics that they fundamentally challenge British understandings of rights. To this end, UK elites typically perceive the ECtHR as being more legitimate, and are thus more willing to comply with its rulings, when the Court takes stances that closely match their own interpretations of rights: individual, intrinsically guaranteed, enhanced and defended by the democratic parliament. This legitimacy diminishes the further Strasbourg's approach moves away from these tenets, while the likelihood that the UK will actively resist complying with the judgment increases.

Conclusion

Cultural politics reifying a distinctly 'British' approach to human rights play a critical role in shaping how compliance actors in the United Kingdom determine the legitimacy of international norms and the judgments of the ECtHR. This approach – used and adapted to various contexts by political,

[121] Hansard (2017b) HC Deb, 2 November 2017, vol 630, col 1012.

[122] Gordon Brown (2004) 'Britishness', British Council Annual Lecture, London, 7 July, reproduced in W. Stevenson (ed) (2006) *Moving Britain Forward: Selected Speeches 1997–2006* (London: Bloomsbury), p 7.

[123] Hansard, HC Deb, 2 November 2017, vol 630, col 1007.

legal, and media actors from conservative and liberal backgrounds alike – is characterized by a particular way of thinking about rights, determined by the distinct nature of legal traditions such as parliamentary sovereignty, political constitutionalism, and weak judicial protection in light of a widely (though certainly not universally) accepted interpretation of rights as Enlightenment-style civil liberties and freedoms rather than modern, codified human rights. The mythology of the British conception of rights as an 800-year-old tradition underpins the UK's interactions with Strasbourg, perpetuating an assumption that although the ECHR is informed by, and closely related to, British conceptions of rights, the UK's own rights culture ultimately remains 'better' at upholding the particular rights needs of the UK.

In this sense, the UK's relationship with Strasbourg is driven by a determination to ensure that 'British rights' are protected first and foremost by the British legal system, rather than by 'foreign' European institutions. British approaches to compliance, then, centre on upholding – if not outright defending – a supposedly superior domestic rights culture against external, European interference. The perception that rights are better protected at home than in Europe is the primary means by which UK actors assess the legitimacy of European human rights rulings and decide to comply with the ECtHR's rulings; the distinction between domestic and European in British cultural politics of rights means any aspect of law with European associations struggles to win domestic legitimacy completely, but the less ECtHR judgments challenge local cultural pillars, the more willing the UK is to comply.

The process of deciding to comply therefore occurs in the context of balancing international commitments and serving as an example of a rights-respecting state with the need to preserve unique British values and traditions. This tension offers insight into why the UK drags its heels on compliance with cases that conflict with British 'common-sense' notions of who is deserving of rights protection, or which are perceived as undermining parliamentary sovereignty and the domestic constitutional order. But it also sheds light on why compliance actors in the UK ultimately take great care to meet most of the obligations set by Strasbourg: if they truly see the UK as the home of human rights, democracy, and the rule of law, respecting its international human rights commitments is an essential component of this identity – provided solutions that align with local notions of legitimacy can be found.

5

Germany: Memory, Transformation, and Openness to International Law

The standard telling of the German human rights story is one of transformation. Reeling from its experience as the perpetrator of some of the most extreme violations of human rights and abuses of state power under the National Socialist regime between 1933 and 1945, postwar Germany has endeavoured to entrench democratic principles as well as respect for human rights and the rule of law in its constitutional order and political culture. This process of 'coping with' or 'working through the past' (*Vergang enheitsbewältigung*)[1] and the total reconstruction of German postwar national identity is widely said to have paid off. The German human rights system is one of the most comprehensive in Europe, while the development of a new, thoroughly Europeanized identity has helped to make the state particularly receptive to participation in the Strasbourg human rights system and to compliance with the judgments of the ECtHR. In practice, Germany has been no more immune to the contemporary human rights challenges facing any other European country – from power struggles over the respective roles of German and European courts to the spread of antirights rhetoric from far-right actors like *Alternativ für Deutschland* (AfD). But the narrative of transformation holds fast, and the constitutional principles and practices that emerged from the immediate postwar era play a powerful foundational role in shaping contemporary understandings of human rights and how to protect them.

1 Jan-Werner Müller (2007) *Constitutional Patriotism* (Princeton, NJ: Princeton University Press), p 17; Timothy Garton Ash (1998) 'The Truth About Dictatorship', *New York Review of Books*, 19 February.

This chapter examines the effects of German cultural politics of human rights on German actors' perceptions of the legitimacy of the Strasbourg system and their decisions to comply with ECtHR judgments. I argue that the postwar German rights cultural context – grounded in notions of postwar transformation, strong judicial oversight to protect democratic values, openness to international cooperation, and pride in the creation of a constitutional order which places respect for human rights at its heart – contributes to understandings of compliance with ECtHR judgments as almost a fait accompli, even with politically sensitive or technically challenging judgments. This understanding is most evident in the fact that – unlike in some other older European democracies with long human rights heritages – debates over the democratic or substantive legitimacy of the ECtHR have not gained traction in the mainstream human rights discourse. Instead, the ECtHR enjoys relatively widespread acceptance among political and legal elites as an extension of the highly respected German judiciary, with compliance viewed as a necessary component of being a rule-of-law-respecting state.

Thus, the German case demonstrates that perceptions of the legitimacy of human rights institutions can become so firmly entrenched that, even when the norms or judgments they pass down are controversial, decisions to comply are the product of a cultural politics that orients actors towards acceptance of the processes of judicial review at both national and international levels. Nonetheless, the careful and nuanced debates among German human rights actors, especially the powerful Federal Constitutional Court, over the precise balance between supranational oversight and sovereign autonomy, as well as over the relationships between human rights law and Holocaust memory, demonstrate that even broad acceptance of Strasbourg and general willingness to comply is contingent on the particular conceptions of human rights and international law that stem from Germany's local cultural human rights context.

The ECHR in German law

The centrepiece of the modern German legal system is the *Grundgesetz* (the constitution or Basic Law). Enacted in the Federal Republic of Germany (*Bundesrepublik Deutschland* (BRD)) in 1949, the Basic Law outlines some of the most comprehensive constitutional rights protections in Europe and is binding on all federal and state authorities. The Basic Law also entrenches the inviolability of human dignity at the core of the German constitutional order,[2] and attributes the inspiration for its creation to 'the determination to

2 *Grundgesetz für die Bundesrepublic Deutschland* [Constitution for the Federal Republic of Germany], 23 May 1949. BGBl. 1949 I, 1. Article 1.

promote world peace as an equal partner in a united Europe'.[3] It is interpreted and protected by the *Bundesverfassungsgericht* (Federal Constitutional Court (BVerfG)). Established in 1951 in the city of Karlsruhe, the BVerfG has exceptionally strong powers of oversight and review of legislation, including being able to overturn legislation that contradicts the Basic Law and to create temporary laws or edicts to fill the gaps left by unconstitutional statutory law. For this reason, although the Federal Parliament (*Deutscher Bundestag*), government agencies, and lower courts are also responsible for upholding and scrutinizing rights, the BVerfG is often viewed as the foremost defender of Germany's constitutional and international rights.

The Federal Republic of Germany signed the European Convention on Human Rights (ECHR) on 4 November 1950 and ratified it on 5 December 1952. It also accepted the jurisdiction of the European Court of Human Rights (ECtHR) on 5 July 1955, and was one of the first states to recognize the right of individual petition at Strasbourg, a feature that closely reflects the right of German citizens to complain to the Federal Constitutional Court for breaches of their constitutional rights established in 1951. Similarities in the text of the Basic Law and the ECHR enabled Germany to accept the Convention and most of its additional Protocols quickly and with few reservations or adjustments to domestic law. But in the shadow of the abuse of human dignity that characterized the Nazi regime, as well as concerns about countering communism, quick and wholehearted implementation of Germany's ECHR commitments was also paramount for being recognized as a 'sovereign equal' in Europe and the wider international community.

Germany's 'moderate dualist' legal system means that incorporating the ECHR entails recognizing international law as a legitimate source of domestic law.[4] The Act on the Convention for the Protection of Human Rights and Fundamental Freedoms 'merely points to the international treaty that is being incorporated', rather than copying the Convention rights into an equivalent piece of domestic legislation.[5] The ECHR thus holds the status of ordinary statute law in the German legal hierarchy, sitting above federal and *Land* law, but subordinate to the Basic Law. The BVerfG recognizes its

---

[3] *Grundgesetz*, preamble.

[4] Hans-Jürgen Papier (2006) 'Execution and Effects of the Judgments of the European Court of Human Rights in the German Judicial System', in Council of Europe, *Dialogue between Judges* (Strasbourg: Publications Unit of the European Court of Human Rights), p 46.

[5] *Gesetz über die Konvention zum Schutze der Menschenrechte und Grundfreiheiten* [Act on the Convention for the Protection of Human Rights and Fundamental Freedoms], 7 August 1952. BGBl. 1952 II, 685; Beate Rudolf (2016) 'Human Rights in Germany – A View from Germany's National Human Rights Institution', *International Journal of Legal Information*, 44(1): 52.

importance as an 'interpretational aid', holding in a landmark decision in 1987 that the ECHR and the case law of the ECtHR 'are also to be taken into account, insofar as this does not lead to a restriction or derogation of basic-rights protection under the Basic Law'.[6] The phrase 'take into account' (*berücksichtigen*), rather than 'comply with' or 'abide by',[7] represents a key source of leeway for domestic courts to disregard Strasbourg jurisprudence if it is deemed necessary. Nonetheless, the BVerfG acknowledges the intention of the German government to uphold its international legal commitments, noting in the same judgment that 'it cannot be assumed that the legislature, insofar as it has not clearly declared otherwise, wishes to deviate from the BRD's international treaty commitments or to facilitate violation of such commitments'.[8] To this end, the BVerfG has established a positive commitment to applying and enforcing the ECHR in German law by elevating the Convention to the jurisdiction of the BVerfG and embedding it firmly in the top tier of the German constitutional hierarchy.

The German human rights cultural context: memory, law, and Europe

Transformation and atonement through rights and law

Cultural politics concerning the meanings of human rights and law in contemporary Germany are inextricable from discourses and practices of Holocaust memorialization. In the political, judicial, and media archives gathered for this case, the Holocaust is routinely portrayed both as the ultimate human rights abuse, and a singular, aberrant moment from which modern democratic Germany has sought complete constitutional rupture. As exiled German legal scholar Hans Kelsen argued in 1945, in order to establish a 'democratic Germany that will join international organizations' there could be 'no continuity between the defeated Nazi state and the new, democratic Germany'.[9] This political and moral imperative for rupture is apparent in the creation of powerful legal institutions like the constitutional court and the Basic Law, whose core democratic structures such as the separation of powers and the weak position of the President cannot be repealed.[10] It also lives on in political narratives presenting the judicialization of human rights as the

6 BVerfGE 74, 358, 26 March 1987, para 370 ('*Unschuldsvermutung*').

7 Christian Tomuschat (2010) 'The Effects of the Judgments of the European Court of Human Rights According to the German Constitutional Court', *German Law Journal*, 11(5): 523.

8 BVerfGE 74, 358, 26 March 1987, para 370.

9 In Ingo Müller (1991) *Hitler's Justice: The Courts of the Third Reich*, translated by Deborah Lucas Schneider (Cambridge, MA: Harvard University Press), p 204.

10 *Grundgesetz*, Article 79(3).

primary source of Germany's transformation, as Angela Merkel demonstrates in a speech marking the sixtieth anniversary of the BVerfG in 2011:

> The fathers and mothers of the Basic Law … set a clear signal for a new beginning as a state of law. … For it was the contempt of law which preceded the unspeakable horrors of the national-socialist tyranny. Therefore, those who created our constitution drew two central lessons from history: Law before power and effective control of power by law.[11]

Elsewhere, Merkel has suggested that 'human rights can only be fully protected in a constitutional system in which the separation of powers and the independence of the judiciary are respected',[12] while former Bundespräzident, Joachim Gauck, has declared that 'after the dark nights of dictatorship, after all the guilt and the later shame and regret, we have been able to formulate a credo that is bright as day. We have done so by restoring the dignity of legal force of justice.'[13]

These articulations of the intrinsic link between law and human rights exist in a broader cultural politics of memory in which the narrative of German postwar rupture and transformation are jealously guarded. For example, the twin debates among academics and public intellectuals in the 1980s and 2020s (dubbed locally *Historkerstreit* and *Historkerstreit 2.0*, or the historians' disputes) about the Holocaust's relation or comparison to other historical and contemporary atrocities, sway so firmly in the direction of reifying the Holocaust as an exception to which nothing else is comparable that genocide scholar, Dirk Moses, describes it as catechism, an almost religious doctrine of German national identity.[14] There is considerably more contestation and variation outside elite political and public discourses. The core memorializing phrase 'Never Again/*Nie wieder*' has contained

---

[11] Angela Merkel (2011) Speech at the ceremony of the 60th anniversary of the Federal Constitutional Court, Karlsruhe, 28 September. Available at: https://www.bundesregierung.de/breg-de/service/newsletter-und-abos/bulletin/rede-von-bundeskanzlerin-dr-angela-merkel-802312 (accessed 29 September 2024).

[12] Angela Merkel (2021) Speech to the Parliamentary Assembly of the Council of Europe, 20 April, video message. Available at: https://www.bundesregierung.de/breg-de/service/bulletin/rede-von-bundeskanzlerin-dr-angela-merkel-1892124 (accessed 8 February 2024).

[13] Joachim Gauck (2015) Speech: Day of Remembrance of the Victims of National Socialism, 27 January, Berlin. Available at: https://www.bundespraesident.de/SharedDocs/Reden/EN/JoachimGauck/Reden/2015/150127-Gedenken-Holocaust.html (accessed 8 February 2024).

[14] Dirk Moses (2021) 'The German Catechism', *Geschichte der Gegenwart*, 23 May. Available at: https://geschichtedergegenwart.ch/the-german-catechism/ (accessed 8 February 2024).

multiple, often conflicting, interpretations since 1945, ranging from gradual recognition of other victims of the Nazis (including Sinti and Roma, queer people, people with disabilities, and political prisoners in addition to the Jews) to the ways the German Democratic Republic (*Deutsche Demokratische Republik* (DDR)) used the phrase to delegitimize fascism and the West.[15] And although the *Bundestag* passed a resolution in 2016 recognizing the Armenian genocide, symbolizing a move away from a previous position that atrocities committed prior to the creation of the Genocide Convention could not be labelled genocide, Germany's colonial genocide of the Nama and Herero people in Namibia did not receive equivalent state recognition until 2021.[16] Nonetheless, among the political and judicial actors responsible for complying with ECtHR decisions, there is little evidence of engagement with what Michael Rothberg calls 'multidirectional memory', that is, memorialization practices that might accommodate more comprehensive and fluid understandings of German national and colonial history.[17] Instead, they hold fast to the transformation narrative, clinging in their compliance practices and justifications to local cultural referents that reinforce the tripartite legitimation of German postwar democracy, Holocaust memory, and Europeanization.

Constitutional patriotism and rights before law

The particular ways that connections between Holocaust memorialization and law play out vary, but are especially evident in shifting understandings of *Rechtstaat*, or the rule-of-law-based state. The concept of *Rechtsstaat* has been present in German legal culture since the late 18th century.[18] Traditionally a narrow, formal principle that government may not interfere unlawfully with the liberty of individuals, it originally bore similarities to the conceptions of negative liberty and rule of law advocated by English Enlightenment scholars. Yet the legitimation of Nazi policies and abuse of power through technically legal methods highlighted the frailty of the concept and its ability to be manipulated for authoritarian and violent means. In the late 1940s, then, West German constitutional theorists,

15 Alf Lüdtke (1993) '"Coming to Terms with the Past": Illusions of Remembering, Ways of Forgetting Nazism in West Germany', *Journal of Modern History*, 65(3): 542–72.

16 Zoé Samudzi (2020) 'Paradox of Recognition: Genocide and Colonialism', *Postmodern Culture*, 31(1&2): 3.

17 Michael Rothberg (2022) 'Lived Multidirectionality: "*Historikerstreit 2.0*" and the Politics of Holocaust Memory', *Memory Studies*, 15(6): 1319.

18 Gernot Sydow (2007) 'Independence of the Judiciary in Germany', in Katja S. Ziegler, Denis Baranger, and Anthony W. Bradley (eds), *Constitutionalism and the Role of Parliaments* (Portland: Hart Publishing), p 225.

lawyers, and political leaders sought to invoke a much stronger notion of the rule of law. While on the surface trying to distance the Bonn Republic from both the Third Reich and the Weimar Republic, they nonetheless reached back to Weimar-era debates about basic rights and judicial review as means to bolster the new constitution against the pitfalls of democracy.[19] Judicial review is therefore one of the core elements of contemporary conceptions of *Rechtsstaat*, forming a front line of defence in terms of enforcing the positive obligations on German government authorities to uphold Basic Law rights and individual liberties.[20] The creation of an 'objective order of values'[21] that placed basic rights 'before the law' and entrenched them as extralegal with an unamendable eternity clause is another.[22] The postwar *Rechtsstaat* and Basic Law, as they have been developed by German courts and constitutional experts, explicitly reject a liberal understanding of rights as negative individual freedoms for citizens to pursue without state interference. Instead, they represent a clear positive duty on the state to not only recognize but provide fundamental rights 'based on a Christian understanding of the human person'.[23]

Discourses reifying human dignity and rule of law also shape and are shaped by a construct known as constitutional patriotism (*Verfassungspatr iotismus*).[24] The term was coined by Dolf Sternberger in 1970, although elements of the concept are apparent in earlier constitutional theory and political discourse.[25] The concept seeks to invoke 'patriotic sentiment in the constitutional state' and 'the love of the laws and common liberties' by encouraging citizens to feel a sense of pride in specific institutions.[26] This meant that expressions of patriotism could be abstract or broad enough to be universally inclusive rather than facilitating the 'othering' of nonconformant groups or individuals. As Jan-Werner Müller explains:

19 Clara Maier (2019) 'The Weimar Origins of the West German *Rechtsstaat*, 1919–1969', *Historical Journal*, 62(4): 1069–91.

20 Geranne Lautenbach (2013) *The Concept of the Rule of Law and the European Court of Human Rights* (New York: Oxford University Press) pp 31–2.

21 BVerfGE 7, 198, 15 January 1958 ('*Lüth*').

22 Maier, 'The Weimar Origins of the West German *Rechtsstaat*', p 1077.

23 Maier, 'The Weimar Origins of the West German *Rechtsstaat*', p 1078.

24 Rudolf, 'Human Rights in Germany', p 50.

25 See, for instance, Karl Jaspers' notion of German cosmopolitanism and collective responsibility for the past, as well as Sternberger's own earlier work on *Staatsfreundschaft* (friendship towards the state). Karl Jaspers (1961) *The Question of German Guilt*, translated by E.B. Ashton (New York: Capricorn Books); Dolf Sternberger (1980) *Staatsfreundschaft [Schriften IV]* (Frankfurt am Main: Suhrkamp). For a history of the concept, see Müller, *Constitutional Patriotism*, pp 15–45.

26 Jan-Werner Müller (2006) 'On the Origins of Constitutional Patriotism', *Contemporary Political Theory*, 5(3): 283.

> Patriotism, then, was not a matter of uncomplicated belonging or a kind of 'feeling at home' that could be taken for granted. Rather, it was based on a political *achievement* and on an explicitly *adversarial* relationship with democracy's enemies. … In the end, loyalty was owed to political and legal institutions as embodiments of a particular constitutional tradition.[27]

The emergence of constitutional patriotism was a direct response to concerns about German citizens returning to more conventional understandings of nationalism. In light of the hypernationalism and white supremacy of the Nazi regime, Jürgen Habermas stressed that 'it is only in the unclouded consciousness of a break with our more fateful traditions that the Federal Republic's unreserved opening to the political culture of the West can mean more than an economically attractive opportunity and politically almost unavoidable choice'.[28] Rather than a return to traditional forms of nationalism and its connotations of violence and power politics, Habermas advocated 'a renewed national self-consciousness' and 'post-national identity tied to the constitutional state'.[29] To this end, Müller argues that the German approach to constitutional patriotism 'has always contained strong doses of 'memory' and 'militancy'; it exists as a consequence of the specific memory of the Holocaust and Nazism, and represents a form of democracy that actively seeks to defend its own values against enemies of democracy.[30] Courts have the authority to defend democratic principles through measures such as banning antidemocratic political parties, balancing free speech with the protection of minorities and individuals, and overturning legislation that undermines democracy. The notion of militant democracy and the protection of democratic values by government institutions can therefore be seen as one of the primary reasons for the emphasis placed on law and judicial review, granting the judiciary a high degree of democratic legitimacy because it has been tasked expressly with protecting that democracy.

However, the extent to which the evolution of the judiciary to become the dominant enforcer of rights is the result of Germany's turn away from Nazism is contested. The process of 'working through the past' and expressions of militant democracy are certainly evident in the early

[27] Müller, 'On the Origins of Constitutional Patriotism', p 286.

[28] Jürgen Habermas (1998) 'Historical Consciousness and Post-Traditional Identity: Remarks on the Federal Republic's Orientation to the West', *Acta Sociologica*, 31(1): 4.

[29] Habermas, 'Historical Consciousness and Post-Traditional Identity', pp 4 and 7.

[30] Müller, 'On the Origins of Constitutional Patriotism', p 283. See also Karl Loewenstein (1937) 'Militant Democracy and Fundamental Rights I', *American Political Science Review*, 31(3): 430–2.

case law of the BVerfG, although explicit evidence of this influence has waned over time.[31] Instead, Michaela Hailbronner argues that the BVerfG has gained such a prominent position in the German constitutional order because of a 'hierarchically ordered and expertise-based' legal culture, grounded in Weberian understandings of law as a rational science to be conducted by experts.[32] To this end, the German judiciary, especially the BVerfG, has built up a form of political legitimacy based on 'constructing law as a logically consistent, gapless system of norms' where 'the imperative of upholding its integrity prevails over case-to-case considerations of what seems right in individual disputes'.[33] This quest for normative consistency is evident in the German judiciary's preference for building coherent legal doctrine to inform its decisions, despite judges not formally being bound by precedent.[34] It is also apparent in the fact that, although judges have been permitted to publish dissenting opinions since 1971, they rarely do so, instead issuing most judgments on behalf of the Court as a single voice.[35]

Debate about the origins of the German judiciary's authority highlights the impact of multiple historical and political influences on the cultural politics of human rights in Germany, as well as drawing attention to some of the limits to the influence of Germany's experience of totalitarianism on its current approach to law and human rights. Nonetheless, memories of Nazism and the Holocaust continue to hold significant power in modern political culture as a reminder of the importance of democracy, human rights, and European integration. They remain prominent threads in narratives surrounding German understandings of law and rights, especially with regard to European-level protection.

---

31 See, for instance, the *Lüth* case, which concerned the applicant's right to protest and boycott the films of a known antisemite as an expression of freedom of speech. The BVerfG upheld Lüth's claim, arguing that the Basic Law contains an 'objective order of values', and that freedom of expression is embedded at the top of this normative order. BVerfGE 7, 198, 15 January 1958.

32 Michaela Hailbronner (2014) 'Rethinking the Rise of the German Constitutional Court: From Anti-Nazism to Value Formalism', *International Journal of Constitutional Law*, 12(3): 628.

33 Hailbronner, 'Rethinking the Rise of the German Constitutional Court', p 642.

34 Ruth Weber and Laura Wittmann (2022) 'The Role of Precedents and Case Law in the Jurisprudence of the German Federal Constitutional Court', in Monika Florczak-Wator (ed), *Constitutional Law and Precedent: International Perspectives on Case-Based Reasoning* (London: Routledge), p 83.

35 Katalin Kelemen (2013) 'Dissenting Opinions in Constitutional Courts', *German Law Journal*, 14(8): 1347–8; E.J. Cohn (1957) 'Dissenting Opinions in German Law', *International and Comparative Law Quarterly*, 6(3): 540–3.

Europeanization

In the wake of Nazism and the collapse of the German state, the creation of a 'European Germany' was seen by West German elites as essential for rebuilding West German national identity.[36] The BRD's first postwar Chancellor, Konrad Adenauer of the Christian Democratic Union (*Christlich Demokratische Union Deutschlands* (CDU)), embraced European integration, influenced by 'the triptych of self-conscious anti-Nazism, Christian values, and dedication to European unity as a means of redemption for past German sins'.[37] The Social Democrats (*Sozialdemokratische Partei Deutschlands* (SPD)) had likewise remained staunchly pro-European throughout the Weimar era and their exile under Nazism, contributing to a centrist political consensus that European integration was in Germany's interest that has remained a consistent influence on German political discourse.[38] Yet gaining entrance into the Council of Europe proved challenging. West Germany's application was initially met with resistance from France and the UK, still wary of the German state and its part in instigating two wars in half a century. Adenauer and the CDU had to fight to convince the Council that Germany should join, drawing on notions of a shared Christian history and expressing a wholehearted commitment to West European values as a means to gain Europe's trust and learn from past mistakes.[39] As Adenauer told the Consultative Assembly in 1951:

> The whole German people, with only a few exceptions, are in favour of European evolution. … A bitter experience has taught our people that it is necessary to expend all one's energies to maintain, develop and defend Western culture if it is to survive. … This fact finds more than symbolic expression in the human rights convention recently

[36] Thomas Mann, cited in Martin Marcussen, Thomas Risse, Daniela Engelmann-Martin, Hans-Joachim Knopf, and Klaus Roscher (1999) 'Constructing Europe? The Evolution of French, British, and German Nation-State Identities', *Journal of European Public Policy*, 6(4): 622.

[37] Ernst Haas (1958) *The Uniting of Europe: Political, Social, and Economic Forces, 1950–57* (Stanford, CA: Stanford University Press), p 127, cited in Marcussen et al, 'Constructing Europe?', p 622.

[38] Thomas Risse (2001) 'A European Identity? Europeanisation and the Evolution of Nation-State Identities', in Maria Green Cowles, James Caporaso, and Thomas Risse (eds), *Transforming Europe: Europeanisation and Domestic Change* (Ithaca, NY: Cornell University Press), pp 198–216.

[39] Marco Duranti (2017) *The Conservative Human Rights Revolution: European Identity, Transnational Politics, and the Origins of the European Convention* (New York: Oxford University Press), pp 192–7.

> established under the auspices of the Council of Europe, and which governments have committed to respect.[40]

More recently, former Chancellor Gerhard Schröder also cast the Nazi era as an aberration in Germany's European history through Franco-German friendship, describing the two countries as 'united by a "culture of doubt"' – that is, a culture 'designed to overcome definitive dogmas' and which upholds 'democracy, pluralism and tolerance in diversity' – that goes back to the Enlightenment era.[41] In 2022, Foreign Minister Annalena Baerbock positioned remembering the Holocaust as foundational to European integration, and as part of the common heritage European institutions claim to uphold, stating that the existence of European integration and liberal democracies 'is tied to the awareness of our dark past' and that 'peace, freedom and democracy in Europe have historical roots that we must preserve'.[42]

To this end, Thomas Banchoff argues that Germany's European identity has been buttressed by 'two interlocking narratives': first, a 'negative narrative [which] drew a link between the German catastrophe of dictatorship, war and genocide, and the irreversibility of Germany's integration into a larger Europe', and second, 'a commitment to Europe through a positive postwar narrative' in which integration 'helped to overcome centuries-old rivalries and conflicts'.[43] Similarly, Lora Wildenthal suggests that Germany's immediate history made it particularly receptive to European integration. Wildenthal notes that this experience had a marked effect on understandings of human rights in German discourses, asserting that 'the complex intertwining of the domestic and the international meant that discussions of (domestic) civil liberties in West Germany have never been far from those of (international) human rights'.[44] These dual narratives structure the human rights cultural

---

[40] Konrad Adenauer (1951) Discours devant le Conseil de l'Europe [Speech before the Council of Europe], Strasbourg, 10 December. Available at: https://www.cvce.eu/content/publication/2003/10/10/0ea92ca7-2add-405e-9b03-047ab6e9b728/publishable_fr.pdf (accessed 18 December 2017).

[41] Gerhard Schröder (2003) Speech at the joint meeting of the German Bundestag and the Assemblée Nationale on the 40th anniversary of the signing of the Elysée Treaty, Versailles, 22 January. Available at: https://www.bundesregierung.de/breg-de/service/bulletin/rede-von-bundeskanzler-gerhard-schroeder-789522 (accessed 8 February 2024).

[42] Annalena Baerbock (2022) Speech at virtual event 'International Holocaust Remembrance Day: Responsibilities for All of Society', hosted by B'nai B'rith International, 24 January. Available at: https://www.auswaertiges-amt.de/en/newsroom/news/baerbock-b-nai-b-rith/2507914 (accessed 8 February 2024).

[43] Thomas Banchoff (1999) 'German Identity and European Integration', *European Journal of International Relations*, 5(3): 273.

[44] Lora Wildenthal (2013) *The Language of Human Rights in West Germany* (Philadelphia, PA: University of Pennsylvania Press), p 6.

environment reciprocally. Protecting the dominant Holocaust memory regime by embedding human rights in judicial and constitutional projects provides legitimization for embracing European and international laws and, in turn, Europeanization provides legitimization for postwar transformation narratives by showing that Germany has been accepted 'back into the community of peoples'.[45]

Socialist human rights in the Deutsche Demokratische Republik

Germany's mainstream postwar rights narratives reflect an almost exclusively West German conception of rights. For the eastern half of the country, that fell under Soviet occupation in 1945 and became the communist DDR from 1949 to 1990, human rights took on radically different meanings and uses to those of West Germany. As early as December 1946, East German legal scholar, Karl Polak, declared that there could be 'no human rights without socialism'.[46] The notion that rights could 'only be realised insofar as socialism has been made a reality' quickly became a key tool for justifying DDR policies.[47] According to the rhetoric of the ruling Socialist Unity Party (*Sozialistische Einheitspartei Deutschlands* (SED)), socialist human rights transcended the 'mere "individual rights" or judicial claims which the individual has against the state', ostensibly offering 'true' liberation from economic struggle and class injustice.[48] Thus, socialist rights were conceived not as an individual defence against excessive state power, but as something provided only as long as the SED remained in power, and bound up with a concomitant duty on citizens to support the socialist cause.[49] In addition to broad structural conceptions of 'freedom from capitalism', the socialist rights narrative emphasized numerous genuine, tangible social and economic rights, such as the rights to work, to a basic standard of living guaranteed by the state, and to holidays. Especially following the DDR's accession to the United Nations and its human rights covenants in 1973, individual citizens

45 Merkel, Speech to the Parliamentary Assembly of the Council of Europe.

46 Karl Polak (1946) 'Gewaltteilung, Menschenrechte, Rechtsstaat: Begriffsformalismus und Demokratie' [Separation of Powers, Human Rights, Rule of Law: Concept Formalism and Democracy], *Einheit*, 7 December. See also Ned Richardson-Little (2014) 'Dictatorship and Dissent: Human Rights in East Germany in the 1970s', in Jan Eckel and Samuel Moyn (eds), *The Breakthrough: Human Rights in the 1970s* (Philadelphia, PA: University of Pennsylvania Press), pp 49–67.

47 Polak, 'Gewaltteilung, Menschenrechte, Rechtsstaat'.

48 Otto Grotewohl (1947) *Deutsche Verfassungspläne* [German Constitutional Plans] (Berlin: Dietz), cited in Richardson-Little, 'Dictatorship and Dissent', p 52.

49 Paul Betts (2013) 'Socialism, Social Rights, and Human Rights: The Case of East Germany', *Humanity: An International Journal of Human Rights, Humanitarianism & Development*, 3(3): 420.

were able to connect socialist ideology to international human rights norms in an attempt to improve the system from within, and as political leverage to gain (slightly) greater personal freedoms.[50]

The ECHR – with its emphasis on individualism, democratic principles, and property rights – was derided as a bourgeois plot, attached to the conservative Christian 'civilizing mission' in western Europe.[51] Socialist human rights narratives thus existed in opposition to the European human rights project – ultimately leaving little room for reconciliation between the two conceptions after reunification in 1990. When the DDR collapsed, calls for liberal rights both from dissenters within the DDR as well as the West, along with the rapid progress of reunification, meant that East German conceptions of rights were subsumed by Western ideas. East Germany acceded to the Federal Republic under Article 23 of the Basic Law, with East German citizens automatically gaining access to the rights of the Basic Law, as well as to the ECHR by virtue of the Federal Republic's existing membership in the Council of Europe.[52] The socialist human rights rhetoric used by the SED to criticize the West and the European human rights system fell to the wayside as former DDR leaders were removed from power and citizens embraced their newly won democratic rights and freedoms. Even the last leader of East Germany as an independent state, Hans Modrow, articulated the desire to shift away from state-provided socialist rights, calling for 'the strict respect for human rights without exception, which demands a new attitude of the state toward the individual'.[53]

Despite extensive historical research on the dual roles of human rights as tools of dissent and dictatorship in the DDR, contemporary legal and political research on Germany's relationship with the ECtHR barely mentions the DDR, except as a historical aberration, or to point out the legal mechanisms by which the DDR merged with the BRD.[54] The most concrete influence of socialist conceptions of rights is in the lasting support for social and economic rights in the constitutions of the former East German *Länder*. In the process of integrating East and West Germany, very few laws – human rights-related or otherwise – were transferred from the DDR legal code to

---

50 Richardson-Little, 'Dictatorship and Dissent', p 57.

51 Betts, 'Socialism, Social Rights, and Human Rights', pp 410–12.

52 Elisabeth Lambert Abdelgawad and Anne Weber (2008) 'The Reception Process in France and Germany' in Helen Keller and Alec Stone Sweet (eds) *A Europe of Rights: The Impact of the ECHR on National Legal Systems* (New York: Oxford University Press), p 114.

53 Hans Modrow, cited in Richardson-Little, 'Dictatorship and Dissent', p 67.

54 Andreas Zimmermann (2001) 'Germany', in Robert Blackburn and Jörg Polakiewicz (eds), *Fundamental Rights in Europe: The European Convention on Human Rights and its Member States, 1950–2000* (New York: Oxford University Press), pp 336–7; Lambert Abdelgawad and Weber, 'The Reception Process in France and Germany', p 114.

the BRD. These absences further highlight the hegemonic nature of West Germany and reunited Germany's transformation narratives in mainstream human rights cultural politics.

Cultural politics in action: Germany's relationship with Strasbourg

The judicial relationship

The relationship between the Strasbourg and Karlsruhe courts can, for the most part, be characterized as cooperative, although this harmony exists partly because in the first several decades of the ECtHR's existence there were few opportunities for judicial dialogue or conflict. The extensive system of rights protections in Germany and the compatibility of Basic Law rights with ECHR rights, especially the BVerfG's individual complaint procedure, meant that by the time the ECtHR delivered its first judgment – *Lawless v Ireland* in 1961 – and began to tentatively develop its own jurisprudence, a solid body of rights-based constitutional law had already been established at Karlsruhe.[55] The BVerfG's reputation as an integral rights-protecting institution helped to ensure that human rights complaints could be addressed before needing to be taken to Strasbourg.[56] Additionally, many of the ECtHR's early judgments against Germany required only individual measures or minor adjustments to the application of law in particular cases, meaning that in the first few decades of their relationship, Karlsruhe and Strasbourg largely avoided the interjudicial conflicts that can arise over more profound structural changes to domestic law.[57] Dialogue between the two courts has increased as the ECtHR has grown in stature and scope, creating more opportunities for new interpretations of the ECHR and divergences from the BVerfG's own jurisprudence, and as the reunification of East and West Germany exposed the Federal Republic to a larger population capable of making complaints.[58]

One of the key instruments guiding the dialogue between Strasbourg and Karlsruhe has been the principle of the Basic Law's *Völkerrechtsfreundlichkeit*, or 'openness towards international law'. As the former President of the

55 See the three landmark cases decided between 1957 and 1961: *Lüth* (BVerfGE 7, 198, 15 January 1958), *Elfes* (BVerfGE 6, 32, 16 January 1957), and *Apothekenurteil* (BVerfGE 7, 377, 11 June 1958).

56 Norman Weiss (2003) 'The Impact of the European Convention on Human Rights on German Jurisprudence', in Esïn Örücü (ed), *Judicial Comparativism in Human Rights Cases* (London: British Institute of International and Comparative Law), p 53.

57 Alice Donald and Philip Leach (2016) *Parliaments and the European Court of Human Rights* (Oxford: Oxford University Press), p 8.

58 Lambert Abdelgawad and Weber, 'The Reception Process in France and Germany', p 124.

BVerfG, Andreas Voßkuhle, notes, the principle 'combines the exercise of state sovereignty with the idea of international cooperation' by enabling German courts to consider international treaties, case law, and customary norms as a natural element of the domestic legal system.[59] The BVerfG has asserted that the Basic Law's 'openness to international law' represents:

> an expression of an understanding of sovereignty, which not only does not oppose integration into international and supranational contexts and their further development, but which presupposes and expects this. Against this background, the 'last word' of the German Constitution is not opposed to an international and European dialogue of the courts, but is its normative basis.[60]

This careful legal balance between sovereign authority and international obligation mirrors political discourses extolling Germany's desire to demonstrate its commitment to European integration and human rights, allowing Germany to build a reputation as a trustworthy, democratic member of the international community by becoming 'embedded in a sphere of international and European references'.[61] This openness to general international law is also complemented by a specific openness to European law (*Europarechtsfreundlichkeit*), which Voßkuhle claims allows Germany to make a unique contribution to a multilevel system of cooperation between national and European courts, and to the creation of a form of legal European integration grounded in cooperation and coherence.[62]

There are limits to Germany's openness towards Strasbourg, though. In the 2004 *Görgülü* case, the BVerfG noted that, as the ECHR holds the status of a federal statute, 'it must be taken into account in the interpretation of domestic law, including fundamental rights and constitutional guarantees'.[63] The court cited the Basic Law's openness to international law and Germany's general commitment to international law as establishing a duty to interpret the Basic Law as much as possible in a manner consistent with Germany's international legal obligations.[64] However, the BVerfG also stressed that this

---

[59] Andreas Voßkuhle (2010a) 'Multilevel Cooperation of the European Constitutional Courts: *Der Europäische Verfassungsgerichtsverbund*', *European Constitutional Law Review*, 6(2): 185.

[60] BVerfGE 128, 326, 4 May 2011, para 89 ('*Preventive Detention I*').

[61] Voßkuhle, 'Multilevel Cooperation', p 179.

[62] Voßkuhle, 'Multilevel Cooperation', p 183; Andreas Voßkuhle (2010b) 'Protection of Human Rights in the European Union. Multilevel Cooperation on Human Rights between the European Constitutional Courts', lecture at Our Common Future, Hannover, 4 November, p 4.

[63] BVerfGE 111, 307, 14 October 2004, para 30 ('*Görgülü*').

[64] BVerfGE 111, 307, 14 October 2004, para 33.

commitment to international law 'takes effect only within the democratic and constitutional system of the Basic Law', asserting that:

> The Basic Law aims to integrate Germany into the legal community of peaceful and free states, *but does not waive the sovereignty* contained in the last instance in the German constitution. There is therefore no contradiction with the aim of commitment to international law if the legislature, exceptionally, does not comply with the law of international agreements, provided this is the only way in which a violation of fundamental principles of the constitution can be averted.[65]

In other words, the last word on the application of international law in Germany belongs to the BVerfG. To this end, *Görgülü* serves as a crucial reminder that as far as domestic courts are concerned, 'national constitutional norms emerge as ultimately superior to European human rights norms and national courts as the final authorities in determining their relationship'.[66] The BVerfG outlined clear limits to the ECtHR's influence in German law, establishing that German courts would only apply the ECHR insofar as it is not considered to violate a principle of the Basic Law, or if legislation is expressly intended to contradict the ECHR. It also remains the remit of the BVerfG to decide whether ECHR principles contradict the Basic Law or not.

Still, the German judiciary recognizes that it shares the goal of protecting fundamental rights with the ECtHR, and is ultimately happy to engage in dialogue with Strasbourg. For instance, in the case *Von Hannover v Germany* – concerning the publication of photos of Princess Caroline of Monaco by German media – the BVerfG and ECtHR reached conflicting conclusions over the right balance to strike between privacy rights and press freedoms. The BVerfG dismissed the Princess' claims on the grounds that photos of her in public were proportionate due to her status as an 'absolute person of contemporary history'.[67] This ruling was consistent with the BVerfG's reluctance to restrict the press in line with the Basic Law's absolute prohibition on censorship – a position that stems directly from Germany's experience of dictatorship.[68] The ECtHR, in contrast, found in favour of Princess Caroline's privacy rights, arguing that although the photos were taken in public, they did not concern activities associated with her official

---

65 BVerfGE 111, 307, 14 October 2004, para 35 [emphasis added].

66 Nico Krisch (2008) 'The Open Architecture of European Human Rights Law', *Modern Law Review*, 71(2): 197.

67 BVerfGE 101, 361, 26 February 2008 ('*Caroline II*').

68 Katja Ziegler (2007) 'The Princess and the Press: Privacy after *Caroline von Hannover v Germany*', in Katja Ziegler (ed), *Human Rights and Private Law: Privacy as Autonomy* (Oxford: Hart Publishing), p 192.

duties and therefore could not 'be deemed to contribute to any debate of general interest to society despite the applicant being known to the public'.[69]

The ECtHR judgment attracted criticism among German legal scholars and practitioners, who viewed the Strasbourg judgment as failing to respect a reasonable margin of appreciation without sufficient justification, especially given that the ECtHR contradicted its own prior case law and application of proportionality tests, deviating from the common (continental) European standard of proportionality to apply a 'reasonableness' test that originates in English law.[70] The BVerfG, however, ultimately shifted away from its original approach when Princess Caroline filed a further constitutional complaint, in order to ensure that its own proportionality test conformed with Strasbourg's – thereby showing itself to be open to cooperation and dialogue even in the face of a potentially controversial judgment.[71] In turn, Strasbourg reaffirmed the importance of the margin of appreciation in its reasoning in *Von Hannover (no 2)*, noting that where the balancing of rights by national courts was consistent with ECtHR case law, 'the Court would require strong reasons to substitute its view for that of the domestic courts'.[72]

The political relationship

In contrast to its interactions with the judiciary, the ECtHR attracts little attention in the German political sphere. Public awareness and discussion of the Strasbourg system has increased over time, especially in the wake of high-profile cases such as *Von Hannover*, and general knowledge of human rights and the German rights protection system are relatively high.[73] At the international level, the Merkel government served as a prominent advocate for the ECtHR, asserting that it is 'resolutely opposed to efforts to weaken the European Court of Human Rights'.[74] German delegates to the Council of Europe have stressed that 'the Court's power to give guidance on the States' obligations' is crucial for ensuring national authorities fulfil their

69 *Von Hannover v Germany*, App no. 59320/00 (ECtHR, 28 July 2005), para 65.

70 Ziegler, 'The Princess and the Press', p 196; Julia Rackow (2015) 'From Conflict to Cooperation: The Relationship Between Karlsruhe and Strasbourg', in Katja S. Ziegler, Elizabeth Wicks, and Loveday Hodson (eds), *The UK and European Human Rights: A Strained Relationship?* (Portland, OR: Hart Publishing), p 381.

71 BVerfGE 120, 180, 26 February 2008 ('*Caroline III*').

72 *Von Hannover v Germany (no. 2)*, App nos. 40660/08 and 60641/08 (ECtHR, 7 February 2012), paras 107 and 105.

73 Christoph Gusy and Sebastian Müller (2008) *Supranational Rights Litigation, Implementation and the Domestic Impact of Strasbourg Court Jurisprudence: A Case Study of Germany*, project report for the JURISTAS project, Bielefeld: Universität Bielefeld, p 28.

74 Christlich Demokratische Union Deutschlands (2013) *Gemeinsam erfolgreich für Deutschland*, Regierungsprogramm 2013–2017 (Berlin: CDU-Bundesgeschäftsstelle), p 75.

obligations.[75] The centre-left SPD has emphasized human rights as 'the obligatory basis of our society' and upholding Germany's international commitments as necessary 'to promote the identity of Germany and Europe as a peacemaker', reflecting the broad cross-partisan support for the European human rights system evident in Germany since it first sought to join the Council of Europe in 1950.[76] High levels of public trust in the BVerfG and understandings of law as a science to be practised by experts facilitate an environment in which government and the *Bundestag* tend to defer to the BVerfG;[77] criticism of the constitutional court is rare, and governments have on occasion waited to hear from the BVerfG before legislating on issues that have implications for constitutional rights.[78]

The emphasis on courts being primarily responsible for dealing with Strasbourg is also apparent in the media's haphazard approach to coverage of Strasbourg cases and developments. National newspapers and weekly magazines cover cases that are considered to be of public interest, such as the *Von Hannover* cases because they concerned a prominent public figure, or *M. v Germany* and *Gäfgen v Germany* because they concerned questions of public safety and the rights of criminals. On the other hand, issues that are not deemed to be of public interest attract almost no media attention, even if they make a significant impact on German law or human rights protections – an approach broadly consistent with the German media's approach to EU and European issues as a whole.[79] Nonetheless, where

---

75 Statement by Head of Delegation for Germany, Dr Max Stadler, in Council of Europe (2012) *Proceedings of the High Level Conference on the Future of the European Court of Human Rights, Brighton, 19–20 April 2012*, p 56.

76 Sozialdemokratische Partei Deutschlands (2013) *Das Wir Entscheidet, Das Regierungsprogramm 2013–2017* (Berlin: SPD-Parteivorstand), p 111.

77 Statista Research Department (2020) *Umfrage in Deutschland zum Vertrauen in Justiz und Rechtssystem 2019*, 9 March. Available at: https://de.statista.com/statistik/daten/studie/153813/umfrage/allgemeines-vertrauen-in-die-justiz-und-das-rechtssystem/ (accessed 1 April 2020); Michael Schlieben (2012) 'Großes Vertrauen in Karlsruhe, wenig in die Regierung', *Zeit Online*, 9 July. Available at: https://www.zeit.de/politik/deutschland/2012-07/umfrage-institutionen-karlsruhe (accessed 1 April 2020); Göran Schattauer (2019) 'Umfrage-Desaster: Nicht einmal 39 Prozent der Deutschen vertrauen unserer Justiz', Focus, 19 December. Available at: https://www.focus.de/politik/gerichte-in-deutschland/exklusive-erhebung-umfrage-desaster-nicht-einmal-39-prozent-der-deutschen-vertrauen-unserer-justiz_id_11474205.html (accessed 1 April 2020); Hailbronner, 'Rethinking the Rise of the German Constitutional Court', p 628.

78 Rackow, 'The Relationship between Karlsruhe and Strasbourg', p 399; Donald and Leach, *Parliaments and the European Court of Human Rights*, p 4.

79 Katrin Voltner and Christiane Eilders (2003) 'The Media Agenda: The Marginalisation and Domestication of Europe', in Kenneth Dyson and Klaus Goetz (eds), *Germany, Europe, and the Politics of Constraint* (Oxford: Oxford University Press/British Academy), p 173; Juan Diez Medrano (2003) *Framing Europe: Attitudes to European Integration in Germany, Spain, and the United Kingdom* (Princeton, NJ: Princeton University Press), pp 179–99.

news outlets do provide coverage of particular issues, the reports tend to be detailed and accurate (with the exception of one or two pieces that reflect some confusion about whether Strasbourg judgments are binding).[80] Editorials about the politics of the European human rights system are rare. This both reflects and contributes to relatively positive, or at least neutral, public perceptions of the ECtHR, although Christoph Gusy and Sebastian Müller note that limited public debate also reflects and reinforces the lack of awareness of the Strasbourg system.[81]

Even among far-right and Eurosceptic actors who might be expected to take a more hostile stance towards human rights or European institutions, criticism of the ECtHR tends to be context-specific. The far-right *Alternativ für Deutschland* party, for example, has criticized the Court for rulings preventing Germany from deporting suspected terrorists.[82] This is in line both with the AfD's hard-line antimigration and anti-Islam platform, and with the pattern of cases concerning crime and national security attracting more aggressive political and media attention evident in the United Kingdom (see Chapter 4). But the party has also endorsed the Court when its rulings suit the AfD agenda. Deputy leader and *Bundestag* member, Beatrix von Storch, released a statement on the party's website in February 2020 praising the Court for a ruling finding that Spain's decision to return two migrants attempting to cross the Spanish (and EU external) border to Morocco did not constitute a violation of the Convention.[83] Von Storch not only extrapolated from the ruling to suggest that Germany could also refuse asylum applications at the German border, she also called for the ECtHR ruling to be used as the basis for justifying the rejection of migrants coming from third countries via the Basic Law.[84] The party's electoral programme for the 2017 federal election similarly referred to (but did not name or cite) a 2014 ECtHR ruling to claim that the party's proposal to ban Islamic religious

---

80 Frank Diering (2004) 'Straßburger Urteile nicht bindend' [Strasbourg Judgments not binding], *Die Welt*, 20 October. Available at: https://www.welt.de/print-welt/article347316/Strassburger-Urteile-nicht-bindend.html (accessed 31 March 2017).

81 Gusy and Müller, *Supranational Rights Litigation, Implementation and the Domestic Impact of Strasbourg Court Jurisprudence*, p 29.

82 Alternative für Deutschland (2017) Facebook post, 2 August. Available at: https://www.facebook.com/alternativefuerde/photos/a.542889462408064/1581236365240030/ (accessed 19 February 2020).

83 The case is *N.D. and N.T. v Spain*, App nos. 8675/15 and 8697/15 (ECtHR, 13 February 2020).

84 Alternativ für Deutschland (2020) 'Beatrix von Storch: Nach dem Urteil des EGMR können illegal Migranten sofort abgeschoben werden' [According to the judgment of the ECtHR, illegal migrants can be deported immediately], AfD, 17 February. Available at: https://www.afd.de/beatrix-von-storch-nach-dem-urteil-des-egmr-koennen-illegale-migranten-sofort-abgeschoben-werden/ (accessed 19 February 2020).

dress would be legal.[85] The ad hoc approach to criticism and support in different contexts indicates that the ECtHR is not a prominent target of Euroscepticism or institutional illegitimacy in its own right, but a tool that can be weaponized to serve specific political agendas and culture wars. At the other end of the political spectrum, members of the left-wing party, *Die Linke*, articulate understandings of human rights that resonate with socialist conceptions, calling for 'a solidary Europe' and the 'fair distribution of rights, wealth and resources'.[86] But while they endorse the ECtHR as an important component of human rights protections in Germany in their party manifesto,[87] their representatives' everyday engagement with the Court tends to focus on compelling other member states – particularly Turkey – to meet their obligations.[88] The tacit assumption is that Germany does not need to be reminded of its commitment to international law.

The overall support for strong judicial oversight grants the ECtHR high levels of institutional and normative legitimacy. The ECtHR is viewed by politicians, judges, and the media as a European extension of the German judiciary and as such is able to 'borrow' legitimacy from the German courts. As long as the German judiciary maintains its status as the pre-eminent institution for defending the Basic Law and ECHR, questions about the legal authority or democratic legitimacy of the Strasbourg system are unlikely to gain traction in the German public sphere. Positive political perceptions of the ECtHR are further bolstered by German support for European integration and Germany's particularly 'open' conception of sovereignty. Broad consensus across the political spectrum that the Europeanization of German politics is in Germany's vital interests has remained a constant overtone in German political discourse since the 1950s,[89] and has helped to foster base-level perceptions of both EU and Council of Europe institutions as legitimate.

---

85 Alternativ für Deutschland (2017) *Programm für Deutschland: Wahlprogramm der Alternativ für Deutschland für die Wahl zum Deutschen Bundestag am 24. September 2017* (Köln: Alternativ für Deutschland), p 35.

86 Die Linke (2021) *Zeit zu handeln! Für soziale Sicherheit, Frieden und Klimagerechtigkeit: Wahlprogramme zur Bundestagswahl 2021* (Berlin: Die Linke), p 113.

87 Die Linke, *Zeit zu handeln!*, p 151.

88 Andrej Hunko (2021) 'Türkiye: Council of Europe Infringement Proceedings against Türkiye Correct', press release, 3 December. Available at: https://www.dielinke-nrw.de/parlament/bundestag/detail-bundestag/tuerkei-vertragsverletzungsverfahren-des-europarates-gegen-tuerkei-richtig/ (accessed 20 February 2024); Bernd Riexinger (2018) 'On the ECHR Judgment on Demirtas/Türkiye', press release, 20 November. Available at: https://www.bernd-riexinger.de/aktuell/detail/bernd-riexinger-zum-egmr-urteil-zu-demirtas-tuerkei/ (accessed 20 February 2024).

89 Simon Bulmer (1989) 'Unity, Diversity and Stability: The "Efficient Secrets" behind West German Public Policy?', in Simon Bulmer (ed), *The Changing Agenda of West German Public Policy* (Aldershot: Dartmouth Publishing), p 32.

These perceptions of the inherent legitimacy of European institutions go hand in hand with widespread public acceptance of judicial intervention to produce a rights culture that views input from international institutions as a natural – even essential – part of the national democratic process. Başak Çalı and Alice Wyss echo this finding, suggesting that German conceptions of the rule of law represent 'a singular concept [where] politicians are under a duty to abide by the rule of law, domestic or international'.[90] Former Chancellor Merkel articulated the idea that international oversight is an extension of the domestic democratic process in a speech to the Parliamentary Assembly of the Council of Europe in 2008, noting that 'there is a duty in Europe to intervene in each other's affairs, where human rights are concerned. In the human rights sphere, a country can have no internal affairs.'[91] Similar sentiments are evident in various public statements by German judges, politicians, and media, expressing concerns that Germany's decisions to comply or not comply reverberate across Europe, potentially sending messages to other states that compliance is optional.[92] This conception of human rights as a regional, rather than exclusively national, responsibility can thus be seen as a reflection of a cultural environment that fosters understandings of international supervision as an intrinsic element of national sovereignty and democracy, rather than as competition or a threat. To this end, it represents one of the core driving forces behind Germany politicians' mostly positive attitudes towards Strasbourg and their willingness to comply with ECtHR judgments.

Smooth political relations are further facilitated by the fact that the Council of Europe and ECtHR reciprocate German formulations of the relationship between memory, law, and human rights. In a statement titled 'Why Remembering the Holocaust is a Human Rights Imperative', the Commissioner for Human Rights, Nils Muižnieks, echoes framings of the Holocaust as an exceptional event by describing it as 'one of the defining moments of history that has shaped the conscience of mankind … unique in its roots, implementation and envisioned totality'.[93] The

[90] Başak Çalı and Alice Wyss (2009) *Why do Democracies Comply with Human Rights Judgments? A Comparative Analysis of the UK, Ireland and Germany*, SSRN Working Paper, 26 August, pp. 20–1.

[91] Angela Merkel (2008) Address to the 2008 Ordinary Session of the Council of Europe Parliamentary Assembly, Strasbourg, 14–18 April. Available at: http://assembly.coe.int/Sessions/2008/Speeches/20080415_Speech-Merkel.htm (accessed 1 April 2017).

[92] See, for example, *Frankfurter Allgemeine Zeitung Archiv* (2004) *Im Ausland mißverständlich* [Misperceptions abroad], 23 October. Available at: https://fazarchiv.faz.net/faz-portal/document?uid=FAZ__FD2200410232525189 (accessed 28 September 2024).

[93] Nils Muižnieks (2016) 'Human Rights Comment: Why Remembering the Holocaust is a Human Rights Imperative', Commissioner for Human Rights, 18 October. Available

ECtHR treats Holocaust denial as running counter to the 'basic values underlying the Convention',[94] using ECHR Article 17 – which prohibits 'any act aimed at the destruction of any of the rights and freedoms set forth herein' – to categorically dismiss any and all cases concerning Holocaust denial as inadmissible.[95]

This alignment between mainstream German and European constructions of the connection between memory, law, and rights is one of the fundamental factors shaping positive political relations between German actors and the ECtHR. In contrast to the United Kingdom, where local practices and ideas concerning the links between rights and law routinely jar with those articulated in Strasbourg, commonalities in German and Strasbourg memory orientations facilitate a broad consensus environment where the legitimacy of the European human rights regime as a whole means the Court has been able to conduct its work to date largely unchallenged. But this harmony is precarious, and depends on both German actors and Strasbourg maintaining similar conceptions of Holocaust memorialization as the bedrock of the contemporary regional human rights order. The speed and ferocity with which German government officials have jumped to intervene in the International Court of Justice (ICJ) case brought by South Africa against Israel provides insight into how the current relationship could fracture. Within hours of Israel's oral hearing, the German government announced its intention to intervene in the case as a third party, citing German history as evidence of their expertise in what constitutes genocide, to dismiss South Africa's argument:

> In view of Germany's history and the crime against humanity of the Shoah, the Federal Government sees itself as particularly committed to the Convention against Genocide … the Federal Government firmly and expressly rejects the accusation of genocide that has now been made against Israel at the International Court of Justice.[96]

at: https://www.coe.int/en/web/commissioner/-/why-remembering-the-holocaust-is-a-human-rights-imperative (accessed 10 February 2024).

94 *Kühnen v Federal Republic of Germany*, App no. 12194/86 (ECtHR, 12 May 1988).

95 Paolo Lobba (2015) 'Holocaust Denial before the European Court of Human Rights: Evolution of an Exceptional Regime', *European Journal of International Law*, 26(1): 239.

96 Steffen Hebestreit (2024) 'Statement by the Federal Government on the Proceedings at the International Court of Justice', Press and Information Office of the Federal Government, 10 January. Available at: https://www.bundesregierung.de/breg-de/aktuelles/erklaerung-der-bundesregierung-zur-verhandlung-am-internationalen-gerichtshof-2252842 (accessed 16 February 2024).

Similarly, Vice-Chancellor Robert Habeck appealed to the exceptionality of the Holocaust, asserting that 'one can criticize the Israeli military for acting too harshly in the Gaza Strip. However, that does not constitute genocide … Accusing Israel of genocide, in my view, is a complete reversal of victims and perpetrators, and is just wrong.'[97] Renowned German international lawyer, Stefan Talmon, lambasted these statements as 'politically motivated',[98] while the government's claim that it 'firmly oppose[s] political instrumentalisation' rang hollow for German-based and international critics alike because the statement was made on the 120th anniversary of the start of the Herero and Nama genocide.[99] The government statement noted Germany's commitment to international law, but the government holds fast to the claim that South Africa's 'accusation has no basis whatsoever', in clear contrast to the facts of the case and the ICJ's own preliminary findings.[100] Germany has not yet had to confront similar tensions with the ECtHR, but the ICJ case illustrates the hegemonic influence the dominant Holocaust memory regime has over how German politicians engage with international law, and how divergences from that regime may jeopardize the broad environment of legitimacy that international courts currently enjoy in Germany.

The effects of the German cultural politics of rights on compliance

The cooperative nature of Germany's relationship with Strasbourg has yielded what is generally regarded as one of the most exemplary compliance records in the European human rights system. Germany acts quickly to comply with ECtHR judgments when they arise, although relatively few cases reach the

---

[97] In Stefan Talmon (2024) 'Germany Rushes to Declare Intention to Intervene in the Genocide Case brought by South Africa against Israel before the International Court of Justice', GPIL – German Practice in International Law, 15 January. Available at: https://gpil.jura.uni-bonn.de/2024/01/germany-rushes-to-declare-intention-to-intervene-in-the-genocide-case-brought-by-south-africa-against-israel-before-the-international-court-of-justice/ (accessed 16 February 2024).

[98] Talmon, 'Germany Rushes to Declare Intention to Intervene'.

[99] Khaled El Mahmoud (2024) 'Measuring with Double Legal Standards: Germany's Intervention in Support of Israel before the ICJ', Verfassungsblog, 25 January. Available at: https://verfassungsblog.de/measuring-with-double-legal-standards-germanys-intervention-in-support-of-israel-before-the-icj/ (accessed 16 February 2024); Presidency of the Republic of Namibia (2024) 'Namibia rejects Germany's Support of the Genocidal Intent of the Racist Israeli State against Innocent Civilians in Gaza', media release dated 13 January, Twitter/X. Available at: https://x.com/NamPresidency/status/1746259880871149956?s=20 (accessed 16 February 2024).

[100] Hebestreit, 'Statement by the Federal Government on the Proceedings at the International Court of Justice'.

judgment stage because they are addressed effectively at home.[101] Between the ECtHR's first judgment finding a violation of the Convention against Germany in 1978 (*König v Germany*) and the creation of the permanent Strasbourg court in 1998, Germany had only been found in violation of the Convention in 14 cases.[102] The number of cases against Germany has increased considerably since 1998, although the total number of violations found remains low overall; in addition to the 14 cases before 1998, the ECtHR delivered 187 judgments finding at least one violation against Germany between 1999 and 2021.[103] The ECtHR receives a relatively high number of individual applications claiming the perpetration of Convention violations by Germany – 27,755 cases were allocated to a judicial formation between 1959 and 2021 – although most of these are struck out or declared inadmissible.[104] Germany also has very few cases pending execution with the Committee of Ministers. Of the 11 cases pending a satisfactory resolution in January 2024, only one was a repetitive case (*Mitzinger v Germany*), and only one is under enhanced supervision (*Basu v Germany*), demonstrating both an institutional capacity and a willingness to comply with ECtHR judgments.[105]

Criticism is one thing, compliance is another

A key illustration of this willingness to comply rests in the series of cases concerning preventive detention. Part of the German criminal justice system for over 80 years, preventive detention (*Sicherungsverwahrung*) allows for the detention – either in prison or in mental health facilities – of dangerous and habitual criminal offenders for preventive purposes after their original prison sentence has expired.[106] It is considered to be a safety measure for both the general public and the offender, and is applied through a separate process from the original prison sentence as it is not viewed as a form of punishment. Legislative reforms in the 1990s expanded the

[101] Çalı and Wyss, *Why do Democracies Comply with Human Rights Judgments*, p 11.

[102] Gusy and Müller, *Supranational Rights Litigation, Implementation and the Domestic Impact of Strasbourg Court Jurisprudence*, p 4.

[103] European Court of Human Rights (2022) *Overview: 1959–2021* (Strasbourg: ECtHR). Available at: https://www.echr.coe.int/documents/d/echr/Overview_19592021_ENG (accessed 10 January 2024).

[104] European Court of Human Rights, *Overview: 1959–2021*.

[105] *Mitzinger v Germany*, App no. 29762/10 (ECtHR, 9 May 2017); *Basu v Germany*, App no. 215/19 (ECtHR, 18 January 2023).

[106] Christopher Michaelson (2012) '"From Strasbourg, with Love" – Preventive Detention before the German Federal Constitutional Court and the European Court of Human Rights', *Human Rights Law Review*, 12(1): 150.

scope of the detention system, lifting the ten-year limit on detention and allowing judges to delay the application of detention orders until the end of prisoners' sentences (meaning that prosecutors had more time to gather evidence to support detention). Following these reforms, a complaint was brought to the BVerfG by an individual known as 'M', convicted of murder and robbery in 1986, claiming that the extension of his detention beyond the ten-year maximum in place at the time of his conviction was a violation of the Basic Law's prohibition of retrospective punishment. The BVerfG dismissed the application as ill-founded in 2004.[107] M took the case to the ECtHR, which found in 2009 that the retrospective extension of his detention constituted a violation of both his Article 5(1) ECHR right to liberty and security, and his Article 7(1) ECHR right not to have a heavier penalty imposed than the one that was applicable at the time of the offence.[108]

Given that the practice of preventive detention has ramifications for public safety, the preventive detention cases have long been the subject of debate in the media and public sphere. Media discourse – in particular from the tabloid *Bild* – has emphasized the potential risks of changes to the preventive detention system through headlines such as 'Are Dangerous Sex Offenders Free Now?'[109] Concerns about the consequences of ending preventive detention have been expressed since reforms to the detention process were first made; as then-Chancellor Gerhard Schröder argued in 2001, 'there can only be one solution' for protecting the public from violent and sexual crimes: that the perpetrators 'be locked away, and indeed forever'.[110] In this context, the government might have been expected to leverage the public safety concerns and general support for the preventive detention system in order to criticize the ECtHR ruling and resist reforms. But the case became neither a compliance issue, nor an opportunity for public figures to question the legitimacy of the Strasbourg court. Instead, the Federal Justice Minister, Sabine Leutheusser-Schnarrenberger, declared that the ECtHR's

[107] BVerfGE 109, 133, 5 February 2004 (*'M'*).

[108] *M. v Germany*, App no. 19359/04 (ECtHR, 17 December 2009).

[109] Although 'M' was convicted of murder, much of the preventive detention debate before and after M's ECtHR case focused more on sexual offenders being released, as there had been a number of similarly high-profile cases concerning such crimes. Bild (2011) 'Kommen jetzt gefährliche Sex-Verbrecher frei?' [Are dangerous sex offenders free now?], Bild, 4 May. Available at: http://www.bild.de/news/inland/sicherungsverwahrung/bundesverfassungsgericht-sicherungsverwahrung-verfassungswidrig-17721950.bild.html (accessed 1 April 2017).

[110] Spiegel Online (2001) 'Sexualstraftäter lebenslang wegsperren' [Sex offenders locked away for life], Spiegel Politik, 8 July. Available at: http://www.spiegel.de/politik/deutschland/gerhard-schroeder-sexualstraftaeter-lebenslang-wegsperren-a-144052.html (accessed 1 April 2017).

ruling was 'final and binding for Germany'.[111] There was some debate at the time about what the appropriate response to the judgment would be – the Attorney General, Kay Nehm, proposed strengthening the preventive detention laws to make them more consistent, rather than abandoning them. Still, there was an overarching recognition that the case would be responded to.[112] Leutheusser-Schnarrenberger emphasized the need for a 'differentiated debate on the consequences and prospects of the verdict', highlighting the distinction between *whether* to comply and *how* to comply, while Nehm noted that 'whatever the solution to this urgent problem, federal and state governments remain committed to cooperation, not least in shaping the transition to a new law'.[113]

Hence, when new preventive detention cases appeared before the BVerfG after the ECtHR's '*M*' judgment, the German court reiterated the approach it has taken since *Görgülü*, clarifying that although the ECHR is subordinate to the Basic Law, the Basic Law nonetheless needs to be interpreted in line with the ECHR.[114] The BVerfG found that indefinite preventive detention was, in keeping with the new ECtHR jurisprudence, incompatible with the Article 2 Basic Law right to liberty, in essence reversing its 2004 decision and toppling a decades-old national practice. The *Bundestag* also worked quickly to present new legislation that would be compatible with the BVerfG and ECtHR rulings, suggesting that political concerns about balancing public safety with human rights were not significant enough to override Germany's legal obligations.[115]

Moreover, where criticism of the case did occur, its primary target was not the ECtHR. Multiple media reports mentioned the ECtHR judgment, but emphasized the responsibility of domestic institutions. For instance, *Der Spiegel* suggested that it was the responsibility of Karlsruhe and ordinary courts to make the changes necessary to comply with Strasbourg's ruling, while the *Süddeutsche Zeitung* and *Frankfurter Allgemeine Zeitung* focused on problems with the original legislation as the cause of the violations found by the ECtHR and BVerfG.[116] These articles indicate a perception that complying

---

111 Spiegel Online (2010) 'Kay Nehm fordert radikale Verschärfung der Sicherungsverwahrung' [Kay Nehm calls for a radical tightening of preventive detention], Spiegel Panorama, 12 May. Available at: http://www.spiegel.de/panorama/justiz/urteil-des-europaeischen-menschenrechtsgerichts-kay-nehm-fordert-radikale-verschaerfung-der-sicherungsverwahrung-a-694486.html (accessed 20 December 2017).

112 Spiegel Online, 'Kay Nehm fordert radikale Verschärfung der Sicherungsverwahrung'.

113 Spiegel Online, 'Kay Nehm fordert radikale Verschärfung der Sicherungsverwahrung'.

114 BVerfGE 128 326, 4 May 2011, paras 86–94.

115 Donald and Leach, *Parliaments and the European Court of Human Rights*, pp 10–12.

116 *Der Spiegel* (2011) 'Späte Erkenntnis' [Late insight], *Der Spiegel*, 7 May. Available at: http://www.spiegel.de/spiegel/print/d-78413701.html (accessed 1 April 2017); Julia Jüttner (2011) '"Ein unerträglicher Zustand"' [An unbearable condition], *Der Spiegel*, 5 May.

with the judgment was a given, and that delays or problems were the fault of domestic institutions, not of Strasbourg. Similarly, although preventive detention has been the subject of heated parliamentary debate, Julia Rackow notes that 'no public figure from any part of the political spectrum questioned the authority of the ECtHR's decision' in *M. v Germany*.[117] This points to the fact that, despite preventive detention clearly being a contested issue, the ECtHR itself was not viewed as the source of that contention, nor was it perceived to be unduly interfering in a domestic issue.

The influence of the German rights cultural environment and notions of legitimacy are evident throughout the process of complying with the preventive detention cases. The lack of criticism of the ECtHR, or indeed the BVerfG, for challenging a widely supported practice reflects the high levels of trust many Germans place in the judiciary and legal professionals as the appropriate experts on constitutional and human rights matters, as well as a recognition of the importance of international law as an extension of the domestic system. One of the only public figures to express doubts about the ECtHR's interpretation in *M. v Germany* was the President of the BVerfG, Andreas Voßkuhle, who had the authority to criticize the ECtHR legitimately as a member of the same branch of government and area of expertise.[118] The President also only critiqued Strasbourg's method of interpretation, suggesting that it had not sufficiently considered all aspects of the case; he did not challenge the authority or legitimacy of the ECtHR in general. The ability of public actors to separate the European human rights system as a legitimate source of international oversight from concerns about the interpretation of specific legal norms therefore illustrates the layers underpinning domestic political and judicial elites' understandings of legitimacy, as outlined in Chapter 2. The German and European judicial systems as a whole were not threatened by debate over the individual case, while altering the longstanding preventive detention practice did not spark more widespread controversy because it neither upset local sensibilities about the larger German constitutional hierarchy, nor came from institutions already struggling with legitimacy problems. Additionally,

---

Available at: https://www.spiegel.de/panorama/justiz/urteil-zur-sicherungsverwahrung-ein-unertraeglicher-zustand-a-760719.html (accessed 1 April 2017); *Süddeutsche Zeitung* (2011) 'Bundesverfassungsgericht kippt Sicherungsverwahrung' [Federal Constitutional Court topples preventive detention], *Süddeutsche Zeitung*, 4 May. Available at: http://www.sueddeutsche.de/politik/urteil-aus-karlsruhe-bundesverfassungsgericht-kippt-sicherungsverwahrung-1.1092944 (accessed 1 April 2017); *Frankfurter Allgemeine Zeitung* (2011) *Sicherungsverwahrung verfassungswidrig* [Preventive detention unconstitutional], 4 May 2011. Available at: http://www.faz.net/aktuell/politik/inland/bundesverfassungsgericht-sicherungsverwahrung-verfassungswidrig-1640218.html (accessed 1 April 2017).

117 Rackow, 'The Relationship between Karlsruhe and Strasbourg', p 387.

118 Rackow, 'The Relationship between Karlsruhe and Strasbourg', p 387.

the debate over how to comply, and later the BVerfG's decision to reverse its own rulings to align with the ECtHR, demonstrate German institutions' openness to dialogue as long as it contributes to the protection of the Basic Law's core rights. To this end, the *M. v Germany* case reflects perceptions that compliance even with difficult judgments is necessary simply because Germany made a commitment that must be respected,[119] and that 'criticising human rights judgments is a separate activity than complying with human rights judgments'.[120]

Germany's cooperative approach to compliance is further evident in the government's response to the 2010 case *Gäfgen v Germany*.[121] The case concerned the use of the threat of torture by German police in order to locate the 11-year-old boy who had been kidnapped and – unbeknown to the police at the time of the threat – murdered by the applicant, Gäfgen, in 2002. The ECtHR Grand Chamber found that the threat of torture by the police constituted inhuman treatment (although not actual torture) and was therefore a violation of Article 3 of the ECHR. The Court also questioned whether the German courts had sufficiently appreciated the severity of the breach of 'one of the core rights of the Convention', given the 'very modest and suspended fines' imposed as punishment on the police officers who committed the violation.[122]

The case (and the earlier domestic proceedings) sparked widespread public debate over whether 'a little bit of torture' could be justified if it were to yield information that could save a life.[123] The debate split public opinion; some sympathized heavily with the police officers, who were seen as doing everything possible to try to rescue the child,[124] while others emphasized the inviolability of human dignity, regardless of the crimes committed by

[119] Donald and Leach, *Parliaments and the European Court of Human Rights*, pp 7–8.

[120] Çalı and Wyss, *Why do Democracies Comply with Human Rights Judgments?*, p 23.

[121] *Gäfgen v Germany*, App no. 22978/05 (ECtHR, 1 June 2010).

[122] *Gäfgen v Germany*, paras 123–4.

[123] Jost Müller-Neuhof (2010) 'Ein bisschen Folter' [A Little Bit of Torture], *Tagesspiegel*, 1 June. Available at: http://www.tagesspiegel.de/weltspiegel/magnus-gaefgen-ein-bissc hen-folter/1849786.html (accessed 27 April 2017).

[124] Thomas Kirn (2012) 'Trauer, Wut und Verachtung sind geblieben' [Grief, anger and contempt have remained], *Frankfurter Allgemeine Zeitung*, 25 September. Available at: http://www.faz.net/aktuell/rhein-main/metzler-entfuehrung-trauer-wut-und-veracht ung-sind-geblieben-11903857-p2.html?printPagedArticle=true#pageIndex_2 (accessed 28 April 2017); Sandra Kegel (2012) 'Anatomies eines moralischen dilemmas' [Anatomy of a moral dilemma], *Frankfurter Allgemeine Zeitung*, 24 September. Available at: http:// www.faz.net/aktuell/feuilleton/kommissar-ennigkeit-zum-fall-anatomie-eines-moralisc hen-dilemmas-11900694-p2.html?printPagedArticle=true#pageIndex_2 (accessed 28 April 2017).

Gäfgen.[125] The Strasbourg ruling was therefore received in Germany in the context of conflicting public discourses and divergence of opinion over how the case should be addressed. The government of the *Land* of Hessen, responsible for paying the compensation ordered by the ECtHR, resisted the order through an attempted appeal in the Frankfurt am Main regional court. The federal government, however, demonstrated no such hesitation. It sent its first action report outlining its plan to comply with the judgment in November 2010, just five months after the judgment was finalized, and disseminated a German translation of the case to all German courts as well as to the federal and *Land* police departments, to be used for education and training.[126] The federal government also placed pressure on the Frankfurt court to speed up the compensation process, which was ultimately paid by the Hessian government in 2013.[127] Additionally, Alice Donald and Philip Leach note that the Human Rights Committee passed a resolution in the *Bundestag* recognizing that the use or threat of torture and inhuman treatment was unacceptable in any circumstances – an act that received some public backlash, and which the *Bundestag* was not under any obligation to undertake, as the general measures required to comply did not include legislative change.[128]

The federal government's actions in complying with the judgment, and the *Bundestag*'s actions in voluntarily reaffirming Germany's commitment to the prohibition of torture therefore point to a determination to comply with ECtHR judgments regardless of domestic perceptions of the case. This determination can be partly explained by the supremacy of the prohibition on torture in the German (and European) normative hierarchy. In both German and ECtHR law, the norm is absolute, and cannot be weighed against competing rights. As Federal Justice Minister Leutheusser-Schnarrenberger asserted in response to the *Gäfgen* judgment: 'the prohibition on torture is absolute. Human dignity is the most precious asset of human rights and is the basis of our entire legal system. This red line must never be crossed.'[129]

[125] *Süddeutsche Zeitung* (2010) 'Folterverbot gilt absolut' [Torture ban is absolute], *Süddeutsche Zeitung*, 1 June. Available at: http://www.sueddeutsche.de/politik/erfolg-fuer-kindes moerder-strassburg-gibt-gaefgen-recht-1.952672 (accessed 27 April 2017).

[126] Committee of Ministers (2011b) Action Report – Communication from Germany Concerning the Case of *Gäfgen against Germany*, to the Secretariat of the Committee of Ministers, DH-DD(2011)647E, 26 April.

[127] *Welt* (2010) 'Kindermörder ist Folteropfer – Kein neuer Prozess' [Child murderer is torture victim – no new trial], *Welt*, 1 June. Available at: https://www.welt.de/aktuell/article7869770/Kindermoerder-ist-Folteropfer-Kein-neuer-Prozess.html (accessed 29 September 2024).

[128] Donald and Leach, *Parliaments and the European Court of Human Rights*, pp 12–13.

[129] Sabine Leutheusser-Schnarrenberger, in *Welt*, 'Kindermörder ist Folteropfer – Kein neuer Prozess'.

But the government's and *Bundestag*'s responses to the *Gäfgen* case also highlight a recognition among German elites of the positive obligation to uphold *Rechtsstaat* principles in all cases, however difficult or politically sensitive. Speaking in the *Bundestag* shortly after the ECtHR's judgment, CDU/CSU member, Frank Heinrich, argued that 'it is a testimony to the true rule of law to accept unpleasant judgments. Those who comply with the judgment of the ECtHR also acquire the mandate to promote and fight for the respect of human rights themselves.'[130] Heinrich's language affirms how highly German elites value references to upholding the rule of law and obeying international commitments, because these actions help to legitimize and strengthen postwar transformation narratives that reify contemporary German culture and identity as fundamentally rights-respecting. It also places the onus to comply on Germany by framing acceptance of ECtHR judgments not as an obligation imposed on the state by Strasbourg, but as a responsibility that German actors themselves must 'fight' for. Thus, the compliance push in this case stems from the duty to uphold the human dignity and rights values at the heart of the postwar *Rechtsstaat*, and to be seen to be doing so.

What is especially noticeable about both the preventive detention and use of torture cases is that there is no indication in either case that the federal government struggled to make a (publicly justified) conscious decision about whether to comply. The clear political challenges and lack of public consensus on the issues could have served as excuses to defy Strasbourg and defend domestic practices, especially for preventive detention, given how long it has been part of the German justice system. Ultimately, however, public criticism and debate over the cases did not seem to influence, or even stall, the government's compliance actions. There is also little indication of the government being pressured to comply by Strasbourg; in both the *Gäfgen* and *M.* cases, the Committee of Ministers' reports expressed satisfaction with the German Ministry of Justice's initial action plans and subsequent progress reports, and the cases were closed by the Committee without controversy.[131]

[130] Frank Heinrich (2010) 'Deutscher Bundestag Stenografischer Bericht 49', Sitzung Plenarprotokoll 17/49, Berlin, 17 June 2010, p 5166, para B.

[131] Committee of Ministers (2012a) 1136 DH meeting, CM/Del/Dec(2012)1136/9, Decision on cases *M group against Germany* (19359/04), 8 March; Committee of Ministers (2014a) 1201 DH meeting, CM/Del/Dec(2014)1201/7, Decision on cases *M group against Germany* (19359/04), 5 June; Committee of Ministers (2014d) Resolution CM/ResDH(2014)290, Execution of the Judgment of the European Court of Human Rights in Thirteen Cases against Germany, 17 December; Committee of Ministers (2014c) Resolution CM/ResDH(2014)289, Execution of the Judgment of the European Court of Human Rights in the Case of *Gäfgen against Germany*, 17 December.

To this end, the core 'legitimacy criteria' or orienting elements present in German cultural politics over the meaning and purpose of rights – respect for the rule of law, commitment to human dignity, respect for the authority of legal decisions, and a perception of the legitimacy of European institutions, driven by a historical need to participate in them – appear to be so firmly entrenched among German elites that the decision to comply with ECtHR rulings is most often a straightforward one. Contemporary compliance choices in specific ECtHR cases rest on a powerful narrative about the foundational decision to accept basic rights and judicial oversight in the 1940s, in the context of needing strong constitutional values and international cooperation to reinvigorate West Germany's own legitimacy as an independent, sovereign democracy. Donald and Leach have made similar findings, noting that their interviewees believe the Convention system was automatically legitimized by virtue of being ratified by the *Bundestag*, while Germany's history means that 'Europe is our future and it's the only one. We have to comply, even if the judgments are sometimes very difficult.'[132]

This does not mean cases are never contentious; debates over the legal substance and social significance of specific rulings are an important part of (re)articulating the principles and practices that give rise to human rights sensibilities in Germany, keeping them in the foreground of discussions on human rights compliance. It also does not mean there will not be cases in the future that challenge Germany's procompliance attitude and require political actors to make more difficult decisions about whether or not to obey a Strasbourg judgment – attempts by the *Bundestag* and the Hessian government to minimize or resist compliance obligations show that unquestioning compliance is standard, but not a given.

Nonetheless, it remains important for understanding how domestic cultural landscapes inform compliance decisions, because it shows how culturally constructed notions of the legitimacy of international law are embedded in Germany through practice. Where British actors rely on cultural referents to rhetorically justify both compliance and noncompliance as evidence of British exceptionalism, German governments and politicians use deeds. Decision-making processes and subsequent implementation of judgments focused on how rather than whether to comply reflect a local cultural–political landscape that, while not entirely homogeneous, nonetheless reifies respect for judicial authority and Europeanization as evidence of memorialization and German transformation. In such a landscape, the foundational legitimacy of the ECtHR is so closely intertwined with elite narratives of German memory and constitutional–patriotic identity that the

[132] Donald and Leach, *Parliaments and the European Court of Human Rights*, p 7.

requirement to comply with its judgments per se is not typically contested, even if the means by which Germany complies are open to debate.

Resistance and noncompliance: the institutions strike back

Although there are no instances in Germany of outright, ongoing refusal to comply with Strasbourg rulings, there are some examples of resistance towards the implementation of judgments. In these cases, tensions over compliance tend to arise over issues concerning how to comply with judgments, rather than whether to comply, either because legislation suggested by Parliament or the executive does not satisfy compliance requirements, or because the BVerfG has deliberately taken a different approach to interpreting the case. As with the examples of Germany's openness to compliance, local knowledges about what makes the law legitimate shape the outcome of the compliance choices made, but questions of the overall legitimacy of the ECtHR or human rights in general rarely come into play.

The most prominent example of this form of tension is Germany's problem with cases concerning the excessive length of judicial proceedings. These cases are a significant compliance issue from Strasbourg's perspective; the ECtHR has found Germany in breach of the Article 6(1) ECHR right in nearly 70 cases, making up almost one third of the total number of violations found against Germany.[133] The right to speedy judicial proceedings as a component of the right to a fair trial is one of the few ECHR rights that is not also enumerated in the Basic Law. Combined with the complicated, multilevel judicial system, this gap in national law renders Germany 'particularly prone to producing long delays in proceedings'.[134] The *Bundestag* has also repeatedly rejected legislation proposed by the Ministry of Justice due to various concerns about the best way to respond to the Strasbourg judgments.

When Germany failed to implement the legislative remedies initially proposed by the Ministry of Justice after the ECtHR's *Sürmeli v Germany* judgment in 2006, the ECtHR instigated Germany's first ever pilot procedure in 2010, *Rumpf v Germany*.[135] The Ministry of Justice had proposed legislative changes to allow a right of appeal to higher courts when the original court was taking too long, but the changes faced resistance from parliamentarians who felt the judiciary was functioning effectively and who were reluctant

[133] European Court of Human Rights (no date b) *HUDOC Case Database*. Available at: https://hudoc.echr.coe.int (accessed 20 December 2017).

[134] Tomuschat, 'The Effects of the Judgments of the European Court of Human Rights According to the German Constitutional Court', p 517.

[135] *Sürmeli v Germany*, App no. 75529/01 (ECtHR, 8 June 2006); *Rumpf v Germany*, App no. 46344/06 (ECtHR, 2 September 2010).

to criticize the courts' procedures.[136] In light of this, the ECtHR issued a stern warning through the *Rumpf* judgment, stating that 'While the Court welcomes the recent legislative initiative, it also notes that the respondent State has failed so far actually to put into effect any measures aimed at improving the situation, despite the Court's substantial and consistent case-law on the matter.'[137] The ECtHR also set a one-year deadline for Germany to produce new remedies for the issue.[138] This is an especially tight time frame given the ECtHR's preference for allowing wide margins of appreciation for states with otherwise consistently efficient compliance records, demonstrating the severity with which Strasbourg viewed Germany's resistance towards its judgments.

The creation of a pilot procedure clearly served as a wake-up call for Germany that it needed to resolve the length of proceedings issue. The government awarded compensation to all the applicants under *Rumpf* and the other outstanding ECtHR cases, and the *Bundestag* passed the Act on Legal Redress for Excessive Length of Court Proceedings and of Criminal Investigation Proceedings in November 2011.[139] The Act established an 'acceleratory remedy' whereby applicants who feel their court proceedings are taking too long can lodge a complaint that permits judges to take action to remedy the situation, as well as a 'compensatory remedy' offering a new category of compensation for people affected by excessive case lengths.[140] The Committee of Ministers expressed its satisfaction with these measures in 2013 and closed its supervision process, although it warned that new cases could still arise depending on how the reforms are implemented and are borne out in case law.[141]

Although the tensions between Germany and Strasbourg over the length of proceedings saga reflect conflicting ideas about how best to address the issue, throughout the debate there was no indication that the resistance was the result of perceptions that the ECtHR was interfering or that its judgments were illegitimate, even when it set the strict time limit for implementing changes. The issue passed by without any noticeable political controversy or media coverage. Resistance from politicians was

[136] Donald and Leach, *Parliaments and the European Court of Human Rights*, p 13.

[137] *Rumpf v Germany*, para 68.

[138] *Rumpf v Germany*, para 73.

[139] Committee of Ministers (2013a) Action Report – Communication from Germany Concerning the *Rumpf* Group of Cases against Germany, to the Secretariat of the Committee of Ministers, DH-DD(2013)1234, 14 November, p 2; *Gesetz über den Rechtsschutz bei überlangen Gerichtsverfahren und strafrechtlichen Ermittlungsverfahren*, 24 November 2011. BGBl. 2011 I S, 2302.

[140] Committee of Ministers, Action Report – DH-DD(2013)1234, p 5.

[141] Committee of Ministers (2011a) 1128 DH meeting, CM/Del/Dec(2011)1128/11, Decision on Cases *Rumpf group against Germany* (46344/06), 2 December 2011.

strong enough to stifle changes to the judicial proceedings system before the *Rumpf* case, but this resistance did not appear to stem from public pressure or from scepticism towards the ECtHR's authority. Rather, it arose from arguments that the judiciary is independent and should not be subject to review by the legislature, as in the preventive detention cases. The remedies ultimately passed by the *Bundestag* in the Act on Legal Redress are a clear indication of this; the measures implemented represent a compromise between the need to comply with the ECtHR's judgments and politicians' reluctance to interfere in the judiciary by offering compensation and complaint mechanisms to applicants instead of addressing the structural factors that facilitate the lengthy proceedings in the first place.

A second compliance issue has occasionally been apparent with the relationship of the ECtHR to the German *Länder*. The federal government is responsible for overseeing compliance with the ECHR and ECtHR judgments in general, but much of the implementation occurs at the state level. The 16 *Länder* have broad jurisdictions and legislative powers, including over police forces and the implementation of certain immigration policies – areas where human rights considerations play a key role.[142] If a *Land* resists the implementation of an ECtHR judgment, or implements legislation incompatible with the ECHR, it can be difficult for the federal government to encourage it to comply.[143] This was the case for the Naumburg Court of Appeal, which, following the ECtHR's *Görgülü* judgment in 2004, explicitly decided to ignore the ECtHR judgment. The Naumburg court argued that ECtHR judgments are binding only on the federal government and that state authorities are free to ignore them:

> the judgment bound only the Federal Republic of Germany as a subject of public international law, but not its bodies, authorities and the bodies responsible for the administration of justice, which are independent under Article 97.1 of the Basic Law. … As a result of the status of the European Convention on Human Rights as ordinary statutory law below the level of the constitution, the ECtHR was not functionally a higher-ranking court in relation to the courts of the States parties. For this reason, neither in interpreting the European Convention on Human Rights nor in interpreting national

142 Gusy and Müller, *Supranational Rights Litigation, Implementation and the Domestic Impact of Strasbourg Court Jurisprudence*, p 14.

143 Zimmermann, 'Germany', p 343.

> fundamental rights could domestic courts be bound by the decision of the ECtHR.[144]

Only when the BVerfG issued an injunction against the Naumburg court and firmly established in its own case law that ECtHR judgments are binding on subnational authorities (by virtue of the fact that regional courts are bound by the Basic Law, which in turn must be interpreted so as to be compatible with the ECHR) did the lower court recognize the binding nature of ECtHR judgments. The superiority of federal courts and the BVerfG over regional courts prevents these clashes from arising frequently – *Görgülü* is the only example of a lower court ignoring the ECtHR so vehemently to date. Smaller attempts at resistance are also apparent, for example, in the Hessian government's attempt to avoid paying compensation in the *Gäfgen* case, as well as in *Jalloh v Germany*, in which the government of Hamburg attempted to argue that the ECtHR's ruling only concerned the *Land* in which the violation had occurred – Nord-Rheine Westfalen – and had no bearing on other *Länder*.[145] These cases reflect case-specific attempts by subnational institutions to test jurisdictional boundaries within the German federal system more than they signal challenges to particular interpretations of human rights or problems with the relative influence of the Convention and ECtHR. Nonetheless, the cases serve as a reminder that broadly procompliance cultural politics in Germany, while strong, is not uniform across the country. Alternative views on the role of the ECtHR and on German human rights protections could gain sufficient traction to challenge the current Germany–Strasbourg relationship and force German elites to more consciously assess the legitimacy of the Strasbourg system and their own decisions to comply with particular judgments.

Conclusion

The cultural politics surrounding compliance with the ECtHR in Germany are underpinned by strong judicial institutions, and political efforts to legitimize narratives of German post-Holocaust transformation. Germany's past and the ways it is remembered in political narratives have had a lasting impact through facilitating the creation of political and legal institutions that fiercely defend democratic values and the rule of law. The intersection of a historical need to regain the respect of the international community through participation in international institutions and human rights mechanisms with an internal determination to develop a postnationalist German identity based

[144] BVerfGE 111, 307, 14 October 2004, paras 312–13.

[145] *Jalloh v Germany*, App no. 54810/00 (ECtHR, 11 July 2006).

on respect for democratic principles, human dignity, and the rule of law, means that in-principle support for compliance with international law and the judgments of the ECtHR has been woven into German national identity and human rights narratives. The related cultural practices of being open to international law have not superseded elite conceptions of sovereignty or national identity, but enhanced them. Compliance with Strasbourg judgments is typically framed as a complement to, or expression of, national sovereignty and identity, rather than a threat, although this dynamic rests heavily on the fact that the ECtHR has rarely ruled in ways that seriously disrupt German judicial and political conceptions of sovereignty.

To this end, German approaches to compliance with the ECtHR are best described as habitual, at least as long as politicians and the BVerfG continue to reify national identity narratives and memory practices that pin the fate of German atonement to the protection of human rights through law. For the most part, this means there are rarely conscious 'decisions' to comply with any given case, in the sense that refusals are given serious consideration. Rather, discussion focuses on how to comply while still allowing space for national practices and autonomous decision making, especially for the Federal Constitutional Court and the norms enumerated in the Basic Law. Andreas von Staden makes a version of this argument too, suggesting that while Germany broadly accepts the normative premise of complying with international obligations, both the government and BVerfG do so along rationalist lines, finding strategies to minimize the work and cost of compliance, and to ensure that the final decisions are made within Germany.[146] What cultural analysis of German compliance practices adds to this is an understanding of the landscape in which such minimizing or sovereignty-protecting decisions occur, and of the local cultural lodestars to which they turn to evaluate the risks and advantages of certain compliance choices. It is here, in the local cultural politics of human rights and law, that political preferences and normative expectations about the legitimacy of law and legal institutions are constituted, and where we can identify the narratives and practices that facilitate smoother or more fractious compliance in particular cases. The German case demonstrates that while local cultural environments can firmly encourage compliance with little fuss, these environments are created and structured by the politics of history and memory all the same, and it is these politics that determine the terms on which compliance will occur.

[146] Andreas von Staden (2018) *Strategies of Compliance with the European Court of Human Rights: Rational Choice within Normative Constraints* (Philadelphia, PA: University of Pennsylvania Press), p 202.

6

Croatia: The Cultural Politics of Rights between Cooperation and Independence

On 5 November 2022, the Republic of Croatia celebrated the 25th anniversary of its ratification of the European Convention on Human Rights (ECHR). Over this time, Croatia has endeavoured to prove that it shares the 'common heritage' of European democracies,[1] attempting to overcome a recent history dominated by authoritarianism and nationalist violence by opening its domestic institutions and society to the rule of law and liberal human rights norms passed down first by the Council of Europe, and later the European Union (EU). But elements of Croatia's 'bad past' (*loše prošlosti*) have proved difficult to let go of,[2] hindering the consolidation of the state's democratic transition and contributing to disjointed understandings of the roles of domestic and international institutions in protecting human rights despite national authorities' 'good faith effort'.[3] Consequently, Croatian interactions with the European human rights system over the past decades have been marked by a generalized acceptance of the European Court of

1 Council of Europe, *Convention for the Protection of Human Rights and Fundamental Freedoms*, European Treaty Series No. 5, Rome, 4 November 1950, Preamble.

2 Nenad Dimitrijević (1996) *Ustavna demokratija shvaćena kontekstualno* [Constitutional democracy understood in context] (Beograd: Prometej Novi Sad), cited in Jasna Omejec (2015) 'Grundrechte in Kroatien' [Fundamental rights in Croatia], in Detlef Merten and Hans-Jürgen Papier (eds), *Handbuch der Grundrechte in Deutschland und Europa* [Fundamental Rights in Germany and Europe], vol xxxiv (Hamburg: C.F. Müller), p 6.

3 Pamela A. Jordan (2003) 'Does Membership Have its Privileges?: Entrance into the Council of Europe and Compliance with Human Rights Norms', *Human Rights Quarterly*, 25(3): 674.

Human Rights (ECtHR) and its obligations on the one hand, and by the challenges of translating acceptance into effective compliance in practice on the other.

In light of this dynamic, this chapter examines the effect of Croatian understandings of human rights and law on Croatian actors' perceptions of the legitimacy of the Strasbourg system and their decisions to comply with ECtHR judgments. I show that cultural politics of human rights in Croatia are structured by outward- or European-facing narratives stressing the importance of liberal democratic conceptions of human rights on the one hand, and on the other by inward-facing political discussion and compliance practices which are more emblematic of contestation across and within different conceptions of Croatian nationalism, formulations of European identity as ethnocultural rather than civic, and memory politics around the 1991–95 war of independence which do not always align with European expectations. At the same time, the Croatian judiciary's understandings of the roles of legal and political institutions in upholding rights remain heavily influenced by socialist-era traditions of formalism and deference to the political elite that foster reluctance to contribute to public debates about the place of local or Convention rights in the Croatian constitutional order.

These factors mean that, while the UK and German cultural contexts have produced certain hegemonic narratives about rights and law that politicians and judges alike find value in acknowledging and drawing on to inform their notions of legitimacy and compliance decisions, in Croatia several competing narratives and understandings of legitimacy pull political and judicial actors in different directions, with mixed results for the state's compliance record. Compliance with 'difficult' or locally sensitive cases often occurs at arm's length, as governments and courts adopt minimizing and avoidance strategies in their efforts to navigate competing understandings of the meanings of rights and the roles of national and European institutions in making them. Thus, the Croatian case demonstrates how the fragmentation of assumptions about rights and law sometimes means more visible cultural politics and contestation over how to engage with European and international law, but can conversely mean no debate at all, as diffuse or incompatible cultural strands make it difficult for compliance actors to weave together meaningful interpretations of what makes the law legitimate for different audiences.

Status of the ECHR in Croatian law

Croatia signed the ECHR on 6 November 1996, on its accession to the Council of Europe. The Council was one of the first international institutions to be joined by the new Republic of Croatia, which had adopted its own first democratic, non-socialist constitution in December

1990,[4] shortly before declaring independence from the Socialist Federal Republic of Yugoslavia (*Socijalistička Federativna Republika Jugoslavija*, or SFRJ) in June 1991. The Convention was ratified, and the jurisdiction of the ECtHR accepted, on 5 November 1997. Croatia's monist legal system means that all international treaties signed, ratified, and made public by the Croatian government automatically have effect in national law, and can be applied directly by domestic courts. The President and government, which sign treaties, and the *Sabor* (parliament), which ratifies them, are responsible for ensuring that any international treaties to which Croatia becomes party are consistent with the Croatian constitution before they are incorporated into the domestic legal order.

The ECHR is given effect in Croatian domestic law primarily by the Constitutional Court (*Ustavni sud Republike Hrvatske*). Along with all the international treaties to which Croatia is party, the ECHR enjoys a quasi-constitutional status in the Croatian legal system, as its 'provisions may be changed or repealed only under conditions and in the way specified by the international treaties themselves, or in accordance with the general rules of international law'.[5] Formally, the provision in Article 141 of the constitution that international treaties are 'above law in terms of legal effects' means that international law, including the ECHR, sits above domestic legislation in the Croatian legal hierarchy, but below the constitution.[6] In practice, international law is frequently used by the Constitutional Court as a means to review national legislation's compatibility with the Croatian legal order. This practice has helped to entrench the ECHR in the Croatian legal system as a core constitutional document; it is the most commonly cited and applied treaty by the Constitutional Court of all the international law to which Croatia is party.[7] The Constitutional Court has explicitly clarified that 'the authority of the Constitutional Court to review the compliance of a law with an international treaty is the logical consequence of the constitutional provision whereby the international treaty ... forms a part of the domestic legal order and is by legal force ranked higher than a law'.[8]

4 *Ustav Republike Hrvatske* [Constitution of the Republic of Croatia], Narodne Novine [Official Gazette], 56/1990. English translation available at Croatian Parliament, 'The Constitution of the Republic of Croatia (Consolidated Text)', https://www.usud.hr/en/the-constitution (accessed 28 December 2024).

5 *Constitution*, Article 141.

6 Ivana Božac and Melita Carević (2015) 'Judicial Application of International and EU Law in Croatia', in Siniša Rodin and Tamara Perišin (eds), *Judicial Application of International Law in Southeast Europe* (Berlin: Springer-Verlag), p 137.

7 Božac and Carević, 'Judicial Application of International and EU Law in Croatia', p 144.

8 Constitutional Court of the Republic of Croatia, Decision U-I-745/1999, 8 November 2000, para 7(1) [English translation]. Available at: http://compendium.itcilo.org/en/compendium-decisions/constitutional-court-of-croatia-8-november-2000-no.-u-i-745-1999 (accessed 17 December 2017).

International law enjoys such a prominent position in part because of the Constitutional Court's 'practice of using international treaties as benchmarks for monitoring domestic law'.[9] As former President of the Constitutional Court, Jasna Omejec, asserts, international treaties 'serve as standards for the review of the national legislation'.[10] This is a particularly important feature of the Croatian legal system, as it means the Constitutional Court not only examines whether Croatian law is consistent with the constitution, but also whether national law is consistent with international standards.

The Croatian human rights cultural context: living the 'thousand-year-old' dream

Modern Croatian conceptions of law, human rights, and the role of European institutions have evolved in the context of a series of political transitions. In less than 30 years, Croatia has gone from a socialist constituent republic of the SFRJ, to an independent though still largely authoritarian presidential state under Franjo Tuđman and his conservative, nationalist party, the Croatian Democratic Union (*Hrvatska demokratska zajednica* (HDZ)), to an increasingly stable parliamentary democracy following Tuđman's death in 1999, and eventually to a full member of the EU in 2013. In the midst of these transitions, Croatia has also had to come to terms with its role in the wars following the breakup of Yugoslavia, including the perpetration of war crimes, while simultaneously responding to pressure from the EU to forge a new identity as a liberal European democracy in the wake of its 20th-century authoritarian experiences.

These transitions and experiences have had profound effects on how Croatian political and legal actors understand human rights and view the role of domestic and international institutions in protecting them, revealing a largely good faith relationship with the ECtHR and international law more broadly. Yet the integration of liberal constitutional ideas and human rights narratives has not been a straightforward, linear process. Rather, the local cultural context remains multifaceted, with liberal democratic, authoritarian, and socialist traditions shifting, interacting, and overlapping in the same environment. To this end, domestic ideas about rights and law are inconsistent, contested, and subject to change, with mixed effects on

[9] Božac and Carević, 'Judicial Application of International and EU Law in Croatia', p 138.

[10] Jasna Omejec (2009) *Legal Framework and Case-Law of the Constitutional Court of Croatia in Deciding on the Conformity of Laws with International Treaties: Report for the European Commission for Democracy Through Law (Venice Commission, Montenegro* (Strasbourg: Venice Commission), p 2.

how Croatia receives, interprets, and decides to comply with Strasbourg human rights norms.

Croatian constitutionalism and the legacies of socialist and authoritarian legal cultures

Croatian legal culture has been characterized by many legal scholars as 'in transition'.[11] It is increasingly open to liberal European conceptions of rule of law and dynamic, purposive interpretation, while still heavily shaped by socialist and nationalist constitutionalisms which emphasize the state, rather than courts, as the supreme guardians of law. The Yugoslav constitution accommodated social and economic rights insofar as they were provided by the state and did not interfere with socialist ideology or the authority of the political elite,[12] but law's purpose was ultimately and explicitly instrumental.[13]

In this context, one of the strongest influences on the cultural politics of rights in Croatia is judicial formalism, a doctrinal method in which judges' purpose is to match the technical facts of a case to the black letter of the law, rather than to evaluate the merits and circumstances of a case or develop law independently. Notions of a deferential, restricted judiciary stem from both the rigid formalism of the 18th-century Austro-Hungarian legal system, as well as communist-era requirements that courts only apply the law according to socialist doctrine.[14] Even the Yugoslav Constitutional Court, established in part to demonstrate the superior freedoms and social-democratic practices of Yugoslav communism relative to Soviet states, was empowered only to review the constitutionality of laws in line with socialist ideology, and did so in an advisory, rather than scrutinizing role.[15] Judges in lower courts, with considerably less autonomy, not only understood their role as narrow and bureaucratic, but relied on the apparatus of communist bureaucracy for their own political survival, adhering to the precise formal wording of the law to avoid responsibility for potentially sensitive decisions, or better yet, delaying and adjourning hearings to avoid making decisions at all.[16]

---

[11] Lana Bubalo (2023) 'An Introduction to the Legal Cultures of Bosnia and Herzegovina, Croatia, and Serbia (Western Balkan)', in Søren Koch and Marius Mikkel Kjølstad (eds), *Handbook on Legal Cultures* (Cham: Springer), p 145.

[12] Article 40, SFRJ Constitution, cited in Branko Pešelj (1963) 'Socialist Law and the New Yugoslav Constitution', *Georgetown Law Journal*, 51(4): 670.

[13] Alan Uzelac (2010) 'Survival of the Third Legal Tradition?', *Supreme Court Law Review*, 49: 378.

[14] Siniša Rodin (2005) 'Discourse and Authority in European and Post-Communist Legal Culture', *Croatian Yearbook of European Law and Policy*, 1(1): 11; Pešelj, 'Socialist Law and the New Yugoslav Constitution', p 664.

[15] Pešelj, 'Socialist Law and the New Yugoslav Constitution', pp 701–3.

[16] Uzelac, 'Survival of the Third Legal Tradition?', p 384.

Courts remained similarly politicized in the 1990s under President Tuđman, who was quick to remind courts that their role was to serve 'the national interests'.[17] Under these instructions, judges – often political appointees with little judicial experience – frequently deferred to the executive and *Sabor* to make important legal decisions.[18]

In the contemporary era, judges maintain a narrow understanding of their role in the Croatian legal system, conceiving of courts as the technocratic 'mouth of the law' and applying statutory legislation in line with the will of the *Sabor* and the executive.[19] Courts may refer legislation to the Constitutional Court, but do not have the power to strike down legislation on constitutional grounds themselves. They also do not recognize case law as a primary source of law and are not bound by precedent, meaning that the judiciary's role is to apply 'authentic', literal interpretations of statutes in line with abstract legal doctrines, rather than to engage in the process of law making by considering the practical social or policy implications of particular cases.[20] Judicial reforms and the appointment of new judges since Tuđman's death in 1999 have helped to address the politicization of the legal system and exposed the judiciary to new understandings of their function and purpose as potential lawmakers. Nonetheless, the notion that the legislature makes laws and courts faithfully apply them is still apparent in judges' reluctance to engage with more dynamic, practical interpretations of the law or to question or critique the legitimacy of legal norms established by the *Sabor*.[21]

Legal professionals hold mixed perceptions of this formalist legacy. Formalism's defenders argue that the method facilitates equality and predictability before the law, providing a buffer against political interference.[22] The continuity of formalism throughout Croatia's many overarching legal systems is also often framed as a proud tradition reflective of Croatian

17 Uzelac, 'Survival of the Third Legal Tradition?', p 382.

18 Christopher Lamont (2011) 'Confronting the Consequences of Authoritarianism and Conflict: The ECHR and Transition', in Antoine Buyse and Michael Hamilton (eds), *Transitional Jurisprudence and the European Convention on Human Rights: Justice, Politics and Rights* (Cambridge: Cambridge University Press), p 88.

19 Tamara Ćapeta (2005) 'Courts, Legal Culture and EU Enlargement', *Croatian Yearbook of European Law and Policy*, 1(1): 7; Jasna Omejec (2010a) 'The Constitutional Development of European Post-Communist and Post-Socialist States', speech delivered at the International Scientific-Practical Conference: The Constitution – A Basis of Democratic Development of the State, 27–28 August, Astana.

20 Ćapeta, 'Courts, Legal Culture and EU Enlargement', p 9; Rodin, 'Discourse and Authority in European and Post-Communist Legal Culture', p 11.

21 Ćapeta, 'Courts, Legal Culture and EU Enlargement', p 10.

22 Bubalo, 'An Introduction to the Legal Cultures of Bosnia and Herzegovina, Croatia, and Serbia', pp 171 and 157.

judicial independence.[23] That the new Constitutional Court, established in 1990, considers itself the descendant of the Yugoslav Constitutional Court even while nationalists have sought to distance Croatia from its federal and communist past by enshrining the 'right of the Croatian nation to self-determination and state sovereignty' in the constitution is a key example of Croatia's complicated understandings of its own national identity and the role of law and courts in maintaining it.[24]

For those invested in Europeanization, formalist traditions and constitutional nationalism are symbolic of Croatia's bad pasts and get in the way of European dynamic interpretation practices. Former President of the Constitutional Court Jasna Omejec suggests that the new rights and political values included in the constitution and Croatian legal order are a 'direct answer to the previous historical experience of repression' and reflect the 'constitutionalisation of fear of the renewal of totalitarianism'.[25] Omejec also emphasizes the necessity of 'accepting the common European constitutional heritage' of liberal, individual rights and respect for the rule of law in moving away from Croatia's illiberal past, pointing to Germany's post-Nazism experience of entrenching constitutional rights and European integration as a model for Croatia's own transition.[26] Hence, as in Germany, entrenching human rights and a sense of openness towards European and international institutions in the Croatian political and legal order have been presented as essential for overcoming Croatia's authoritarian and conflict-ridden history. But Croatia's progress towards these European normative expectations is ongoing, and attempts to sever independent Croatia from its legal history are not comprehensive. Despite reforms, judicial formalism remains the dominant mode of legal interpretation, and the state is still largely understood as the ultimate determiner of law. As Croatian Judge at the Court of Justice of the European Union (CJEU), Siniša Rodin, asserts, 'while it cannot be said that the Croatian judiciary or the Constitutional

---

[23] Péter Cserne (2020) 'Discourses on Judicial Formalism in Central and Eastern Europe: Symptom of an Inferiority Complex?', *European Review*, 28(6): 885.

[24] Ksenija Turković and Jasna Omejec (2016) 'Commitment to Reform: Assessing the Impact of the ECtHR's Case Law on Reinforcing Democratisation Efforts in Croatian Legal Order', in Iulia Motoc and Ineta Ziemele (eds), *The Impact of the ECHR on Democratic Change in Central and Eastern Europe* (Cambridge: Cambridge University Press), p 111; Robert M. Hayden (1992) 'Constitutional Nationalism in the Formerly Yugoslav Republics', *Slavic Review*, 51(4): 658.

[25] Omejec, 'The Constitutional Development of European Post-Communist and Post-Socialist States'.

[26] Omejec, 'The Constitutional Development of European Post-Communist and Post-Socialist States'.

Court are hostile to fundamental rights, the fact remains that their proper social function still needs to be discovered'.[27]

Croatian, European, innocent: the politics of national identity and memory

Finally, Croatia's perceptions of the European human rights system (and the European project in general) are influenced by the mythologies and memory politics surrounding Croatia's national and European identities. In particular, two interlocking – at times both complementary and contradictory – narratives have played a critical role in shaping how Croatia views its place in Europe and its participation in European institutions.

The first narrative portrays Croatia as an independent nation, distinct from other Balkan and Eastern European cultures. In this tale, Croatia's independence dates back over a millennium, to the medieval Kingdom of Croatia, which stood as an independent kingdom from 925 to 1102, when it formed a union with the Kingdom of Hungary and was eventually folded into the Austro-Hungarian realm in 1527. The notion of Croatia as one of the oldest civilizations in Europe is a fundamental element of Croatian national identity and political mythology, helping to construct 'over centuries a sense of uniqueness and distinctness of Croats from their South Slavic neighbours and a deeply rooted desire for sovereign statehood'.[28] Having existed only as a constituent state or region within larger polities for centuries – the Hapsburg Empire, the Kingdom of Slovenes, Croats and Serbs, the Kingdom of Yugoslavia, the Nazi puppet Independent State of Croatia, and the SFRJ – the Croatian declaration of independence from Yugoslavia in 1991 represented an important turning point in Croatian nationalist history. President Tuđman announced that Croatia had finally fulfilled its 'thousand year old dream',[29] while recognition of Croatian statehood by Germany in 1991 and other European states in 1992 helped to bolster the belief that Croatia deserved to be a sovereign state. This narrative is also reflected in the constitution: the document's opening section on historical foundations speaks of Croatia's 'millennial national identity' and the 'continuity of its statehood'.[30] In reality, having been subsumed under other states and empires for centuries means that almost all of the legal and political traditions that continue to have any effect in the contemporary system come from non-Croatian sources,

[27] Siniša Rodin (2013) 'Croatia: Developing Judicial Culture of Fundamental Rights', in Rainer Arnold (ed), *The Universalism of Human Rights* (Dordrecht: Springer), p 403.

[28] Jelena Subotić (2011) 'Europe is a State of Mind: Identity and Europeanisation in the Balkans', *International Studies Quarterly*, 55(2): 315.

[29] Franjo Tuđman, cited in Marcus Tanner (2010) *Croatia: A Nation Forged in War* (3rd edn, New Haven, CT: Yale University Press), p ix.

[30] *Ustav Republike Hrvatske*, chapter 1.

particularly the Austro-Hungarian Empire and the SFRJ.[31] Nonetheless, narratives emphasizing Croatia's independence still play a powerful role in senses of Croatian national identity, informing Croatia's determination to be recognized as an equal sovereign actor through membership in European and international institutions.

The second narrative intersects with Croatia's independence tale to suggest that Croatia is – and always has been – thoroughly European, and that the nation's inclusion in Yugoslavia in the 20th century was, as President Tuđman declared, 'just a short episode in Croatian history'.[32] This narrative stresses Croatia's 'European' traits and close cultural and historical connections to Central Europe through the Austro-Hungarian Empire, as well as to its Mediterranean/Adriatic neighbours, while simultaneously seeking to distance Croatia from its profoundly different, if not outright inferior, Balkan neighbours. In this view, Croatia is Catholic, democratic, prosperous, uses the Roman (rather than Cyrillic) alphabet, and shares the sensible, pragmatic culture of its Germanic, Central European neighbours. In contrast, the Balkan states and their South Slavic peoples are predominantly Orthodox and Muslim, and painted as being poor, primitive, and preoccupied with religious and national tribalism.[33] Thus, Croatia's European identity is as much about establishing the state as naturally belonging to Europe as it is about distancing itself from its Balkan, Yugoslav past and its pejorative associations.[34] To this end, the 'Croatia as European' narrative has in large part served a strategic purpose, being used to try to position Croatia as a stable, liberal democracy whose natural status is as an independent, equal, sovereign member of the European institutions. It has also had a lasting negative impact on the nature of rights protections in terms of underpinning nationalist tensions between Croats and minority ethnic groups, especially Serbs.[35]

---

31 Branko Smerdel (2014) 'In Quest of a Doctrine: Croatian Constitutional Identity in the European Union', *Zbornik Pravnog fakulteta u Zagrebu* [Collected papers of the Zagreb Law Faculty], 64(4): 514; Rodin, 'Discourse and Authority in European and Post-Communist Legal Culture', p 11.

32 Franjo Tuđman (1997) Address of the President of the Republic of Croatia on the State of the Nation, cited in Nicole Lindstrom (2003) 'Between Europe and the Balkans: Mapping Slovenia and Croatia's "Return to Europe" in the 1990s', *Dialectical Anthropology*, 27(3–4): 325.

33 Jelena Subotić (2013) 'Stories States Tell: Identity, Narrative and Human Rights in the Balkans', *Slavic Review*, 72(2): 322; Lindstrom, 'Between Europe and the Balkans', p 317.

34 Subotić, 'Europe is a State of Mind', pp 311–12; Maple Rasza and Nicole Lindstrom (2004) 'Balkan is Beautiful: Balkanism in the Political Discourse of Tuđman's Croatia', *East European Politics and Societies*, 18(4): 630.

35 Brad K. Blitz (2008) 'Democratic Development, Judicial Reform and the Serbian Question in Croatia', *Human Rights Review*, 9(1): 123–35.

This self-image of Croatia as culturally, historically, naturally belonging to Europe is often at odds with the image of the political, cosmopolitan Europe which the EU and Council of Europe expect their members to adopt. As Jelena Subotić has shown, European narratives of Holocaust remembrance which centre Jewish victimhood and demand acknowledgement of past culpability from European states have been profoundly unsettling for Croatia and other former communist states. Here, Holocaust remembrance was first absorbed into larger narratives about 'communist triumph over fascism' and then into postcommunist narratives about the crimes of communism perpetrated against – not by – the peoples of those states.[36] The obligations arising from the Council of Europe and ECtHR occasionally rub up against local identity narratives and political memory in similar ways, especially with cases concerning state investigations into deaths during the 1991–95 war or other challenges to national identities.

Nonetheless, the belief that there are close underlying cultural and historical similarities between independent Croatia and the rest of Europe has also helped to open Croatia to joining European institutions and accepting European norms with relatively little conflict.[37] Croatian political notions of legitimacy are thus profoundly connected to the pursuit of statehood, and the pursuit of recognition as culturally and historically European. These views intersect to produce elite political narratives that, on one hand, suggest that the only way to achieve legitimate statehood for Croatia is through participation in European institutions, but, on the other hand, foster Euroscepticism and nationalism due to fears about national identity and culture being subsumed under supranational entities in light of the memory of negative experiences with Yugoslav federalism and communism. Consequently, Croatia's political and judicial interactions with Strasbourg reflect discourses of rights and law that broadly frame Strasbourg as legitimate for its role in reifying Croatia's European and national identities, but play out differently as various actors navigate (or avoid) different conceptions of what those identities mean and whom they include.

Cultural politics in action: Croatia's relationship with Strasbourg

The judicial relationship

The tension between being open to European human rights norms in principle and struggling to incorporate them domestically in practice

[36] Jelena Subotić (2019) *Yellow Star, Red Star: Holocaust Remembrance after Communism* (London and Ithaca, NY: Cornell University Press).

[37] Subotić, 'Europe is a State of Mind', pp 309–30.

is clearest in the relationship between Croatia's domestic courts and Strasbourg. The Croatian Constitutional Court has afforded the ECHR a 'quasi-constitutional' status in Croatian law, and has the potential to provide a highly effective standard of human rights protections in line with Strasbourg. The Constitutional Court has also acknowledged the 'binding interpretive authority' of the ECtHR's judgments, including judgments concerning other countries, and has 'explicitly accept[ed]' the ECtHR as the creator of 'European constitutional standards'.[38] This indicates that the Constitutional Court holds the ECtHR in high esteem, and recognizes a seemingly unconditional obligation to incorporate the Convention and Strasbourg case law into constitutional proceedings.

In practice, however, the actual application of Convention rights and Strasbourg case law by the Croatian judiciary – especially by the ordinary courts – has been, as Siniša Rodin asserts, 'scarce and inconclusive'.[39] While the Constitutional Court often applies the Convention in its decisions and uses it as a legal basis for striking down both parliamentary legislation and subordinate courts' judgments, these decisions are not always consistent with the case law of the ECtHR.[40] The Constitutional Court often treats the Convention as a standalone document, developing its own interpretations and jurisprudence, independent of the ECtHR's case law and interpretations of the ECHR. This parallel jurisprudence does not necessarily diminish or damage domestic legal protections of rights – Rodin argues that the Constitutional Court is a 'sophisticated interpreter of fundamental rights and a national leader in the application of the ECHR'[41] – but it does reflect domestic courts' practice of only recognizing statutory codes as sources of law, and their corresponding inexperience with case law. This means that, for the most part, the Constitutional Court is not engaging with the understandings of the Convention rights expressed by the ECtHR, or participating in dialogue with the ECtHR over the meanings and applications

[38] Jasna Omejec (2010b) *Ways and Means to Recognise the Interpretive Authority of Judgments Against Other States – the Experience of the Constitutional Court of Croatia: Report to the Conference on the Principle of Subsidiarity, Skopje, 1–2 October*, reproduced in Committee on Legal Affairs and Human Rights, Parliamentary Assembly of the Council of Europe (2010) *Strengthening Subsidiarity: Integrating the Strasbourg Court's Case-Law into National Law and Judicial Practice*, Conference on the Principle of Subsidiarity, Skopje, 1–2 October, p 17. Available at: https://assembly.coe.int/committeedocs/2010/20101125_skopje.pdf (accessed 24 September 2024).

[39] Siniša Rodin (1999) 'Application of the European Human Rights Convention in the Republic of Croatia – an Element of Constitutional Checks and Balances', *European Studies*, 36(5): 108.

[40] Rodin, 'Application of the European Human Rights Convention in the Republic of Croatia', p 107.

[41] Rodin, 'Croatia: Developing Judicial Culture of Fundamental Rights', p 391.

of Convention rights as they evolve over time. It also means that when the Constitutional Court does refer to Strasbourg case law, it tends to do so in a 'troubleshooting nature', quoting 'de-contextualized normative parts as a justification of decisions in individual cases' without fully engaging with or internalizing the particular rights, norms, and understandings of human rights law which have been developed by Strasbourg and are taking hold in other European states.[42]

Similarly, judicial application of the Convention by the nonconstitutional judiciary has, to date, been extremely limited. The Supreme Court has cited the Convention (though again, not the ECtHR's case law) relatively frequently in recent years, although Jasna Omejec notes that 'there is no other national court in Croatia [other than the Constitutional Court] today which directly applies the Convention law'.[43] This means that, despite the Convention's formal constitutional status, there is little depth to the Convention's influence in Croatian law, as lower-level courts do not refer to constitutional documents in ordinary practice.

Ordinary courts' reluctance to hear human rights cases is further perpetuated by a historically rigid perception, confirmed in a 2004 Supreme Court judgment, that the adjudication of human rights claims under the ECHR (or any rights-based law) 'does not fall within the jurisdiction of the ordinary courts', but is solely the responsibility of the Constitutional Court.[44] This reflects the courts' narrow interpretation of their role as appliers, rather than makers, of the law; the ECHR and Strasbourg jurisprudence often require creative, dynamic interpretation and consideration of a wide range of possible social and political consequences of the application of Convention rights in given cases – practices which do not easily mesh with the abstract legal doctrines applied in formalist legal systems, and which Croatian judges believe to be beyond the scope of their authority and expertise. As such, the extent to which Strasbourg judgments and practices have permeated Croatian legal culture and day-to-day legal protection of human rights is limited and relatively superficial. The absence of regular dialogue between the Croatian judiciary and ECtHR, in particular, limits the extent to which the Constitutional and national courts can debate and contextualize the fit of European human rights standards within the domestic legal system, because

42 Rodin, 'Croatia: Developing Judicial Culture of Fundamental Rights', p 392.

43 Jasna Omejec (2016) 'Challenges of Implementation of the ECHR in the Post-Yugoslav Context – The Lessons of Experience of Croatian Constitutional Court', speech delivered at Regional Challenges in Implementation of the European Convention on Human Rights Conference, European Humanities University, Vilnius, 8–9 December. Available at: https://www.youtube.com/watch?v=DOVZkn3okbU&t=306s (accessed 18 August 2017).

44 Supreme Court of the Republic of Croatia, Decision 1840/01-2, 27 October 2004.

there is no discussion about what Convention rights mean and how they might be applied in particular circumstances.

The lack of dialogue between the Croatian courts and Strasbourg, and the Croatian judiciary's inconsistent use of Convention law, may be partially explained by the fact that only cases brought to the ECtHR against Croatia are translated into the Croatian language. Cases concerning other member states tend only to be available in the language in which the case was decided (English or French), and the official languages of the States Party to the case. ECtHR cases that produce new interpretations of Convention rights or apply the Convention to new areas of law, but are brought against states other than Croatia, are therefore not always accessible for Croatian judges, lawyers, and legal scholars. Even when European law is translated into Croatian, the process of translating complex legal language from English and French can produce interpretations that do not automatically make sense in Croatian or do not reflect the original purpose of the text.[45] As Omejec notes, the fact that European laws often introduce new legal concepts into the Croatian system means that 'there are often no appropriate Croatian expressions for them'.[46] This makes it difficult to develop a comprehensive knowledge of the broader body of Strasbourg case law, and acts as a barrier to the flow and contestation of human rights norms and interpretations between the ECtHR and the Croatian legal system. States that joined the Strasbourg system later in the ECtHR's timeline are also disadvantaged with regard to the internalization of European human rights norms, relative to founding members of the Court, because they must catch up on a huge body of existing case law rather than following a gradually developing body from its beginnings. The Croatian Constitutional Court and Ministry of Justice recognize that understanding ECtHR judgments is important for ensuring the correct application of the Convention and its standards at the national level, as well as for reducing the number of claims against Croatia at the ECtHR.[47] They thus both produce Croatian translations of relevant Strasbourg case law, although this is a relatively recent initiative.[48] It is unclear

[45] Omejec, 'Fundamental Rights in Croatia', p 13.

[46] Omejec, 'Fundamental Rights in Croatia', p 13.

[47] Constitutional Court of the Republic of Croatia (no date) *Case-Law of the European Court of Human Rights Concerning the Republic of Croatia*. Available at: https://www.usud.hr/en/echr-case-law (accessed 18 December 2017); Ministry of Justice, Office of the Agent of the Government of the Republic of Croatia (2017) *Judicial Practice: Review of Judgments and Decisions of the European Court of Human Rights*. Available at: https://uredzastupnika.gov.hr/sudska-praksa/148 (accessed 18 December 2017).

[48] The Constitutional Court Records and Documents Department also employs a senior legal adviser who monitors ECtHR case law and provides written summaries, as well as oral advice, to judges on important cases concerning other states that may have implications

whether they will translate only new cases, or also provide Croatian versions of some of the ECtHR's historical landmark decisions.

The Croatian judiciary has also struggled to adapt to the dynamic, evolutive approach to legal interpretation used by the ECtHR (and the CJEU). Concepts that require a broad understanding of how to balance competing social and legal needs across different circumstances such as proportionality, equal opportunity, and indirect discrimination (where discrimination is the consequence, but not the deliberate intention, of an action) have only recently been introduced into Croatian law, incorporated via legislation passed by the *Sabor* and inspired by the practices of the European courts as well as the German BVerfG.[49] As Tamara Ćapeta notes, these concepts require 'a certain measure of creativity from judges', which has proven challenging for Croatian judges who are used to more straightforward and narrowly applicable principles.[50] Similarly, Rodin suggests that the practice of applying the law precisely as the state intends it means that former communist states in Central and Eastern Europe, including Croatia, are not used to dialogue or discourse between different courts or between courts and the legislature as a means to agree on the definitions and interpretations of laws.[51]

Despite these challenges, Ćapeta suggests that Croatian judges' formalism and unquestioning application of the law may actually make them 'good European judges' who apply European and international law willingly and without contestation.[52] In the context of preparing for EU accession prior to 2013, Croatian judges simply needed the 'right measure of "European indoctrination"', via seminars and training in the technicalities of EU law, in order to apply it unquestioningly.[53] Indeed, without local concepts to compete with, some legal norms from both the EU and ECtHR can be slotted into existing law without disrupting any prior understandings about 'right' ways to interpret the norm. This openness may help with overcoming judicial formalism by enabling Croatia to gradually adopt European rights norms and legal practices, and to build local understandings of rights that evolve in tandem with European-level practices and traditions. But in the absence of contestation or dialogue between national courts and Strasbourg, Croatian courts are struggling to engage with the ECtHR and Convention rights in the subsidiarity-oriented manner envisioned by Strasbourg, leaving

for Croatia. Omejec, *Ways and Means to Recognise the Interpretive Authority of Judgments Against Other States*, p 19.

49 Rodin, 'Croatia: Developing Judicial Culture of Fundamental Rights', pp 391–403.

50 Ćapeta, 'Courts, Legal Culture and EU Enlargement', p 4.

51 Rodin, 'Discourse and Authority in European and Post-Communist Legal Culture', p 2.

52 Ćapeta, 'Courts, Legal Culture and EU Enlargement', p 16.

53 Ćapeta, 'Courts, Legal Culture and EU Enlargement', p 16.

a significant gap between the judiciary's stated determination to Europeanize and its actual practice. As Jasna Omejec notes, 'officially, there is unbroken and very loud support for Croatia to join the European integrations', and the Constitutional Court in particular 'is already open to European integrations and concepts of "transnational constitutionalism"'. Nonetheless, there remain 'severe democratic deficits in the ability [of Croatia] to accept the European constitutional heritage on all levels'.[54]

The judiciary's reluctance to move away from formalist legal doctrine creates a rigid constraint on the 'cultural flows'[55] in and out of Croatian institutions. The judiciary, and the Constitutional Court in particular, has the potential to play a powerful role in terms of defining human rights locally, including contesting or accepting ideas flowing from the ECtHR, but does not do so precisely because local doctrinal practices constrain the dynamic approaches to interpretation that might facilitate more active contestation. Although legal scholars fill part of this role through academic debates (and the education of new generations of more Europe-literate lawyers),[56] questions about what rights are and who they are for are still largely the preserve of the political sphere. Thus, while the domestic judiciary broadly embraces the legitimacy of the ECtHR in principle, there is little space for judges to develop their own notions of what that legitimacy entails and where its limits lie in practice.

The political relationship

Croatia's political engagement with the Council of Europe officially began in 1992, with the submission of an application for membership. As one of the wealthiest constituent republics in the former Yugoslavia, with close historical connections to Central Europe through the Hapsburg Empire, Croatia, along with neighbouring Slovenia, initially appeared well placed to make the transition from former communist state to liberal European democracy.[57] The Parliamentary Assembly of the Council of Europe (PACE) granted Croatia special guest status in May 1992 in recognition of this position and to help facilitate a smooth application process.[58]

---

[54] Omejec, 'The Constitutional Development of European Post-Communist and Post-Socialist States'.

[55] Ulf Hannerz (1992) *Cultural Complexity: Studies in the Social Organisation of Meaning* (New York: Columbia University Press), p 14.

[56] Bubalo, 'An Introduction to the Legal Cultures of Bosnia and Herzegovina, Croatia, and Serbia', p 171.

[57] Razsa and Lindstrom, 'Balkan is Beautiful', p 629.

[58] Parliamentary Assembly of the Council of Europe (1996a) 'Application by Croatia for Membership of the Council of Europe', Opinion 195, 24 April (12th sitting).

What followed, however, was a deeply controversial accession process, throughout which repeated human rights abuses and illiberal governmental practices made it increasingly uncertain that Croatia would be able to join the Council at all. In particular, Croatia's attempts to expel ethnic Serbs from Croatia and ongoing involvement in the war in Bosnia-Herzegovina forced the Council of Europe to suspend Croatia's application mere months after it was lodged in September 1992.[59] Accession negotiations were not reopened until 1994, when Croatia ended its involvement in the conflict and signed the Dayton Agreement. Parliamentary elections held in October 1995 and deemed (with some reservations) 'to have been free and fair' by the PACE's ad hoc monitoring committee also helped to restore faith in the accession process, although the Council of Europe remained wary about Croatia's progress and imposed a number of new requirements on the state.[60]

Thus, on 15 March 1996, the Croatian government committed to undertaking 21 specific requirements for accession, including signing and ratifying the ECHR; accepting the compulsory jurisdiction of the ECtHR and the right of individual petition to the European Commission on Human Rights; ratifying other Council of Europe treaties such as the Framework Convention on the Protection of Minorities, the Convention for the Prevention of Torture, and the European Social Charter; and full cooperation with the Dayton-Paris Agreements and the Prosecutor for the International Criminal Tribunal for the Former Yugoslavia (ICTY).[61] But the accession process was suspended for a second time in May 1996 because of the Croatian government's ongoing restrictions on the media and interference in Zagreb's local council elections. The PACE noted 'with dismay' that the Croatian authorities 'have since acted in blatant disregard of their commitments', asserting that the Croatian government's noncompliant behaviour since March had 'cast severe doubt on their good faith'.[62] This second suspension was lifted in October 1996, and Croatia acceded to the Council, as well as to the jurisdiction of the Strasbourg human rights system, shortly thereafter.

Croatia's accession to the Council of Europe was rather unusual in that, unlike most other Central and Eastern European states seeking Council

59 Lamont, 'Confronting the Consequences of Authoritarianism and Conflict', p 91.

60 Parliamentary Assembly of the Council of Europe, 'Application by Croatia for Membership of the Council of Europe'.

61 Parliamentary Assembly of the Council of Europe, 'Application by Croatia for Membership of the Council of Europe'.

62 Parliamentary Assembly of the Council of Europe (1996b) 'Implementation by Croatia of its Commitments in the Framework of the Procedure of Accession to the Council of Europe', Resolution 1089, 29 May.

membership in the 1990s, which either attempted to democratize before seeking membership or used their Council membership to aid their transition, Croatia appeared to become more authoritarian and illiberal after joining. The process drew attention to Tuđman's selective and inconsistent interest in joining the Council, especially given that, despite rhetoric proclaiming that accession meant Croatia was 'returning to Europe',[63] Tuđman backed away from the process when it meant relinquishing presidential powers and accepting culpability for war crimes.[64] The accession thus highlights Tuđman-era Croatia's instrumental use of regional institutions for political gain and to legitimize Croatian statehood – an approach that could have marked the beginning of a relationship driven by instrumental cooperation and selective compliance, in line with similar postcommunist and postconflict states in the Balkans and Eastern Europe.[65]

Croatia's relationship with Strasbourg has improved considerably since President Tuđman's death in December 1999 and the subsequent power shift that resulted from parliamentary elections in January 2000. The newly elected moderate President, Stjepan Mesić, sought to reverse the political isolation created by Tuđman, arguing that 'the opening of Croatia towards Europe is crucial. … Croatia's isolation damages Croatia only, and there will be no steps forward if it stays this way.'[66] This pro-European approach provided the impetus for more constructive engagement with the Council of Europe, allowing the Parliamentary Assembly to end its formal monitoring of Croatia's compliance with its accession agreement in September 2000.[67] Democratic reforms and political leaders' recognition of the importance of constructive participation in European institutions have yielded an overall cooperative relationship between Croatia and the ECtHR. For pro-Europe and liberal politicians, much of the ECtHR's ongoing legitimacy in Croatia stems from recognition that the Court played a crucial role in facilitating the country's transition to liberal democracy, through the adjudication of cases and by establishing clear international human rights standards for Croatia

63 Rasza and Lindstrom, 'Balkan is Beautiful', p 629; Lindstrom, 'Between Europe and the Balkans', p 313.

64 Lamont, 'Confronting the Consequences of Authoritarianism and Conflict', pp 91–4.

65 Deputy Secretary General of the Council of Europe, Peter Leuprecht, accused the Council of pursuing 'opportunistic and unprincipled "Realpolitik"' and of lowering its standards in allowing Croatia and Russia to accede, suggesting that concerns about instrumental cooperation went both ways. See Peter Leuprecht (1998) 'Innovations in the European System of Human Rights Protection: Is Enlargement Compatible with Reinforcement', *Transnational Law and Contemporary Problems*, 8(2): 313.

66 Cited in Subotić, 'Europe is a State of Mind', p 316.

67 Parliamentary Assembly of the Council of Europe (2000) 'Honouring of Obligations and Commitments by Croatia', Resolution 1223, 26 September.

to adopt. Mesić asserted in a speech in 2009, after his presidency, that the Council of Europe and ECtHR have:

> made an extraordinary contribution to the building of democratic values which found their expression in the rule of law, high standards of protection of human rights and promotion of democracy at the state, local and social level. … [W]e appreciate all the efforts whereby the Council of Europe have helped to restore the acceptance of democracy in Croatia.[68]

This support exists alongside recognition that Croatian authorities have more work to do to translate stated perceptions of the European human rights system as legitimate and valuable into meaningful compliance. As Deputy Prime Minister and Minister for Foreign and European Affairs, Marija Pejčinović Burić, noted in a speech marking the 20th anniversary of Croatia's ratification of the ECHR in November 2017, there remains a discrepancy between accepting the ECtHR's authority and acting on it:

> Croatia's support to the Court's work is beyond question … regardless of their content, the Court's decisions encourage positive changes in the way domestic law and court and administrative practice are interpreted. … There is, however, still room for a far better implementation of the Convention in Croatia, which is the responsibility of us all.[69]

For nationalists, conservatives, and Eurosceptics, Strasbourg's legitimacy is slightly more tenuous. The ECtHR does not attract the same degree of ire from far-right politicians as the EU or ICTY, suggesting that the concerns about those institutions undermining hard-won Croatian sovereignty and unsettling national identities are not generally attached to Strasbourg in the same way.[70] Instead, Croatian far-right politicians tend to refer to European and Croatian courts and to the concept of human rights strategically, appropriating the language of law and rights to appeal to domestic nationalist

---

68 Stjepan Mesić (2009) Address of the President of the Republic of Croatia to the Summer University for Democracy, Strasbourg, 8 July. Available at: https://www.coe.int/t/dgap/Source/Croatia_President%20Mesic-speech.doc (accessed 7 September 2017).

69 Marija Pejčinović Burić (2017) 'Croatia – 20 Years Before the ECHR', press release, Zagreb, 9 November, reproduced in Ministry of Foreign and European Affairs, Republic of Croatia. Available at: https://mvep.gov.hr/press-22794/fm-pejcinovic-buric-attends-round-table-on-croatia-20-years-before-the-echr/195945 (accessed 28 September 2024).

70 Marko Stojic (2006) 'Between Europhobia and Europhilia: Party and Popular Attitudes Towards Membership of the European Union in Serbia and Croatia', *Perspectives on European Politics and Society*, 7(3): 392.

audiences. The recently founded Homeland Movement (*Domovinski pokret*) party, for instance, cites the wide margin of appreciation the ECtHR gives to states concerning how they ensure representation of minority populations in national parliaments, to campaign for abolition of guaranteed minority seats in the *Sabor*.[71] Elsewhere, the party's leader, Ivan Penava, has demanded respect for the 'fundamental rights' of the 'huge silent majority who still live in Vukovar and silently wait for justice' – a reference to Croatian victims of the massacre by Serb forces in the border town in 1991, and a common dog whistle for anti-Serb sentiment.[72] More established nationalist parties are subtler – even during the tumultuous accession era, HDZ politicians typically did not openly criticize the ECtHR, but nor do they actively defend it. Their apathy suggests tolerance, rather than acceptance, of the ECtHR, as compliance with it is necessary for EU membership and international recognition of Croatian sovereignty. But apathy also facilitates a permissive environment at home for human rights abuses – particularly concerning migrants, Serb and Roma minority communities, and LGBTQ+ communities – to flourish unchecked. Strasbourg's political legitimacy among Croatian nationalists and Eurosceptics is in this sense contingent on not disrupting this tolerance, and is jeopardized by cases where right-wing politicians cannot appropriate or quietly ignore the rulings.

Among these competing visions of Strasbourg's legitimacy and appropriations of its purpose, there is little public debate about what this support actually entails, or how the ECtHR fits into existing constitutional and human rights debates in Croatia. For much of the public, the Strasbourg Court represents a safeguard against corruption and inefficiency in the national legal system. Croatians have among the lowest levels of confidence in their national political and legal institutions in Europe.[73] This is evident in

[71] Domovinski Pokret (2021) Program Djelovanja [Action Program], February, p 29.

[72] Branimir Bradarić (2019) 'Penava: Situacija u Vukovaru nije zrela za iskorake, ne možemo prijeći preko nepravde iz 91' [Penava: The situation in Vukovar is not ripe for a breakthrough, we cannot overcome the injustice of 1991], *Večernji List*, 14 July. Available at: https://www.vecernji.hr/vijesti/vukovarci-su-osjetili-najgore-iz-rata-kao-i-nepravdu-koju-i-danas-osjecaju-1332185 (accessed 8 March 2024).

[73] Parliamentary Assembly of the Council of Europe Committee on the Honouring of Obligations and Commitments by Member States of the Council of Europe (2015) *The Progress of the Assembly's Monitoring Procedure (October 2014–August 2015): Periodic Review Report of Countries not under the Monitoring Procedure sensu stricto or Engaged in a Post-Monitoring Dialogue: Croatia*, Document 13868 part 4, 14 September (Strasbourg: Council of Europe), p 7. Available at: http://assembly.coe.int/nw/xml/XRef/Xref-DocDetails-en.asp?FileID=22028&lang=en (accessed 12 November 2015); Davorka Matić (2008) 'Political Culture, Socio-Cultural Values and Democratic Consolidation in Croatia', in Sabrina P. Ramet, Konrad Clewing, and Reneo Lukić (eds), *Croatia Since Independence: War, Politics, Society, Foreign Relations* (Munich: De Gruyter), pp 171–88.

the high numbers of inadmissible and struck out applications to the ECtHR and in perceptions of the ECtHR as a fourth instance court for appealing national judgments,[74] and reflects limited public discussion of either the ECtHR's purpose or homegrown human rights solutions. Croatian news outlets, likewise, are inconsistent in their coverage of European human rights issues and ECtHR cases. In the cases the media does cover, journalists tend to provide detailed coverage about the facts of ECtHR cases concerning Croatia and neighbouring states, but rarely engage in analysis or commentary. When it comes to reporting the consequences or obligations arising from cases, the press focuses primarily on individual compensation. The media also do not tend to include comments from relevant government ministers, members of parliament, or local human rights advocates in their reporting, meaning that articles detailing Strasbourg rulings often lack political and social context about how the judgments are received.[75] This contrasts with the closer public scrutiny applied to judgments made by national courts and the Constitutional Court, as well as with media coverage of domestic human rights issues,[76] and perhaps reinforces public perceptions of the ECtHR as a supervisory institution that exists to critique and improve Croatian human rights practices, not to be criticized by domestic actors.

The absence of discourses concerning the European human rights system raises a distinct limitation regarding the 'active making of culture'.[77] In short, the surface-level openness to cooperation with the ECtHR expressed by the Constitutional Court and in the discourses of the liberal political elite does not translate consistently into effective human rights practices – not

---

74 Turković and Omejec, 'Commitment to Reform', p 133.

75 A recent exception is a piece in *Novilist* which reports the number of Croatian cases still pending execution before the Committee of Ministers. The article stresses the need for domestic authorities to recognize the importance of responding to the ECtHR's judgments. It also acknowledges the resistance towards the ECtHR's judgments and authorities present in the United Kingdom, Denmark, and Russia, but suggests that nonexecution of judgments in Croatia stems from lack of awareness of the 'binding force' of ECtHR judgments 'at all levels and across all branches of government', rather than from criticism of the Strasbourg Court. Jasmin Klarić (2017) 'Hrvatska još nije provela čak 182 presude Europskog suda' [Croatia has not yet implemented 182 ECtHR judgments], *Novilist*, 2 November. Available at: http://www.novilist.hr/Vijesti/Hrvatska/STO-UOPCE-ZNACI-SUD-U-STRASBOURGU-Hrvatska-jos-nije-provela-cak-182-presude-Europskog-suda?meta_refresh=true (accessed 3 November 2017).

76 See, for example: Snježana Krnetić (2014) 'HDSSB želi promjene: Ustavni sud krši i Ustav i ljudska prava' [HDSSB wants changes: Constitutional Court violates the Constitution and human rights], 24stata, 10 December. Available at: https://www.24sata.hr/news/hdssb-zeli-promjene-ustavni-sud-krsi-i-ustav-i-ljudska-prava-397720 (accessed 7 September 2017).

77 Sally Engle Merry (2012) 'What is Legal Culture? An Anthropological Perspective', *Journal of Comparative Law*, 5(2): 42.

because of the diversity of legitimacy perceptions, but because of a lack of ongoing debate about how to navigate diversity. Debates about human rights and Croatia's place in Europe obviously exist, but the ECtHR largely sits outside them, kept at arm's length by actors who want international oversight and those who want to avoid it in equal measure. This distance results in a mixed compliance record, as Croatian political (and to a lesser extent judicial) actors turn to different cultural touchstones to contextualize and justify their compliance choices.

The effects of Croatian cultural politics of rights on compliance

Between Croatia recognizing the jurisdiction of the ECtHR in 1997 and the ECtHR's most recent statistical overview in 2021, the Court has made a total of 474 judgments concerning Croatia, 380 of which found one or more violations of the Convention.[78] As with the UK and Germany, the number of cases that make it to a judgment is relatively small compared to the total number of applications lodged against Croatia. In the 1997–2021 period, 17,491 applications were allocated to a judicial formation, meaning that the vast majority of cases – approximately 97 per cent – were struck out before they reached the decision stage.[79]

In January 2024, 61 cases were pending execution under the supervision of the Committee of Ministers.[80] This includes 25 lead cases and 35 repetitive cases, as well as one friendly settlement. Of these cases, eight are currently being supervised under the enhanced supervision procedure: *M.H. and Others v Croatia*, concerning inadequate investigations into the death of a child, and *Statileo v Croatia* and its associated repetitive cases, concerning disproportionate restrictions on property rights, are under enhanced supervision due to their classifications as a complex problem and structural problem, respectively.[81] These figures mean that Croatia has a higher number

[78] European Court of Human Rights (2022) *Overview: 1959–2021*, Strasbourg: ECtHR. Available at: https://www.echr.coe.int/documents/d/echr/Overview_19592021_ENG (accessed 10 January 2024).

[79] European Court of Human Rights, *Overview: 1959–2021*.

[80] Council of Europe (no date a) HUDOC-EXEC Case Database, Department for the Execution of Judgments of the ECHR, Strasbourg. Available at: https://hudoc.exec.coe.int (accessed 10 January 2024).

[81] *M.H. and Others v Croatia*, App nos. 15670/18 and 43115/18 (ECtHR, 18 November 2021); *Statileo v Croatia*, App no. 12027/10 (ECtHR, 10 October 2014); *Mirošević-Anzulović v Croatia*, App no. 25815/14 (ECtHR, 4 October 2016); *Bego v Croatia*, App no. 35444/12 (ECtHR, 15 November 2016); *Gosovic v Croatia*, App no. 37006/13 (ECtHR, 4 April 2017); *Skelin-Hrvoj and Đuričić v Croatia*, App no. 23414/15 (ECtHR,

of total cases than those pending against the UK or Germany, but still a considerably lower number than those of the ECtHR's more obstinate Contracting States.[82] This indicates that despite broad support from elites for the ECHR, Croatia continues to face some hurdles when it comes to preventing lead cases from arising, and implementing the measures required by the Committee of Ministers to prevent repetitive cases.

Collateral noncompliance: prioritizing European and nationalist identities

The interplay of Croatia's multifaceted European and nationalist identities and their constitutive effects on the legitimacy of (non)compliance decisions are particularly apparent in the case *M.H. and Others v Croatia*.[83] The case was brought by the family of then 6-year-old Afghani, Madina Hussiny, who was killed in 2017 when she was hit by a train within hours of being turned back into Serbia by Croatian border guards. The applicants claimed that by turning the family back, ordering them to follow the train tracks in the dark, the Croatian authorities were responsible for Madina's death. In addition to the violation to the right to life, the case claimed Croatian police failed to adequately investigate her death, and that the family were then subject to degrading treatment and denied adequate legal support in an immigration centre in the Croatian border town of Tovarnik.

The ECtHR First Section (seven-judge chamber) unanimously held that there had been a procedural violation of Article 2, and that while there had been no violation of Article 3 regarding the adult family members, the trauma of losing a sibling at a young age and having to process the loss in detention conditions constituted a violation for the child applicants. The Chamber also found several violations concerning the applicants' access to justice, and unanimously ordered Croatia to pay nonpecuniary damages of €40,000 plus €16,700 in costs.

Due to its complex nature, the case has remained under the Committee of Ministers' enhanced supervision procedure since the judgment was rendered final in April 2022. The government has not yet paid the damages (already significantly lower than the applicants' originally requested €650,000), on

---

10 June 2021); *Hegediš v Croatia*, App no. 41306/18 (ECtHR, 23 June 2022); *Arambašin v Croatia*, App no. 48981/17 (ECtHR, 23 June 2022).

[82] The states with the highest number of cases pending execution as of January 2024 are Russia (2580), Ukraine (768), Turkey (428), Romania (465), Azerbaijan (300), and Italy (246). All other Contracting States have fewer than 200 cases pending, with an average of 35 cases. Council of Europe, HUDOC-EXEC Case Database.

[83] *M.H. and Others v Croatia*, App nos. 15670/18 and 43115/18 (ECtHR, 18 November 2021).

the grounds that, since the applicants left Croatia for Slovenia in 2018, Croatian authorities were unaware of their whereabouts.[84] The Office of the Representative of the Republic of Croatia before the ECtHR also claims that the applicants' representative had not provided bank account details and the original power of attorney document (only a copy) within the three-month payment deadline.[85] Regarding general measures, the Committee of Ministers has welcomed the reopening of the criminal investigation and the creation of an independent border monitoring mechanism to more systematically provide 'genuine and effective access to procedures for legal entry into Croatia'.[86] However, the Committee also noted several measures still in need of improvement, inviting the Croatian authorities to ensure the investigations are conducted in 'a fully Convention-compliant manner' by improving training for police, prosecutors, and judges, making use of Council of Europe training courses, encouraging local courts to develop more Convention-compliant case law to support ongoing review of the effectiveness of investigations, and providing adequate legal assistance to migrants in languages they can understand and with access to lawyers of their own choice.[87]

The case sparked significant consternation in Croatia, playing into both local and European politics of migration and discourses delegitimizing 'irregular' migration. The Interior Minister, Davor Božinović, acknowledged that Madina's death was a 'tragedy' but was quick to stress that the Croatian government was not responsible.[88] Božinović also referred to the importance of following international law, but not in relation to the ECHR or human rights but Croatia's EU migration obligations and supposedly 'legitimate' ways of seeking asylum:

> We, and the EU, took the position that it's necessary to prevent illegal entry into Croatia and the EU and that those who believe that, under international law, they have the option to exercise asylum rights should apply for it. This means coming before institutions, in the specific case

[84] Committee of Ministers (2023b) Action Plan – Communication from Croatia concerning the case of *M.H. and Others against Croatia*, to the Secretariat of the Committee of Ministers, DH-DD(2023)758, 21 June, s 26.

[85] Committee of Ministers, Action Plan – DH-DD(2023)758, s 27.

[86] Committee of Ministers (2023a) 1475 DH meeting, CM/Del/Dec(2023)1475/H46-14, decision on case *M.H. and Others v Croatia* (15670/18), 19–21 September, s 4.

[87] Committee of Ministers, 1475 DH meeting, ss 4–10.

[88] N1 Zagreb (2021) 'Interior Minister: Migrant Girl's Death is "Tragic", but I Will Not Step Down', N1 News, 19 November. Available at: https://n1info.hr/english/news/interior-minister-migrant-girls-death-is-tragic-but-i-will-not-step-down/ (accessed 24 February 2024).

> to a border crossing. … Receiving and talking with those people, that's international law.[89]

The government made the same argument in the original case, submitting that 'as a European Union member State with the prospect of joining the Schengen Area in the near future, Croatia had the right to control the entry of aliens to its territory and had the obligation to protect the State borders from illegal crossings'.[90] Even the applicants themselves adhered to a conception of Croatia as European rather than Balkan, noting in their submission to the ECtHR that Serbia was, in their view, 'in Asia', with fewer work and education opportunities than in 'European' Croatia and their eventual goal destination, the United Kingdom.[91] Coming from outside Croatia, the applicants' own understandings of what and where Europe is are not grounded in the same cultural environment as those of the Croatian authorities, but their statement and eventual departure to Slovenia served to reinforce Božinović's perception of Croatia as a European frontier and through route, which on the one hand 'should prevent illegal entry into its territory, and on the other, prevent … migration to other states'.[92]

These responses tread a fine line through Croatia's multifaceted European and nationalist identities. At first glance, references to the rule of law and the tragedy of a child's death speak to Croatian legal discourses about being committed to the Council of Europe and the liberal human rights norms contained in the ECHR. At the same time, framing commitments to EU border control as a stronger obligation enables the Croatian government to distance itself from a Balkan identity by painting itself instead as an integral European frontier. That this framing reflects local sensibilities about Croatia as culturally and historically European (rather than as meeting standards of a civic identity) is evident in the fact that other (western) EU member states have distanced themselves from the Croatian government's position. Regional courts in both Germany and the Netherlands have raised concerns about 'systemic deficiencies' in Croatia's turnback practices.[93]

---

89 N1 Zagreb, 'Interior Minister: Migrant Girl's Death is "Tragic", but I Will Not Step Down'.

90 *M.H. and Others v Croatia*, App nos. 15670/18 and 43115/18, para 291.

91 *M.H. and Others v Croatia*, para 49.

92 N1 Zagreb, 'Interior Minister: Migrant Girl's Death is "Tragic", but I Will Not Step Down'.

93 Committee of Ministers (2023c) Communication from an NGO (Centre for Peace Studies and the Human Rights House Zagreb) (18/07/2023) in the Case of *M.H. and Others v Croatia* (App no. 15670/18) and Reply from the Authorities (26/07/2023), DH-DD(2023)891, 27 June, s 40.

Finally, the government's line also speaks to nationalist conceptions of border sovereignty and antimigration attitudes. It therefore appeals to a range of local sensibilities about law enforcement and Croatia's place in Europe, using commitment to an EU obligation both to legitimize Croatian conceptions of Europeanness, and to skirt the ECHR obligation by trying to frame it as an undesired but ultimately necessary form of 'collateral noncompliance'.[94] Of course, not everyone bought into the government's approach – local NGOs Human Rights House Zagreb and the Centre for Peace Studies described the Ministry of Interior's response to the judgment as reflective of a 'culture of cover-up' and impunity for the police officers involved in border turnbacks.[95] Their submission explicitly criticizes the ministry's actions as 'behaviour prohibited by the Convention', reflecting perceptions among Croatian legal and human rights professionals that the ECHR provides an important check on less trustworthy local institutions. Nonetheless, the case highlights how Croatian government officials rely on the same formulations of Croatia's European geography and prioritization of EU obligations to speak to a range of local audiences and to navigate competing obligations to the EU and ECHR.

Quiet, reluctant compliance: the cultural politics of necessity

In September 2022, 11 years after the case was first referred for supervision, the Committee of Ministers adopted its final resolution on the group of cases *Skendžić and Krznarić v Croatia*, closing its supervision satisfied that Croatia had sufficiently complied with its obligations.[96] The ECtHR had found Croatia in violation of the Article 2 ECHR right to life due to the Croatian police's failure to adequately investigate the disappearance of the applicants' family members during the 1991–95 war.[97]

The government's response to the group of cases has been mixed. On the one hand, the government has implemented a range of individual and

[94] Zoë Jay and Matt Killingsworth (2024) 'To Arrest or Not Arrest: South Africa, the International Criminal Court, and New Frameworks for Assessing NonCompliance', *International Studies Quarterly*, 68(2): 1–13.

[95] Committee of Ministers, Communication from an NGO (Centre for Peace Studies and the Human Rights House Zagreb), s 8.

[96] Committee of Ministers (2022c) Resolution CM/ResDH(2022)248, Case of *Skendžić and Krznarić against Croatia* and Four Other Cases, 22 September.

[97] *Skendžić and Krznarić v Croatia*, App no. 16212/08 (ECtHR, 20 April 2011); *Jularic v Croatia*, App no. 20106/06 (ECtHR, 20 April 2011); *Jelić v Croatia*, App no. 57856/11 (ECtHR, 12 October 2014); *B. and Others v Croatia*, App no. 71593/11 (ECtHR, 19 October 2015); *M. and Others v Croatia*, App no. 50175/12 (ECtHR, 13 November 2017).

general measures to improve the efficacy of its war crimes investigations.[98] It paid damages to the applicants and passed legislation intended to strengthen the independence of criminal investigations. This included transferring cases to independent police units when it was suspected that investigated offences had been committed by members of the police, expanding the authority of prosecutors to issue binding orders to the police, and granting four domestic courts and county prosecutors' offices exclusive competence for handling war crimes cases. The Criminal Procedure Code was amended to introduce strict deadlines for investigations and complaints, and to broaden the scope of the rights of victims to ensure ongoing communication and public scrutiny of investigations. To respond to the increase in cases that arose following these legislative changes (mostly made between 2011 and 2013), the Constitutional Court was vested with new powers to review the effectiveness of investigations and order prosecuting authorities to carry out specific investigatory steps within time limits and award damages to complainants. Finally, the government cooperated with the International Commission on Missing Persons and with state authorities in Serbia and Bosnia and Herzegovina to more effectively account for missing persons, and introduced the Act on Missing Persons in the Homeland War in July 2019 to better protect the family members of missing persons and enhance identification processes.

On the other hand, progress slowed after 2013 (when Croatia joined the EU), and many of the measures implemented after 2013 only occurred at the urging of the Committee of Ministers.[99] The NGOs Documenta and Human Rights House Zagreb specifically criticized the government's measures concerning missing persons as 'ineffective and conducive to [a] climate of impunity for war crimes' for still being too slow and opaque.[100]

---

[98] Committee of Ministers (2022a) Action Report – Communication from Croatia Concerning the Group of Cases *Skendžić and Krznarić against Croatia*, Addendum to the Action Report, DH-DD(2022)730, 12 July.

[99] Committee of Ministers (2014b) 1208 DH meeting, CM/Del/Dec(2014)1208/5, Decision on Cases *Skendžić and Krznarić against Croatia* (16212/08), 25 September; Committee of Ministers (2016a) 1259 DH meeting, CM/Del/Dec(2016)1259/H46-10, Decision on Cases *Skendžić and Krznarić group against Croatia* (1621/08), 7–8 June; Committee of Ministers (2017a) 1280 DH meeting, CM/Del/Dec(2017)1280/H46-10 Decision on Cases *Skendžić and Krznarić group against Croatia* (16212/08), 10 March; Committee of Ministers (2019a) 1348 DH meeting, CM/Del/Dec(2019)1348/H46-7 Decision on Cases *Skendžić and Krznarić group v Croatia* (16212/08), 6 June; Committee of Ministers (2020) 1390 DH meeting, CM/Del/Dec(2020)1390/H46-6, Decision on Cases *Skendžić and Krznarić group v Croatia* (16212/08), 3 December.

[100] Committee of Ministers (2019b) Rule 9.2 Communication from a NGO (Human Rights House Zagreb and Documenta – Centre for Dealing with the Past) and Response from the Croatian Authorities (14/05/2019) in the *Skendžić and Krznarić* Group of Cases against Croatia (16212/08), DH-DD(2019)546, 15 May, s 4.

Milan Skendžić, whose family brought the original case, is still listed in the Ministry of Interior's Register of Missing Persons, though not in the Ministry of Croatian Veterans' Affairs Book of Missing Persons, indicating that records and criteria for tracing missing persons are inconsistent, and the two exhumations carried out yielded no results.[101]

Outside of its progress reports, the Croatian government has provided no further public explanation or discussion of why it has taken so long to implement some measures or why it considers those measures sufficient. There is also virtually no evidence of coverage or scrutiny of the government's mixed compliance efforts by the media or other political actors, despite opposition to the closure of the case from local and international human rights NGOs and wide-ranging coverage of missing persons investigations in general.[102]

The government's silence on these cases also jars with the significant coverage and debate that surrounded similar cases brought before the ICTY. Conservative politicians, church groups, victims, and victim advocacy groups alike criticized and distanced themselves from ICTY verdicts,[103] and while several Croatian prime ministers and presidents framed compliance with the ICTY as necessary in order to 'build [Croatia's] future in the company of the democratic world and united Europe',[104] it was not until Prime Minister Ivo

---

[101] Committee of Ministers, Rule 9.2 Communication from a NGO (Human Rights House Zagreb and Documenta – Centre for Dealing with the Past), s 10.

[102] Searches on the websites of national daily newspapers and in the Nexis newspaper database for the names of ECtHR cases, individual applicants, and broader phrases such as 'Homeland War + European Court of Human Rights' (*Domovinski rat + Europski sud za ljudska prava*) and 'Missing persons (*Nestale osobe*) + European Court of Human Rights' all return no results. One right-wing nationalist online paper, *Dnevno*, published an opinion piece one month before the Council of Europe closed the *Skendžić and Krznarić* cases, which claimed that Serbian leaders were trying to 'cast a stain and stigma that Croatia was created on crime, that Croats are genocidal and Ustaše' *(nastoje baciti ljagu i stigmu da je Hrvatska stvorena na zločinu, da su Hrvati genocidni i ustašoidni*) and use the ECtHR to demand compensation from Croatia. However, the piece does not refer to any actual cases concerning Croatia, nor does it appear to have triggered any broader discussion of the ECtHR's role in relation to how Croatia handles its past. Iva Međugorac (2022) 'DOSTA JE "ČETNIČKE PROPAGANDE" O OLUJI! Pravnik iznio sve detalje: Sustavno se stvara stigma da je Hrvatska stvorena na zločinu' [ENOUGH OF 'CHETNICA PROPAGANDA' ABOUT A STORM! The lawyer presented all the details: A stigma is being systematically created that Croatia was created on the basis of crime], Dnevno.hr, 6 August. Available at: https://www.dnevno.hr/vijesti/hrvatska/dosta-je-cetnicke-propagande-o-oluji-pravnik-iznio-sve-detalje-sustavno-se-stvara-stigma-da-je-hrvatska-stvorena-na-zlocinu-2004050/ (accessed 27 February 2024).

[103] Jelena Subotić (2014) 'Legitimacy, Scope, and Conflicting Claims on the ICTY: In the Aftermath of *Gotovina, Haradinai* and *Perišić*', *Journal of Human Rights*, 13(2): 180.

[104] In Subotić, 'Europe is a State of Mind', p 318.

Sanader framed cooperation with the ICTY as an opportunity to exert more homegrown influence over the justice process that progress began to be made. Cooperation with the ICTY, Sanader argued, would 'protect the historical truth about the Homeland War, helping suspects, allowing suspects to defend themselves while on bail, and transferring ICTY cases to Croatian courts'.[105] But where Sanader clearly relied on formulations of homegrown justice to legitimize meeting difficult international obligations with the ICTY, there have been no such attempts to interpret or contextualize Croatia's obligations in the *Skendžić and Krznarić* cases. They therefore pose something of a challenge for the theory of culturally informed compliance articulated in this study, and for the methodological focus on 'contentious' cases. Why have ECtHR cases concerning investigations into war crimes committed during the 1991–95 war, which elsewhere are the subject of considerable political and legal contestation, as well as of national embarrassment,[106] not received significant public attention, and why – despite mixed outcomes – did compliance occur relatively smoothly?

There is undoubtedly an instrumental dimension to Croatia's compliance with cases relating to the war, both in terms of compliance (originally) being necessary for EU membership, and in terms of EU membership being considered a valuable token of Croatia's Europeanness. That the government's progress towards comprehensive general measures slowed after 2013 speaks to the strategic politics and external pressures at play. Nonetheless I suggest that, rather than ending the explanation here, exploring the cultural constitutive environment in which local perceptions of the legitimacy (or illegitimacy) of international law are constructed can provide clearer insight into the patterns of silence and contestation apparent in Croatian human rights politics, to understand why the Croatian government aimed to keep quiet about its motives in the *Skendžić and Krznarić* cases but has been more vocal about others.

Specifically, compliance with the *Skendžić and Krznarić* cases is best understood through the intersection of Croatia's European identity and memory politics. Membership in and smooth relations with European institutions are important for Croatian politicians' local conceptions of Croatian statehood and national identity as culturally and historically European. But EU and Council of Europe narratives of human rights and genocide frequently run counter to local memories of the war of independence. The intrinsic connection between genocide and fascism present in dominant European memory narratives is complicated in Croatia

[105] *Novi list*, 3 July 2004, in Subotić, 'Stories States Tell', p 324.

[106] Jelena Subotić and Ayşe Zarakol (2012) 'Cultural Intimacy in International Relations', *European Journal of International Relations*, 19(4): 927.

(and the former Yugoslavia) by memory politics that associate genocide and war crimes with communism, and downplays atrocities committed by the Ustaše regime, in order to venerate independent Croatian statehood.[107] European expectations about compliance with war crime proceedings – to comply fully, swiftly, and apologetically – are difficult in light of local conceptions of the necessity of Croatian independence, while local memory politics that (try to) absolve Croatia of responsibility for atrocities perpetrated in the war are an uncomfortable fit with (German-inspired) European conceptions of memory and human rights as acts of atonement.

In order to keep these competing and incongruous legitimacies separate, the Croatian government quietly set about doing the minimum necessary to satisfy their obligations to the ECtHR without drawing attention to the measures among local audiences. Media silence and limited scrutiny both helped to maintain the separation, and reflected the limited available content from government actors (in contrast to British politicians, who relish opportunities to take credit for meeting difficult obligations as evidence of British superiority and the failings of Strasbourg in one fell swoop). From this angle, it becomes clear that understanding Croatia's compliance with the *Skendžić and Krznarić* cases as instrumental only tells us one half of the story; we need cultural politics to understand why certain choices are considered instrumental in the first place, and to understand the variation in states' compliance patterns.

The cultural causes of structural problems

Local understandings of the purpose of law and the nature of rights also affect which types of cases reach the ECtHR in the first place. The Croatian judiciary's narrow conception of its role within the legal system, and its literal, formalist approach to statutory interpretation are core contributors to the immense number of excessive length of proceedings cases brought to Strasbourg against Croatia – nearly one third of all cases in which the ECtHR has found violations by Croatia since 1997.[108] The bulk of these length of proceedings cases are repetitive, accumulating before the Committee of Ministers because Croatia has not responded to the lead judgments effectively enough to prevent similar cases.[109]

Formalist tendencies in Croatian judicial culture have contributed to this swell of cases in two key ways. First, because judges tend to read the law

107 Subotić, *Yellow Star, Red Star*, p 145.

108 European Court of Human Rights (2017) *Violations by Article and State 1959–2016: Annual Report 2016* (Strasbourg: ECtHR); Council of Europe, HUDOC-EXEC Case Database.

109 See for example *Horvat v Croatia*, App no. 51585/99 (ECtHR, 26 October 2001).

literally and with limited consideration of the practical intent or effect of the law, the notion that a trial must be completed within a reasonable time for it to be fair did not exist in Croatia until it ratified the ECHR and until the Croatian constitution was amended in 2000 to include the reasonable time requirement in its text.[110] Second, even after the reasonable time requirement was explicitly incorporated into the constitution, the Constitutional Court continued to interpret its own jurisdiction over such cases so narrowly that most individual complaints were declared inadmissible.[111] In failing to recognize the opportunity to expand its jurisdiction and take a more flexible approach to statutory interpretation, the Constitutional Court, as the ECtHR ruled in *Debelić v Croatia*, 'rendered an otherwise effective remedy ineffective'.[112] The *Sabor* amended the constitution again in 2002 to provide more flexible admissibility criteria and more effective domestic remedies for fair trial complaints, in response to the ECtHR's judgment in *Horvat v Croatia*,[113] but two decades later the ECtHR is still finding Convention violations stemming from 'excessive formalism', and backlogs of cases are still pending before both national courts and the ECtHR.

Failure to comply with and prevent length of proceedings cases is usually understood purely as due to capacity problems: what the ECtHR calls 'excessive formalism' is such a widespread issue in its member states that the Council of Europe provides factsheets and training to help overcome it.[114] But as Alan Uzelac argues, lack of training and exposure to European interpretive methods does not explain why formalism persists in Croatia and other former socialist states three decades after these states' transitions and accessions.[115] Instead, I suggest that these institutional problems are better understood as the products of a cultural environment that allows formalism to persist because the judiciary clings to an understanding of its role as an impartial applier of law made elsewhere. Judges' sensibilities about the legitimacy of law are shaped by a centuries-long tradition that, one the one hand, values consistency and predictability, and, on the other hand, has

[110] Ćapeta, 'Courts, Legal Culture and EU Enlargement', pp 12–13.

[111] Lamont, 'Confronting the Consequences of Authoritarianism and Conflict', pp 94–6; Rodin, 'Croatia: Developing Judicial Culture of Fundamental Rights', p 393.

[112] *Debelić v Croatia*, App no. 2448/03 (ECtHR, 26 August 2005), para 46.

[113] *Ustavni zakon o izmjenama i dopunama Ustavnog zakona o Ustavnom sudu* [Constitutional Act Amending and Supplementing the Constitutional Act on Constitutional Court], Official Gazette 29/2002, 22 March 2002; see also Rodin, 'Croatia: Developing Judicial Culture of Fundamental Rights', p 393; Turković and Omejec, 'Commitment to Reform', p 124.

[114] Council of Europe (2023) *Excessive Formalism by Courts: Thematic Factsheet* (Strasbourg: Department for the Execution of Judgments of the European Court of Human Rights), April.

[115] Uzelac, 'Survival of the Third Legal Tradition?', p 378.

endured (but also contributed to) several different authoritarian regimes by evading and delaying decision-making responsibility.[116] The Constitutional Court and pro-European politicians put more faith in the liberal human rights and dynamic interpretation of the Strasbourg system as a means not simply to endure the political regime of the day but to actively contribute to building a new one that affirms Croatia's 'one thousand-year-old' European identity. But the nature of formalist reasoning, coupled with the legacy of a socialist constitutionalism that vested all the substantive law-making authority in the state, means the courts themselves have not been willing to participate in the cultural politics that might more effectively align Croatian judicial practice with Strasbourg's expectations.

The compliance problem here is not so much about questioning the legitimacy of the ECtHR itself, but a disconnect between two different perceptions of the legitimate purpose of domestic courts, and institutional structures that make the disconnect difficult to reconcile or move past. The inability of the Croatian judiciary to interpret legislation and its own jurisdiction flexibly enough to provide effective domestic remedies therefore highlights the way two-way channelling of culture through institutions and institutions through cultural production[117] – as the cultural-institutional context of judicial formalism – both causes violations of the right to a fair trial and hinders effective solutions to resolve or prevent them. As long as restrictive interpretive practices and assumptions that the judiciary should be 'politically objective'[118] breed reluctance within the judiciary to discuss the role of courts in protecting and creating rights, Croatia is likely to continue to struggle to effectively comply with the types of procedural rights that require not only legislative but judicial solutions, despite stated intentions from governments and the Constitutional Court that they want to do so.

Conclusion

Croatia's record of compliance with the ECtHR is the product of a human rights cultural context shaped by several different conceptions of human rights, the roles of judicial, political, and international institutions in protecting them, and European and national identities. In the judicial sphere, practices of formalism and reluctance to be seen engaging in human rights debates traditionally understood as the preserve of politics – although criticized by some as relics of authoritarian and communist pasts that denied

[116] Uzelac, 'Survival of the Third Legal Tradition?', p 384.

[117] Hannerz, *Cultural Complexity*, p 14.

[118] Jernej Letnar Černič (2018) 'The European Court of Human Rights in the States of the Former Yugoslavia', *East European Yearbook on Human Rights*, 1(1): 32–54.

Croatia its sovereign independence – continue to have consistent significant effects on the state's compliance record. These effects appear both in terms of limiting effective judicial solutions when the ECtHR finds violations, and in terms of shaping the types of cases that reach Strasbourg in the first place, by flooding courts with cases concerning fair trials and the length of proceedings. Politically, cultural touchstones including identity narratives that paint Croatia as ethnoculturally European and as an independent nation distinct from its Balkan neighbours provide powerful incentives and justificatory tools for legitimizing the Strasbourg system. But since they also serve to legitimize domestic nationalisms and memory politics that largely denies Croatian responsibility for atrocities committed during the Second World War and breakup of Yugoslavia, the same cultural tools often jar with specific ECtHR obligations concerning war crime investigations and the rights of applicants who are not ethnically Croatian.

In both spheres, then, compliance decisions are the products of attempts to maintain the dissonance between recognition of the legitimacy of the Strasbourg system in the abstract, and the legitimacy of local Croatian identity narratives which are not always compatible with European conceptions of rights. The same cultural touchstones that serve several fragmented legitimacies and identities – judicial formalism, socialist constitutionalism, and dual narratives of Croatian Europeanism and nationalism – also enable flexible, strategic compliance and noncompliance decisions. This explains why the Constitutional Court faithfully states its commitment to European rights and interpretive practices while lower courts continue their age-old practice of avoiding decisions with real political impact. It also explains why Croatian politicians deploy interpretations of the purpose of law and Croatia's place in Europe that help them to both quietly go about meeting minimal Strasbourg obligations unnoticed and boldly shirk them as needed.

Conclusion

Legitimacy is as much a local cultural phenomenon as it is an international social one. Whatever the ideas and systems created among members of a regional or international community, the shared understandings of legitimacy they build through cooperation, persuasion, reciprocity, and even coercion, are mediated by the personal, local interpretations and assumptions that each actor brings with them from home. But for the most part, explanations of legitimacy's relationship to compliance have overlooked or underplayed these local dynamics – the unique ideas about what is good or right or fair that evolve both in conversation with, and independently from, ideas present in international spaces. In doing so, these explanations have also overlooked the challenge of variation: why similar states have different relationships with Strasbourg, and why they comply with most of the rulings of the European Court of Human Rights (ECtHR), but not all. Yet both variation and legitimacy are central to human rights protection in Europe. The European human rights system relies on its status as a legitimate arbiter of rights standards in Europe and the good faith efforts of its members to elicit compliance with the Convention and Court, and deliberately allows its members considerable leeway to implement their responses to ECtHR rulings according to local constitutional and cultural traditions. A comprehensive explanation of compliance in the European human rights system thus needs an understanding of legitimacy that accommodates – indeed, expects – variation.

This book responds to the variation puzzle, and to the socially constructed approaches to legitimacy that have so far struggled to engage with it, by offering a new, localized account of the origins of legitimacy. Treating the concept of legitimacy as grounded in dynamic cultural and historical contexts, not just those shared among members of a regional or international order, but those produced at home in domestic contexts, this book has shown how ideas about human rights and law can hold very different meanings for seemingly similar actors, with significant consequences for how different democracies within the European human rights system respond to their obligations under the ECtHR. Drawing on insights from anthropology and sociology about how culture shapes behaviour, and with the help of interpretive analysis of the United Kingdom, Germany, and Croatia, the book set out to explore three questions. What makes state actors perceive international law as legitimate enough to comply with in the first place? How do those perceptions translate into decisions to comply with particular judgments of the ECtHR? And what types of ECtHR cases are states likely to comply with or resist? This final chapter addresses each question in turn, and concludes by drawing out some of the key implications of a cultural approach to legitimacy for understanding the European human rights system.

Taking as a starting point the well-established constructivist assumption that states feel a 'pull towards compliance' when they believe the law is legitimate,[1] the first question this book set out to explore is: where does the sense that international law is legitimate enough to comply with come from? Following the work of Clifford Geertz and others, I have argued here that legitimacy is a type of local knowledge, contextualized by dynamic, overlapping, and interconnected collections of ideas and experiences that provide the foundations for interpreting the meanings and consequences of actions.[2] For law and human rights specifically, this knowledge emerges and evolves through the 'cultural politics of human rights'[3] – debates, practices, and expectations about what human rights are, what they should be, who they are for, and how and by whom they are protected, inflected by historical experiences and memory practices, political narratives, and institutional structures and constitutional traditions. These understandings and expectations are fluid, variable, and often internally inconsistent or contradictory, but they are crucial for understanding domestic actors' perceptions of the legitimacy of international law, as they provide orienting ideas and points of reference that contextualize how actors interpret the law and how they bear the weight of their obligations to it.

The cultural politics and local knowledges of law and human rights facilitate the translation of legitimacy ideas into compliance action by providing toolkits: habits, ideas, and practices that domestic actors can draw on when responding to their international legal obligations. These local knowledges and toolkits do not tell actors what to do in a strictly causal sense. But they are also more than background knowledge, passively waiting to fill gaps in actors' world views when shared understandings produced through social interaction fail. Rather, as cultural specialists from sociology and anthropology conclude, cultures are active, dynamic

[1] Thomas M. Franck (1990) *The Power of Legitimacy Among Nations* (New York: Oxford University Press), p 234.

[2] Clifford Geertz (1983) *Local Knowledge: Further Essays in Interpretive Anthropology* (New York: Basic Books), p 215.

[3] Kate Nash (2009) *The Cultural Politics of Human Rights: Comparing the US and UK* (Cambridge: Cambridge University Press), p 7.

landscapes, environments in which actors both translate new ideas into the local vernacular, and bring their vernacular understandings to bear on their interactions with the world around them. The cultural politics of human rights therefore inform actors' sense of the possible, first by creating local knowledge of what is good or right about law and human rights – what I have (loosely) called legitimacy criteria – and then by providing the tools to enact that knowledge and react to new information and contexts.

Seeing culture as the source of a range of possible actions is crucial for understanding variation in compliance. There is no one right way to respond to a legal obligation for an actor with a given identity. Instead, in each of the case studies we see different actors drawing on the same narrative devices, political memories, institutional rules, and cultural signposts to make completely different compliance choices. In Croatia, for example, habits of judicial formalism sometimes make national judges happy adopters of new European norms, but these habits can also sometimes lead to resistance or slow compliance because judges are reluctant to engage in direct discussions about how they see incoming ECtHR judgments fitting within the local legal order. In the UK, politicians from across the political spectrum draw on narratives of Britain's longstanding rights tradition to push themselves to adhere to politically sensitive rulings, and then turn around and use the same myths of Magna Carta and parliamentary sovereignty to decry judicial activism when they feel the ECtHR has gone too far. The relationship between culturally informed perceptions of legitimacy and compliance actions is therefore inherently flexible, as domestic actors pick and choose from within their toolkits to respond to different obligations.

But if the ways legitimacy perceptions translate into compliance are fluid enough to be used across multiple contexts, which types of cases are states likely to comply with or resist? This question is especially important if we want to move beyond the generalized references to domestic salience and rule of law culture that currently underpin the dominant explanations of compliance and noncompliance, to understand variation within and across countries with rule of law cultures and strong commitments to human rights. It is also crucial for understanding the types of human rights issues and ECtHR cases that might need extra attention or advocacy to guarantee compliance in practice. After all, one of the core puzzles that has driven this book is compliance 'sticking points': the difficult cases where states with otherwise solid compliance records push back against their obligations under the European human rights system, the cases where questions about legitimacy – either of the specific case or of the ECtHR and Convention as a whole – are strongest.

Part of the answer will be unsurprising to many; in each of the states studied here, the ECtHR rulings that caused the most friction tended to push the limits of local ideas about who deserves rights. From attempts to deport terror suspects to debates about whether 'a little bit of torture' is ever justifiable, cases concerning national security, the rights of prisoners or minorities, or the balancing of one person's rights against those of another tap into fundamentally human insecurities about safety or 'others'. The details regarding whose security is (perceived to be) at stake and who is being othered by whom are inflected by both cultural and power politics, but these types of cases are united by the fact that they force us into uncomfortable realizations about just how limited our belief in supposedly universal rights can be. Governments, media, and civil society actors stoke, exploit, and exacerbate these insecurities for various strategic and normative reasons, so they easily become part of mainstream public debate. This, in turn, sparks direct consideration of the rights at stake and brings competing cultural mindsets to the fore as different domestic actors attempt to justify their arguments about why someone does not deserve a right or why a certain act is not a human rights violation. In the coming years, as the effects of the COVID-19 pandemic, climate emergency, forced migration, and other global challenges push people with competing rights and needs even further into conflict with each other, arguments about which people or communities deserve what rights, or about how to proportionately and justly balance conflicting rights, are likely to be the sources of further sticking points – not just for the ECtHR but for human rights everywhere.

But there are also plenty of examples of states complying with rulings on issues of deserving and undeserving rights quickly and with comparatively little consternation. At the same time, cases concerning the length of judicial proceedings in Croatia and Germany show that states are just as likely to resist compliance with issues that do not necessarily challenge ideas about the deservingness of claimants, and which are not, for want of a better term, exciting enough to attract mainstream public attention.

The bigger indicator for whether a case is likely to be resisted, then, is how much the obligations stemming from a judgment rub up against local sensibilities about who should be protecting rights, in what ways, and for whom. These cases are not just politically sensitive at a particular moment in time or context, but strike at the institutions and ideas at the very heart of compliance actors' senses of their local culture and national identity. The prisoner voting case in the UK, for example, clearly played into British assumptions that there are 'common-sense' limits to who deserves or is entitled to rights, but it was the *Hirst* judgment's implications for parliamentary sovereignty and concerns that the ECtHR was subverting national authority that sparked the fiercest criticisms and a decade-long standoff between Westminster and Strasbourg. The *Hirst* case also demonstrates how difficult it can be for Strasbourg to elicit compliance from states once perceptions of national authority being undermined are established – in the end, it took a compromise that did not require Parliament to go back on its previous refusal to consider prisoner suffrage for the UK to finally comply with the *Hirst* ruling, while barely expanding the scope of the voting rights actually available to imprisoned people.

In Germany, a historically grounded conception of the *Rechtsstaat* entrenching fundamental rights *before* the law and obligating the state to provide them in concrete, meaningful ways means wholesale defiance of ECtHR rulings is less likely. Still, the legitimacy of the European human rights system depends largely on both the historical alignment between German and European Holocaust memory practices, and the Constitutional Court's openness to the Convention – a status that is reflected in the fact that the *Bundesverfassungsgericht* (Federal Constitutional Court) retains the 'last word' on human rights in Germany, even if that word is amicable.

Resistance to human rights rulings in Europe is therefore best understood as a failure to find a way to reconcile legal obligations with local sensibilities about what is legitimate or reasonable. This is more than a generic reference to domestic salience though; it is an active, ongoing process of making and remaking ideas about legitimacy. The flexibility and hybridity of culture and cultural politics mean that any actor can hypothetically find the tools they need to justify a choice to comply with or defy an obligation. The trick is to understand what those tools and sensibilities are, and how and when they are used by different domestic actors – something that requires detailed, historicized interpretation by researchers to make concrete. But in the end, these same processes of making legitimacy also give us the answer to why compliance eventually emerges after initial resistance. By drawing on their local knowledge and cultural toolkits – interpreting and reshaping cultural symbols, bringing old stories to bear on new situations – domestic actors find the justifications and motivations they need to push themselves towards compliance.

What are the implications of understanding the relationship between legitimacy and compliance from a domestic culture perspective? For starters, it offers a way to round out our knowledge of the connections between domestic and international politics. I have focused on the domestic dimensions in this book to highlight the local politics that contribute to varied understandings of legitimacy, but the interactions between domestic actors and Strasbourg – particularly the dialogue between national courts and the ECtHR – show how much national and European cultural environments intersect with each other, and how conversations or interpretations in one space routinely spark conversations and interpretations in another. To this end, my focus on the cultural politics of human rights and local understandings of legitimacy is specifically intended as a complement to the idea of international socially constructed shared understandings, rather than an alternative. In closing, I outline two areas of study in particular where rights cultures and localized understandings of legitimacy can work with international-level approaches to enhance our knowledge of international law and human rights regimes, and draw out some of the key implications for the European human rights system.

First, it is worth emphasizing that this was a study of a European court in a European context; I have no interest in claiming its findings are universal, even within Europe itself. At the risk of stating the obvious, different regions, states, and communities have different cultural politics; the same issues, ideas, and structures will not apply everywhere, at least not in the same ways. As Marie-Bénédicte Dembour reminds us, in human rights regimes premised on both common standards and subsidiarity, 'minimal common standards are never entirely *common*: they always stand in the way of more peculiar, or particular, norms'.[4] To the extent that this work is generalizable, then, it is through a call to pay attention to particularism. Studying the cultural politics of human rights and variation in compliance patterns empirically requires attention to detail, time, and cultural competence. This type of scholarship must be thorough and deep, but a theoretical approach that embraces cultural hybridity and the power dynamics that underpin cultural influences on political behaviour can help scholars identify where to start.

With that in mind, one field of study this book speaks to concerns the growing national backlash against international legal institutions. From proposals to weaken the authority of the ECtHR through subsidiarity reforms, to withdrawals by the Philippines, Burundi, and Russia from the International Criminal Court and Rome Statute, to Israel's refusal to adhere to the International Court of Justice's interim measures and the UN Security Council's resolutions calling for a ceasefire in Palestine, the legitimacy of these institutions, and their ability to elicit compliance, is far from secure. And if the stakes are high for the institutions themselves, they are higher still for the people and communities affected by their failures to constrain state power. Now more than ever, understanding the motivations that inform states' responses to international legal systems and the norms they promote is vital. Well-established research agendas exploring noncompliance and backlash against international courts offer valuable prescriptions and frameworks for understanding different forms of criticism and resistance.[5] But we will also always need to flesh out the specifics if we want to understand particular cases, especially if we want to understand what particular status

4 Marie-Bénédicte Dembour (2006) *Who Believes in Human Rights?: Reflections on the European Convention* (New York: Cambridge University Press), p 155.

5 Karen J. Alter and Michael Zürn (2020) 'Conceptualising Backlash Politics: Introduction to a Special Issue on Backlash Politics in Comparison', *British Journal of Politics and International Relations*, 22(4): 563–84; Courtney Hillebrecht (2021) *Saving the International Justice Regime: Beyond Backlash against International Courts* (New York: Cambridge University Press).

quo backlash movements hope to revert to, or the emotional or institutional dynamics that accompany backlash.[6] A cultural approach to legitimacy can complement the backlash framework by helping to contextualize the sensibilities and environments that shape perceptions of legitimacy, giving us better indications of the sticking-point issues or procedures that might trigger or exacerbate a backlash. There are also connections to be made between the backlash literature and the layered approach to legitimacy outlined in this book. Knowing whether a country's criticisms are predominantly case-by-case issues, or part of broader structural or foundational problems, and identifying the points where the different layers overlap or feed into each other, can add to conversations about where the backlash threshold might fall, or where institutions face tipping points for legitimacy crises.

Meanwhile, subtler forms of resistance, such as doing the bare minimum necessary to comply or proposing reforms to the ECtHR system that shift authority away from the Court, allow states to reduce or shirk their obligations with their own legitimacy as members of the international community intact, but can have damaging effects on how European and international institutions, not to mention the human rights norms they aim to uphold, are perceived and valued in the long term. As compliance scholars turn their focus to different forms of noncompliance, resistance, and evasion, studying how ideas about legitimacy are constructed will help to identify the types of cases that lead to these behaviours, and the ways they might be addressed, prevented, or at the very least anticipated.

The second area of study the book speaks to is the recent shift in constructivist scholarship towards more sophisticated arguments about the nature of culture and its relationships to international political orders. These works draw on scholarship from anthropology, sociology, and history to demonstrate that cultures are not coherent, bounded entities with direct causal effects on their members, but dynamic, hybrid collections of meanings and practices which shape action by contextualizing how actors interpret the world around them and providing ranges of skills and knowledge to help them move through it. By revealing how cultural politics of human rights generate shifting and evolving local ideas about legitimacy, this book complements this cultural turn. In particular, understanding local conceptions of human rights as emerging from dynamic *cultural politics* rather than from static, monolithic *culture* addresses the gap where explanations of compliance have so far deferred to states' 'rule of law cultures' or 'cultural matches'. The variations in what it means to be a rule of law state or to have a democratic tradition across the UK, Germany, and Croatia, and the ways these concepts are interpreted or applied by the actors responding to ECtHR judgments,

6 Alter and Zürn, 'Conceptualising Backlash Politics', p 14.

demonstrate the importance of engaging with the specifics of the 'politics of culture' – the debates and processes through which ideas about legitimacy are constructed, the ways stories and institutions are mobilized so that particular ideas triumph while others are silenced or forgotten.[7]

For the European human rights system as a whole, too, there is knowledge to be gained by combining the practicalities of local-level compliance processes and cultural politics with the theoretical insights offered by work on culture in large-scale international orders to study the mid-level politics of regional human rights orders. Seeking to further discussions about the relationship between culture and international order, Andrew Phillips and Christian Reus-Smit suggest that 'we should start by assuming existential cultural diversity'.[8] This conversation is no less necessary for understanding the European human rights system. As Chapter 3 has shown, the Convention and Court are fundamentally designed in recognition of regional diversity – a series of compromises somewhere between traditional state-based concerns about sovereignty and genuine differences in the institutional, legal, and social structures of the Council of Europe's many members. The idea of Europe's 'common heritage' is foundational to regional-level ideas about rights and justificatory narratives for European cooperation, but it is inextricably woven with Europe's uncommon heritages.

The ongoing challenge for the European human rights system and its members is – and always has been – working out how to accommodate differing approaches and expectations while maintaining a coherent pan-European set of human rights standards. Members of the Council of Europe are continuing to push for reforms of the ECtHR that place renewed emphasis on subsidiarity and deference to national authorities (and threatening to withdraw if they do not get their way). Although the ECtHR and Council of Europe have often capitulated to these demands by offering wider margins of appreciation and accepting minimalist compliance measures from recalcitrant states,[9] newer scholarship on the concept of European consensus shows that the ECtHR is fighting back, drawing on ideas about common European values to shape discussions about both specific rights issues and the European public order at large.[10] Recognizing

---

7 Christian Reus-Smit (2018) *On Cultural Diversity: International Theory in a World of Difference* (Cambridge: Cambridge University Press), p 5.

8 Andrew Phillips and Christian Reus-Smit (eds) (2020) *Culture and Order in World Politics* (Cambridge: Cambridge University Press), p 320.

9 Janneke Gerards (2018) 'Margin of Appreciation and Incrementalism in the Case Law of the European Court of Human Rights', *Human Rights Law Review*, 18(3): 495–515; Øyvind Stiansen and Erik Voeten (2020) 'Backlash and Judicial Restraint: Evidence from the European Court of Human Rights', *International Studies Quarterly*, 64(4): 770.

10 Claerwen O'Hara (2021) 'Consensus, Difference and Sexuality: Que(e)rying the European Court of Human Rights' Concept of "European Consensus"', *Law and*

what different states believe these concepts and balances entail, and what assumptions or sensibilities lie behind them, will be a valuable source for understanding the future evolution of the ECtHR, and the future of rights protection in Europe more broadly. So too will be understanding the ECtHR's own conceptions of how the balance should be struck, and the roles it plays in structuring and accommodating diversity among its Contracting States. For now, it helps to remember that although the ECtHR and Council of Europe speak in a language of common European rights, at home their member states frequently speak in dialect, and the translations are not always literal.

Cultural theorist, Stuart Hall, once argued that 'cultural difference doesn't mean that I am totally different from you. But I come to the present, to who I am, by a different route from yours; and therefore our conversation has to recognize that different histories have produced us, different histories have made this conversation possible.'[11] Our conversations about the legitimacy of international law and regional human rights institutions should similarly recognize the different paths that lead the politicians, judges, and other actors responsible for meeting states' international obligations to view law and human rights as legitimate or not. The aim of this book was to cast a brighter light on the differences within the European human rights system, to show how different traditions and experiences with rights and law create and shape particular local knowledges about the legitimacy of international law, and how they are central in pushing states towards (non)compliance, especially with more challenging cases. It is my hope that the book opens up additional lines of thinking and new ways of contextualizing the concepts of legitimacy, compliance, and the role of culture in influencing how state actors interact with international human rights law. The local cultural politics of human rights show us more about where beliefs that international human rights law is legitimate come from. It is here, in the unshared understandings of legitimacy, that we are able to unlock new insights into patterns of variation in states' records of compliance or resistance, and ultimately to better protect human rights.

Critique, 32(1): 91–114; Jens Theilen (2021) *European Consensus between Strategy and Principle: The Uses of Vertically Comparative Legal Reasoning in Regional Human Rights Adjudication* (Baden: Nomos Verlagsgesellschaft); Kanstantsin Dzehtsiarou (2021) *Can the European Court of Human Rights Shape European Public Order?* (Cambridge: Cambridge University Press).

11 Stuart Hall (2007) 'Living with Difference: Stuart Hall in Conversation with Bill Schwarz', *Soundings: A Journal of Politics and Culture*, 37(2): 151.

References

Abbott, K.D. and D. Snidal (2000) 'Hard and Soft Law in International Governance', *International Organization*, 54(3): 421–56.

Adenauer, K. (1951) Discours devant le Conseil de l'Europe [Speech before the Council of Europe], Strasbourg, 10 December, CVCE. Available at: https://www.cvce.eu/content/publication/2003/10/10/0ea92ca7-2add-405e-9b03-047ab6e9b728/publishable_fr.pdf (accessed 18 December 2017).

Adler, E. (1997) 'Seizing the Middle Ground: Constructivism in World Politics', *European Journal of International Relations*, 3(3): 319–63.

Adler, E. (2008) 'The Spread of Security Communities: Communities of Practice, Self-Restraint, and NATO's Post-Cold War Transformation', *European Journal of International Relations*, 14(2): 195–230.

Adler, E. and V. Pouliot (2011) 'International Practices', *International Theory*, 3(1): 1–36.

Adu, A. and K. Stacey (2023) 'Rishi Sunak "Won't Allow Foreign Court to Block" Rwanda Plan', *Guardian*, 1 December. Available at: https://www.theguardian.com/uk-news/2023/dec/01/rishi-sunak-wont-allow-foreign-court-to-block-rwanda-plan (accessed 23 January 2024).

Alexander, J. (2003) *The Meanings of Social Life: A Cultural Sociology*, Oxford: Oxford University Press.

Allan, D. (2008) *Making British Culture: English Readers and the Scottish Enlightenment, 1740–1830*, New York: Routledge.

Allen, R. (2017) 'The Great Revolution in Prisoner Voting will Affect … a Few Dozen People', *Guardian*, 30 October. Available at: https://www.theguardian.com/commentisfree/2017/oct/30/prisoner-voting-government-proposal-european-court-human-rights (accessed 23 March 2024).

Alter, K.J. (2014) *The New Terrain of International Law: Courts, Politics, Rights*, Princeton, NJ: Princeton University Press.

Alter, K.J. and M. Zürn (2020) 'Conceptualising Backlash Politics: Introduction to a Special Issue on Backlash Politics in Comparison', *British Journal of Politics and International Relations*, 22(4): 563–84.

Alternative für Deutschland (2017) Facebook post, 2 August. Available at: https://www.facebook.com/alternativefuerde/photos/a.542889462408064/1581236365240030/ (accessed 19 February 2020).

Alternativ für Deutschland (2017) *Programm für Deutschland: Wahlprogramm der Alternativ für Deutschland für die Wahl zum Deutschen Bundestag am 24. September 2017*, Köln: Alternativ für Deutschland.

Alternativ für Deutschland (2020) 'Beatrix von Storch: Nach dem Urteil des EGMR können illegal Migranten sofort abgeschoben werden', AfD, 17 February. Available at: https://www.afd.de/beatrix-von-storch-nach-dem-urteil-des-egmr-koennen-illegale-migranten-sofort-abgeschoben-werden/ (accessed 19 February 2020).

Altwicker, T. (2016) 'Switzerland: The Substitute Constitution in Times of Popular Dissent', in P. Popelier, S. Lambrecht, and K. Lemmens (eds), *Criticism of the European Court of Human Rights – Shifting the Convention System: Counter-Dynamics at the National and EU Level*, Cambridge: Intersentia Ltd, pp 385–412.

Amnesty International (2012) 'UK: Abu Qatada Still at Risk of Torture and Unfair Trial', public statement issued 9 May, AI Index EUR 45/010/2012/.

Amos, M. (2012) 'The Dialogue between United Kingdom Courts and the European Court of Human Rights', *International and Comparative Law Quarterly*, 61(3): 557–84.

Amos, M. (2013) 'Transplanting Human Rights Norms: The Case of the United Kingdom's Human Rights Act', *Human Rights Quarterly*, 35(2): 386–407.

ANSA.it (2015) 'Strasbourg Court "Useless" says Salvini', ANSA, 9 April. Available at: https://www.ansa.it/english/news/politics/2015/04/09/strasbourg-court-useless-says-salvini_07b1abed-c340-443f-b073-776d80562b81.html (accessed 31 March 2024).

Ash, T.G. (1998) 'The Truth About Dictatorship', *New York Review of Books*, 19 February.

Asthana, A. and R. Mason (2016) 'UK Must Leave European Convention on Human Rights, says Theresa May', *Guardian*, 26 April. Available at: https://www.theguardian.com/politics/2016/apr/25/uk-must-leave-european-convention-on-human-rights-theresa-may-eu-referendum (accessed 20 January 2017).

Badescu, C.G. and T.G. Weiss (2010) 'Misrepresenting R2P and Advancing Norms: An Alternative Spiral?', *International Studies Perspectives*, 11(4): 354–74.

Baerbock, A. (2022) Speech at virtual event 'International Holocaust Remembrance Day: Responsibilities for All of Society', hosted by B'nai B'rith International, 24 January. Available at: https://www.auswaertiges-amt.de/en/newsroom/news/baerbock-b-nai-b-rith/2507914 (accessed 8 February 2024).

Banchoff, T. (1999) 'German Identity and European Integration', *European Journal of International Relations*, 5(3): 259–89.

Barkhuysen, T. and M.L. van Emmerik (2005) 'A Comparative View on the Execution of Judgments of the European Court of Human Rights', in T. Christou and J.P. Raymond (eds), *European Court of Human Rights: Remedies and Execution of Judgments*, London: British Institute of International and Comparative Law, pp 1–24.

Bates, E. (2010) *The Evolution of the European Convention on Human Rights: From its Inception to the Creation of a Permanent Court of Human Rights*, New York: Oxford University Press.

Bates, E. (2012) 'British Sovereignty and the European Court of Human Rights', *Law Quarterly Review*, 128 (July): 382–411.

Bates, E. (2014) 'Analysing the Prisoner Voting Saga and the British Challenge to Strasbourg', *Human Rights Law Review*, 14(3): 503–40.

Baudet, T. (2011) 'The Anti-Democratic Impulses of the ECHR', Spiked, 19 January. Available at: https://www.spiked-online.com/2011/01/19/the-anti-democratic-impulses-of-the-echr/ (accessed 31 March 2024).

BBC (2012) '"Unacceptable" UK can't Deport Abu Qatada – Theresa May', BBC News, 7 February. Available at: http://www.bbc.com/news/uk-politics-16923527 (accessed 9 August 2017).

BBC (2017a) 'Human Rights Lawyer: Prisoner Votes Plan is "Cynical"', BBC News, 30 October. Available at: https://www.bbc.com/news/uk-41803722 (accessed 23 March 2024).

BBC (2017b) 'Prisoner Voting Compromise Ends Dispute with European Court', BBC News, 7 December. Available at: https://www.bbc.com/news/uk-42271100 (accessed 23 March 2024).

Becker Lorca, A. (2020) 'Universal and European: Cultural Diversity in International Law', in A. Phillips and C. Reus-Smit (eds), *Culture and Order in World Politics*, Cambridge: Cambridge University Press, pp 207–31.

Bellamy, R. (2007) *Political Constitutionalism: A Republican Defence of the Constitutionality of Democracy*, New York: Cambridge University Press.

Berrey, E. (2020) 'When Liberal States Bite Back: The Micro-Politics of Culture', in A. Phillips and C. Reus-Smit (eds), *Culture and Order in World Politics*, Cambridge: Cambridge University Press, pp 159–81.

Besson, S. (2008) 'The Reception Process in Ireland and the United Kingdom', in H. Keller and A. Stone Sweet (eds), *A Europe of Rights: The Impact of the ECHR on National Legal Systems*, New York: Oxford University Press, pp 31–106.

Besson, S. (2016) 'Subsidiarity in International Human Rights Law – What is Subsidiary about Human Rights?', *American Journal of Jurisprudence*, 61(1): 69–107.

Betts, P. (2013) 'Socialism, Social Rights, and Human Rights: The Case of East Germany', *Humanity: An International Journal of Human Rights, Humanitarianism and Development*, 3(3): 407–26.

Bild (2011) 'Kommen jetzt gefährliche Sex-Verbrecher frei?', Bild, 4 May. Available at: http://www.bild.de/news/inland/sicherungsverwahrung/bundesverfassungsgericht-sicherungsverwahrung-verfassungswidrig-17721950.bild.html (accessed 1 April 2017).

Blitz, B.K. (2008) 'Democratic Development, Judicial Reform and the Serbian Question in Croatia', *Human Rights Review*, 9(1): 123–35.

Bloomfield, A. (2016) 'Norm Antipreneurs and Theorising Resistance to Normative Change', *Review of International Studies*, 42(2): 310–33.

Bodansky, D. (2013) 'Legitimacy in International Law and International Relations', in J.L. Dunoff and M.A. Pollack, *Interdisciplinary Perspectives on International Law and International Relations: The State of the Art*, New York: Cambridge University Press, pp 321–41.

Bowcott, O. (2014) 'Conservatives Pledge Powers to Ignore European Court of Human Rights Rulings', *Guardian*, 3 October. Available at: http://www.theguardian.com/politics/2014/oct/03/conservatives-ignore-european-court-human-rights-rulings (accessed 14 May 2016).

Bowcott, O. (2015) 'Strasbourg Court has Backed Off over Rights Rulings, says Jack Straw', *Guardian*, 21 May. Available at: https://www.theguardian.com/law/2015/may/21/strasbourg-court-backed-off-human-rights-jack-straw (accessed 18 January 2024).

Božac, I. and M. Carević (2015) 'Judicial Application of International and EU Law in Croatia', in S. Rodin and T. Perišin (eds), *Judicial Application of International Law in Southeast Europe*, Berlin: Springer-Verlag, pp 135–63.

Bradarić, B. (2019) 'Penava: Situacija u Vukovaru nije zrela za iskorake, ne možemo prijeći preko nepravde iz 91', *Večernji List*, 14 July. Available at: https://www.vecernji.hr/vijesti/vukovarci-su-osjetili-najgore-iz-rata-kao-i-nepravdu-koju-i-danas-osjecaju-1332185 (accessed 8 March 2024).

Bratza, N. (2012) Speech at the opening of the Brighton Conference, Council of Europe, Proceedings of the High Level Conference on the Future of the European Court of Human Rights, Brighton, 19 April.

Braun, V. and V. Clark (2022) *Thematic Analysis: A Practical Guide*, London: Sage.

Brown, G. (2004) 'Britishness', British Council Annual Lecture, London, 7 July, reproduced in W. Stevenson (ed) (2006) *Moving Britain Forward: Selected Speeches 1997–2006*, London: Bloomsbury,.

Brunnée, J. and S.J. Toope (2010) *Legitimacy and Legality in International Law: An Interactional Account*, Cambridge: Cambridge University Press.

Brunnée, J. and S.J. Toope (2011) 'History, Mystery, and Mastery', *International Theory*, 3(2): 348–54.

Bubalo, L. (2023) 'An Introduction to the Legal Cultures of Bosnia and Herzegovina, Croatia, and Serbia (Western Balkan)', in S. Koch and M.M. Kjølstad (eds), *Handbook on Legal Cultures*, Cham: Springer, pp 145–96.

Bueger, C. and F. Gadinger (2015) 'The Play of International Practice', *International Studies Quarterly*, 59(3): 449–60.

Bukovansky, M. (2002) *Legitimacy and Power Politics: The American and French Revolutions in International Political Culture*, Princeton, NJ: Princeton University Press.

Bull, H. (2002) *The Anarchical Society: A Study of Order in World Politics*, 3rd edn, New York: Columbia University Press.

Bulmer, S. (1989) 'Unity, Diversity and Stability: The "Efficient Secrets" behind West German Public Policy?', in S. Bulmer (ed), *The Changing Agenda of West German Public Policy*, Aldershot: Dartmouth Publishing, pp 13–39.

Burić, M.P. (2017) 'Croatia – 20 Years Before the ECHR', press release, Zagreb, 9 November, reproduced in Ministry of Foreign and European Affairs, Republic of Croatia. Available at: https://mvep.gov.hr/press-22794/fm-pejcinovic-buric-attends-round-table-on-croatia-20-years-before-the-echr/195945 (accessed 28 September 2024).

Burke, E. (1790) *Reflections on the Revolution in France*, London: Dent, Everyman's Library.

Búzás, Z.I. (2017) 'Evading International Law: How Agents Comply with the Letter of the Law but Violate its Purpose', *European Journal of International Relations*, 23(4): 857–83.

Çalı, B. and A. Wyss (2009) *Why do Democracies Comply with Human Rights Judgments? A Comparative Analysis of the UK, Ireland and Germany*, SSRN Working Paper, 26 August, pp 1–34.

Çalı, B. and A. Koch (2014) 'Foxes Guarding the Foxes? The Peer Review of Human Rights Judgments by the Committee of Ministers of the Council of Europe', *Human Rights Law Review*, 14(2): 301–25.

Cameron, D. (2012) Speech on the European Court of Human Rights, delivered to the Parliamentary Assembly of the Council of Europe, 25 January. Available at: https://www.gov.uk/government/speeches/speech-on-the-european-court-of-human-rights (accessed 9 August 2017).

Cameron, D. (2015) Magna Carta 800th anniversary: Prime Minister's speech, Runnymede, Surrey, 15 June. Available at: https://www.gov.uk/government/speeches/magna-carta-800th-anniversary-pms-speech (accessed 29 May 2021).

Ćapeta, T. (2005) 'Courts, Legal Culture and EU Enlargement', *Croatian Yearbook of European Law and Policy*, 1(1): 1–21.

Carr, E.H. (1946) *The Twenty Years' Crisis, 1919–1939: An Introduction to the Study of International Relations*, London: Macmillan.

Černič, J.L. (2018) 'The European Court of Human Rights in the States of the Former Yugoslavia', *East European Yearbook on Human Rights*, 1(1): 32–54.

Chayes, A. and A.H. Chayes (1995) *The New Sovereignty: Compliance with International Regulatory Agreements*, Cambridge, MA: Harvard University Press.

Checkel, J. (1999) 'Norms, Institutions and Identity in Contemporary Europe', *International Studies Quarterly*, 43(1): 83–114.

Checkel, J. (2001) 'Why Comply? Social Learning and European Identity Change', *International Organization*, 55(3): 553–88.

Checkel, J. (2004) 'International Institutions and Socialisation in Europe: Introduction and Framework', *International Organization*, 59(4): 801–26.

Christlich Demokratische Union Deutschlands (2013) *Gemeinsam erfolgreich für Deutschland*, Regierungsprogramm 2013–2017, Berlin: CDU-Bundesgeschäftsstelle.

Christys, P. (2017) 'British Bill of Rights Shelved as Country "Can't Handle" Even More Constitutional Change', *Express*, 25 February. Available at: http://www.express.co.uk/news/uk/771924/EU-Human-Rights-Act-Brexit-Artic-Britain-Theresa-May-Liz-Truss-politics-Brexit-Article-50 (accessed 26 February 2017).

Clark, I. (2005) *Legitimacy in International Society*, Oxford: Oxford University Press.

Clark, I., S. Kaempf, C. Reus-Smit, and E. Tannock (2018) 'Crisis in the Laws of War? Beyond Compliance and Effectiveness', *European Journal of International Relations*, 24(2): 319–43.

Clayton, R. (2015) 'Should the English Courts under the HRA Mirror Strasbourg Case Law?', in K.S. Ziegler, E. Wicks, and L. Hodson (eds), *The UK and European Human Rights: A Strained Relationship?*, Portland, OR: Hart, pp 95–113.

Cohn, E.J. (1957) 'Dissenting Opinions in German Law', *International and Comparative Law Quarterly*, 6(3): 540–3.

Commission on a Bill of Rights (2012) *A UK Bill of Rights?: The Choice Before Us*, vol 1. London: Ministry of Justice.

Committee of Ministers (2010) 'Supervision of the Execution of Judgments and Decisions of the European Court of Human Rights: Implementation of the Interlaken Action Plan – Modalities for a Twin-Track Supervision System', CM/Inf/DH(2010)37, 6 September. Available at: https://rm.coe.int/16804a327f (accessed 29 December 2017)

Committee of Ministers (2011a) 1128 DH meeting, CM/Del/Dec(2011)1128/11, Decision on cases *Rumpf group against Germany* (46344/06), 2 December.

Committee of Ministers (2011b) Action Report – Communication from Germany Concerning the Case of *Gäfgen against Germany*, to the Secretariat of the Committee of Ministers, DH-DD(2011)647E, 26 April.

Committee of Ministers (2012a) 1136 DH meeting, CM/Del/Dec(2012)1136/9, Decision on cases *M group against Germany* (19359/04), 8 March.

Committee of Ministers (2012b) High Level Conference on the Future of the European Court of Human Rights, 'Brighton Declaration', Brighton, 19–20 April.

Committee of Ministers (2013a) Action Report – Communication from Germany Concerning the *Rumpf* Group of Cases against Germany, to the Secretariat of the Committee of Ministers, DH-DD(2013)1234, 14 November.

Committee of Ministers (2013b) Action Report – Communication from the United Kingdom Concerning the Case of *Othman (Abu Qatada) against the United Kingdom*, DH-DD(2013)315, 20 March.

Committee of Ministers (2013c) Resolution CM/ResDH(2013)114, *A and others against the United Kingdom*, 6 June.

Committee of Ministers (2014a) 1201 DH meeting, CM/Del/Dec(2014)1201/7, Decision on cases *M group against Germany* (19359/04), 5 June.

Committee of Ministers (2014b) 1208 DH meeting, CM/Del/Dec(2014)1208/5, Decision on Cases *Skendžić and Krznarić against Croatia* (16212/08), 25 September.

Committee of Ministers (2014c) Resolution CM/ResDH(2014)289, Execution of the Judgment of the European Court of Human Rights in the Case of *Gäfgen against Germany*, 17 December.

Committee of Ministers (2014d) Resolution CM/ResDH(2014)290, Execution of the Judgment of the European Court of Human Rights in Thirteen Cases against Germany, 17 December.

Committee of Ministers (2015a) High Level Conference on the Implementation of the European Convention on Human Rights, Our Shared Responsibility, 'Brussels Declaration', Brussels, 27 March.

Committee of Ministers (2015b) *Supervision of the Execution of Judgments and Decisions of the European Court of Human Rights 2014*, 8th Annual Report of the Committee of Ministers, Strasbourg: Committee of Ministers.

Committee of Ministers (2016a) 1259 DH meeting, CM/Del/Dec(2016)1259/H46-10, Decision on Cases *Skendžić and Krznarić group against Croatia* (1621/08), 7–8 June.

Committee of Ministers (2016b) Communication from the Authorities (05/02/2016) Concerning the Cases of *Hirst No 2* and *Greens and M.T. against the United Kingdom* (74025/01, 600041/08), DH-DD(2016)188, 5 February.

Committee of Ministers (2017a) 1280 DH meeting, CM/Del/Dec(2017) 1280/H46-10, Decision on Cases *Skendžić and Krznarić group against Croatia* (16212/08), 10 March.

Committee of Ministers (2017b) Action Plan – Communication from the United Kingdom Concerning the Case of *Hirst (No 2) v the United Kingdom*, DH-DD(2017)1229, 2 November.

Committee of Ministers (2017c) *Supervision of the Execution of Judgments and Decisions of the European Court of Human Rights 2016*, 10th Annual Report of the Committee of Ministers, Strasbourg: Committee of Ministers.

Committee of Ministers (2018a) 1331 DH meeting, CM/Notes/1331/ H46-35, Notes on the Agenda, *Hirst No 2 group v United Kingdom* (74025/ 01), 4–6 December.

Committee of Ministers (2018b) High Level Conference: Continued Reform of the European Human Rights Convention System – Better Balance, Improved Protection, 'Copenhagen Declaration', Copenhagen, 12–13 April.

Committee of Ministers (2019a) 1348 DH meeting, CM/Del/ Dec(2019)1348/H46-7, Decision on Cases *Skendžić and Krznarić group v Croatia* (16212/08), 6 June.

Committee of Ministers (2019b) Rule 9.2 Communication from a NGO (Human Rights House Zagreb and Documenta – Centre for Dealing with the Past) and Response from the Croatian Authorities (14/05/2019) in the *Skendžić and Krznarić* Group of Cases against Croatia (16212/08), DH-DD(2019)546, 15 May.

Committee of Ministers (2020) 1390 DH meeting, CM/Del/Dec(2020)1390/ H46-6, Decision on Cases *Skendžić and Krznarić group v Croatia* (16212/ 08), 3 December.

Committee of Ministers (2022a) Action Report – Communication from Croatia Concerning the Group of Cases *Skendžić and Krznarić Against Croatia*, Addendum to the Action Report, DH-DD(2022)730, 12 July.

Committee of Ministers (2022b) Resolution CM/Res(2022)2 on the Cessation of the Membership of the Russian Federation to the Council of Europe, 16 March, 1428 meeting of the Ministers' Deputies.

Committee of Ministers (2022c) Resolution CM/ResDH(2022)248, Case of *Skendžić and Krznarić against Croatia* and Four Other Cases, 22 September.

Committee of Ministers (2023a) 1475 DH meeting, CM/Del/ Dec(2023)1475/H46-14, decision on case *M.H. and Others v Croatia* (15670/18), 19–21 September.

Committee of Ministers (2023b) Action Plan – Communication from Croatia Concerning the Case of *M.H. and Others Against Croatia*, to the Secretariat of the Committee of Ministers, DH-DD(2023)758, 21 June.

Committee of Ministers (2023c) Communication from an NGO (Centre for Peace Studies and the Human Rights House Zagreb) (18/07/2023) in the Case of *M.H. and Others against Croatia* (App no 15670/18) and Reply from the Authorities (26/07/2023), DH-DD(2023)891, 27 June.

Congress of Europe (1948) *Message to Europeans*, The Hague, London, Paris: International Committee of the Movements for European Unity.

Conservative Party (1997) *Conservative Party Manifesto 1997*, London: Conservative Party. [Online copy] Available at: http://www.conservativemanifesto.com/1997/1997-conservative-manifesto.shtml (accessed 31 July 2016).

Conservative Party (2014) *Protecting Human Rights in the UK: The Conservatives' Proposal for Changing Britain's Human Rights Laws*, London: Conservative Party.

Conservative Party (2015) *The Conservative Party Manifesto*, London: Conservative Party.

Constitutional Court of the Republic of Croatia (no date) *Case-Law of the European Court of Human Rights Concerning the Republic of Croatia*. Available at: https://www.usud.hr/en/echr-case-law (accessed 18 December 2017).

Coogle, A. (2014) 'Abu Qatada Case is No Victory for London', Human Rights Watch, 27 October. Available at: https://www.hrw.org/news/2014/10/27/abu-qatada-case-no-victory-london (accessed 23 January 2024).

Cortell, A.P. and J.W. Davis (2000) 'Understanding the Domestic Impact of International Norms: A Research Agenda', *International Studies Review*, 2(1): 65–87.

Costa, J. (2011) 'On the Legitimacy of the European Court of Human Rights' Judgments', *European Constitutional Law Review*, 7(2): 173–82.

Council of Europe (1975) *Collected Edition of the 'Travaux Préparatoires' of the ECHR*, ed A. Robertson, The Hague: M. Nijhoff, 1975–85.

Council of Europe (no date a) HUDOC-EXEC Case Database, Department for the Execution of Judgments of the ECHR, Strasbourg. Available at: https://hudoc.exec.coe.int (accessed 10 January 2024).

Council of Europe (no date b) 'Presentation of the Department', Department for the Execution of Judgments of the European Court of Human Rights, Strasbourg. Available at: https://www.coe.int/en/web/execution/presentation-of-the-department (accessed 29 March 2024).

Council of Europe (2012) *Proceedings of the High-Level Conference on the Future of the European Court of Human Rights, Brighton, 19–20 April.*

Council of Europe (2023) *Excessive Formalism by Courts: Thematic Factsheet*, Strasbourg: Department for the Execution of Judgments of the European Court of Human Rights.

Courea, E. (2022) 'London Playbook: Return of the Pyjama Judges – Inside Tory WhatsApp Groups – Brussels Sues', Politico, 15 June. Available at: https://www.politico.eu/newsletter/london-playbook/return-of-the-pyjama-judges-inside-tory-whatsapp-groups-brussels-sues/ (accessed 31 March 2024).

Cowan, J.K., M. Dembour, and R.A. Wilson (eds) (2004) *Culture and Rights: Anthropological Perspectives*, New York: Cambridge University Press.

Cserne, P. (2020) 'Discourses on Judicial Formalism in Central and Eastern Europe: Symptom of an Inferiority Complex?', *European Review*, 28(6): 880–91.

Dale, W. (1976) 'Human Rights in the United Kingdom: International Standards', *International and Comparative Law Quarterly*, 25(2): 292–309.

Danish Chairmanship of the Committee of Ministers (2018) 'Draft Copenhagen Declaration', Copenhagen, 5 February.

David, L. (2020) *The Past Can't Heal Us: The Dangers of Mandating Memory in the Name of Human Rights*, Cambridge: Cambridge University Press.

de Búrca, G. (2011) 'The Road Not Taken: The European Union as a Global Human Rights Actor', *American Journal of International Law*, 105(4): 649–93.

Deitelhoff, N. (2020) 'What's in a Name? Contestation and Backlash against International Norms and Institutions', *British Journal of Politics and International Relations*, 22(4): 715–27.

Deitelhoff, N. and L. Zimmermann (2019) 'Norms Under Challenge: Unpacking the Dynamics of Norm Robustness', *Journal of Global Security Studies*, 4(1): 2–17.

Deitelhoff, N. and L. Zimmermann (2020) 'Things We Lost in the Fire: How Different Types of Contestation Affect the Robustness of International Norms', *International Studies Review*, 22(1): 51–76.

Dembour, M. (2004) 'Following the Movement of a Pendulum: Between Universalism and Relativism', in J.K. Cowan, M. Dembour, and R.A. Wilson (eds), *Culture and Rights: Anthropological Perspectives*, New York: Cambridge University Press, pp 56–79.

Dembour, M. (2006) *Who Believes in Human Rights?: Reflections on the European Convention*, New York: Cambridge University Press.

Der Spiegel (2011) 'Späte Erkenntnis', *Der Spiegel*, 7 May. Available at: http://www.spiegel.de/spiegel/print/d-78413701.html (accessed 1 April 2017).

Dicey, A.V. (1915) *Introduction to the Study of the Law of the Constitution*, 8th edn, London: Macmillan.

Die Linke (2021) *Zeit zu handeln! Für soziale Sicherheit, Frieden und Klimagerechtigkeit: Wahlprogramme zur Bundestagswahl 2021*, Berlin: Die Linke.

Diering, F. (2004) 'Straßburger Urteile nicht bindend', *Die Welt*, 20 October. Available at: https://www.welt.de/print-welt/article347316/Strassburger-Urteile-nicht-bindend.html (accessed 31 March 2017).

Diez Medrano, J. (2003) *Framing Europe: Attitudes to European Integration in Germany, Spain, and the United Kingdom*, Princeton, NJ: Princeton University Press.

Dixon, J.M. (2017) 'Rhetorical Adaptation and Resistance to International Norms', *Perspectives on Politics*, 15(1): 83–99.

Domovinski Pokret (2021) Program Djelovanja [Action Programme], February.

Donald, A. and P. Leach (2016) *Parliaments and the European Court of Human Rights*, Oxford: Oxford University Press.

Donald, A., J. Gordon, and P. Leach (2012) *The UK and the European Court of Human Rights*, Manchester: Equality and Human Rights Commission.

Downs, G.W., D.M. Rocke, and P.N. Barsoom (1996) 'Is the Good News About Compliance Good News About Cooperation?', *International Organization*, 50(3): 379–406.

Duranti, M. (2012) 'Curbing Labour's Totalitarian Temptation: European Human Rights Law and British Postwar Politics', *Humanity: An International Journal of Human Rights, Humanitarianism and Development*, 3(3): 361–83.

Duranti, M. (2017) *The Conservative Human Rights Revolution: European Identity, Transnational Politics, and the Origins of the European Convention*, New York: Oxford University Press.

Dworkin, R. (2004) 'Hart's Postscript and the Character of Political Philosophy', *Oxford Journal of Legal Studies*, 24(1): 1–37.

Dyer, C., M. White, and A. Travis (2004) 'Judges' Verdict on Terror Laws Provokes Constitutional Crisis', *Guardian*, 18 December. Available at: https://www.theguardian.com/uk/2004/dec/17/terrorism.humanrights3 (accessed 20 January 2017).

Dyson, J. (2015) 'Delay Too Often Defeats Justice', speech at the Law Society, London, 22 April.

Dzehtsiarou, K. (2011) 'European Consensus and the Evolutive Interpretation of the European Convention on Human Rights', *German Law Journal*, 12(10): 1730–45.

Dzehtsiarou, K. (2021) *Can the European Court of Human Rights Shape European Public Order?*, Cambridge: Cambridge University Press.

Dzehtsiarou, K. (2024) 'The United Kingdom and the European Convention on Human Rights: Together Until the End?', *European Convention on Human Rights Law Review*, 5(1): 1–7.

Eimer, T.R., S. Lütz, and V. Schüren (2016) 'Varieties of Localisation: International Norms and the Commodification of Knowledge in India and Brazil', *Review of International Political Economy*, 23(3): 450–79.

El Mahmoud, K. (2024) 'Measuring with Double Legal Standards: Germany's Intervention in Support of Israel before the ICJ', Verfassungsblog, 25 January. Available at: https://verfassungsblog.de/measuring-with-double-legal-standards-germanys-intervention-in-support-of-israel-before-the-icj/ (accessed 16 February 2024).

Ensor, J. and Z. Weise (2016) 'Turkey Suspends European Convention on Human Rights Amid Fears of Further Crackdown', *Telegraph*, 21 July. Available at: http://www.telegraph.co.uk/news/2016/07/21/turkey-suspends-european-convention-on-human-rights-as-it-enacts/ (accessed 5 February 2018).

European Court of Human Rights (no date a) *History of the Court's Reforms*. Available at: https://www.echr.coe.int/documents/d/echr/Reforms_history_ENG (accessed 29 September 2024).

European Court of Human Rights (no date b) *HUDOC Case Database*. Available at: https://hudoc.echr.coe.int (accessed 11 May 2024).

European Court of Human Rights (2014) *Practical Guide on Admissibility Criteria*, Strasbourg: ECtHR.

European Court of Human Rights (2017) *Violations by Article and State 1959–2016: Annual Report 2016*, Strasbourg: ECtHR.

European Court of Human Rights (2022) *Overview: 1959–2021*, Strasbourg: ECtHR. Available at: https://www.echr.coe.int/documents/d/echr/Overview_19592021_ENG (accessed 10 January 2024).

European Union Committee (2016) *The UK, the EU and a British Bill of Rights: 12th Report of Session 2015–16*, HL Paper 139, London: House of Lords.

Falkner, G. and O. Treib (2008) 'Three Worlds of Compliance or Four? The EU-15 Compared to New Member States', *Journal of Common Market Studies*, 46(2): 293–313.

Feldman, D. (2005) 'The Impact of the Human Rights Act 1998 on English Public Law', keynote address delivered at the conference European Influences on Public Law: 5 Years of the Human Rights Act 1998 in English Law and Recent Developments in France, British Institute of International and Comparative Law, London, 7 October.

Finnemore, M. and K. Sikkink (1998) 'International Norm Dynamics and Political Change', *International Organisation*, 52(4): 887–917.

Finnemore, M. and S.J. Toope (2001) 'Alternatives to "Legalisation": Richer Views of Law and Politics', *International Organization*, 55(3): 743–58.

Føllesdal, A. (2013) 'Much Ado About Nothing? International Judicial Review of Human Rights in Well-Functioning Democracies', in A. Føllesdal, J. Karlsson Schaffer, and G. Ulfstein (eds), *The Legitimacy of International Human Rights Regimes: Legal, Political and Philosophical Perspectives*, Cambridge: Cambridge University Press, pp 272–99.

Foucault, M. (1984) 'Neitzsche, Genealogy, History', in P. Rabinow (ed), *The Foucault Reader*, New York: Pantheon Books, pp 76–100.

Franck, T.M. (1990) *The Power of Legitimacy Among Nations*, New York: Oxford University Press.

Franck, T.M. (1995) *Fairness in International Law and Institutions*, Oxford: Clarendon Press.

Frankfurter Allgemeine Zeitung (2011) *Sicherungsverwahrung verfassungswidrig*, 4 May. Available at: http://www.faz.net/aktuell/politik/inland/bundesverfassungsgericht-sicherungsverwahrung-verfassungswidrig-1640218.html (accessed 1 April 2017).

Frankfurter Allgemeine Zeitung Archiv (2004) *Im Ausland mißverständlich*, 23 October. Available at: https://fazarchiv.faz.net/faz-portal/document?uid=FAZ__FD2200410232525189 (accessed 28 September 2024).

Fuller, L.L. (1958) 'Positivism and Fidelity to Law – A Reply to Professor Hart', *Harvard Law Review*, 71(4): 630–72.

Fuller, L.L. (1977) *The Morality of Law*, rev edn, New Haven, CT: Yale University Press.

Gauck, J. (2015) *Speech: Day of Remembrance of the Victims of National Socialism*, 27 January, Berlin. Available at: https://www.bundespraesident.de/SharedDocs/Reden/EN/JoachimGauck/Reden/2015/150127-Gedenken-Holocaust.html (accessed 8 February 2024).

Gearty, C. (2016) *On Fantasy Island: Britain, Europe, and Human Rights*, Oxford: Oxford University Press.

Gee, G. and G. Webber (2013) 'Rationalism in Public Law', *Modern Law Review*, 76(4): 708–34.

Geertz, C. (1973) *The Interpretation of Cultures: Selected Essays*, New York: Basic Books.

Geertz, C. (1983) *Local Knowledge: Further Essays in Interpretive Anthropology*, New York: Basic Books.

George, A.L. and A. Bennett (2004) *Case Studies and Theory Development in the Social Sciences*, Cambridge, MA: MIT Press.

Gerards, J. (2016) 'The Netherlands: Political Dynamics, Institutional Robustness', in P. Popelier, S. Lambrecht, and K. Lemmens (eds), *Criticism of the European Court of Human Rights – Shifting the Convention System: Counter-Dynamics at the National and EU Level*, Cambridge: Intersentia, pp 327–60.

Gerards, J. (2018) 'Margin of Appreciation and Incrementalism in the Case Law of the European Court of Human Rights', *Human Rights Law Review*, 18(3): 495–515.

Gibson, J.L. and G.A. Caldeira (1996) 'The Legal Cultures of Europe', *Law and Society Review*, 30(1): 55–85.

Gies, L. (2015) *Mediating Human Rights: Media, Culture and Human Rights Law*, Abingdon: Routledge.

Gilpin, R. (1981) *War and Change in World Politics*, Cambridge: Cambridge University Press.

Glenn, H.P. (2004) 'Legal Cultures and Legal Traditions', in M. Van Hoeck (ed), *Epistemology and Methodology of Comparative Law*, Oxford: Oxford University Press, pp 7–20.

Goldsmith, J. and E. Posner (2005) *The Limits of International Law*, New York: Oxford University Press.

Goldstein, J., M. Kahler, R.O. Keohane, and A.-M. Slaughter (2000) 'Introduction: Legalisation and World Politics', *International Organization*, 54(3): 385–99.

Goodman, R. and D. Jinks (2004) 'How to Influence States: Socialisation and International Human Rights Law', *Duke Law Journal*, 54(3): 621–703.

Goodman, R. and D. Jinks (2008) 'Incomplete Internalisation and Compliance with Human Rights Law', *European Journal of International Law*, 19(4): 725–48.

Gordon, J. (2010) 'A Developing Human Rights Culture in the UK? Case Studies of Policing', *European Human Rights Law Review*, 6: 609–20.

Greer, S. and L. Wildhaber (2013) 'Revisiting the Debate about "Constitutionalising" the European Court of Human Rights', *Human Rights Law Review*, 12(4): 655–87.

Grieve, D. (2011) 'European Convention on Human Rights – Current Challenges', speech at Lincoln's Inn, London, 24 October.

Griffith, J.A.G. (1979) 'The Political Constitution', *Modern Law Review*, 42(1): 1–21.

Guardian (2013) 'Prisoners "Damn Well Shouldn't" be Given Right to Vote, says David Cameron', *Guardian*, 14 December. Available at: http://www.theguardian.com/politics/2013/dec/13/prisoners-right-to-vote-david-cameron (accessed 9 May 2016).

Guardian (2016) 'Patrick Stewart: What has the ECHR Ever Done for Us? – Video', *Guardian*, 25 April. Available at: https://www.theguardian.com/culture/video/2016/apr/25/patrick-stewart-sketch-what-has-the-echr-ever-done-for-us-video (accessed 23 January 2024).

Gupta, A. and J. Ferguson (1997) 'Beyond "Culture": Space, Identity, and the Politics of Difference', *Cultural Anthropology*, 7(1): 6–23.

Gusy, C. and S. Müller (2008) *Supranational Rights Litigation, Implementation and the Domestic Impact of Strasbourg Court Jurisprudence: A Case Study of Germany*, project report for the JURISTAS project, Bielefeld: Universität Bielefeld.

Habermas, J. (1987) *The Theory of Communicative Action*, vol 2: *Lifeworld and System: A Critique of Functionalist Reason*, translated by T. McCarthy, Boston, MA: Polity Press.

Habermas, J. (1998) 'Historical Consciousness and Post-Traditional Identity: Remarks on the Federal Republic's Orientation to the West', *Acta Sociologica*, 31(1): 3–13.

Hafner-Burton, E.M., E.D. Mansfield, and J.C.W. Pevehouse (2015) 'Human Rights Institutions, Sovereignty Costs and Democratisation', *British Journal of Political Science*, 45(1): 1–27.

Hailbronner, M. (2014) 'Rethinking the Rise of the German Constitutional Court: From Anti-Nazism to Value Formalism', *International Journal of Constitutional Law*, 12(3): 626–49.

Hall, S. (2007) 'Living with Difference: Stuart Hall in Conversation with Bill Schwarz', *Soundings: A Journal of Politics and Culture*, 37(2): 148–58.

Halme-Tuomisaari, M. (2010) *Human Rights in Action: Learning Expert Knowledge*, Leiden: Brill.

Hannerz, U. (1969) *Soulside: Inquiries into Ghetto Culture and Community*, New York: Columbia University Press.

Hannerz, U. (1992) *Cultural Complexity: Studies in the Social Organisation of Meaning*, New York: Columbia University Press.

Hansard (2010) HC Deb, 3 Nov 2010, volume 517, column 921. Available at: https://publications.parliament.uk/pa/cm201011/cmhansrd/cm101103/debtext/101103-0001.htm#10110358000023 (accessed 14 May 2024).

Hansard (2011a) HC Deb, 10 Feb 2011, volume 523, columns 493 and 502. Available at: https://publications.parliament.uk/pa/cm201011/cmhansrd/cm110210/debtext/110210-0001.htm#11021059000001 (accessed 14 May 2024).

Hansard (2011b) HC Deb, 10 Feb 2011, volume 523, column 583. Available at: https://publications.parliament.uk/pa/cm201011/cmhansrd/cm110210/debtext/110210-0001.htm#11021059000001 (accessed 14 May 2024).

Hansard (2012a) HC Deb, 17 April 2012, volume 543, column 174. Available at: https://publications.parliament.uk/pa/cm201212/cmhansrd/cm120417/debindx/120417-x.htm (accessed 14 May 2024).

Hansard (2012b) HC Deb, 22 Nov 2012, volume 553, columns 745–62. Available at: https://publications.parliament.uk/pa/cm201213/cmhansrd/cm121122/debtext/121122-0002.htm#12112237000006 (accessed 14 May 2024).

Hansard (2013a) HC Deb, 8 July 2013, volume 566, columns 23–4. Available at: https://publications.parliament.uk/pa/cm201314/cmhansrd/cm130708/debtext/130708-0001.htm#13070810000003 (accessed 14 May 2024).

Hansard (2013b) HC Deb, 16 Oct 2013, volume 568, column 736. Available at: https://publications.parliament.uk/pa/cm201314/cmhansrd/cm131016/debtext/131016-0001.htm#13101671000010 (accessed 14 May 2024).

Hansard (2016) HL Deb, 24 May 2016, volume 733, column 281. Available at: https://hansard.parliament.uk/lords/2016-05-24/debates/70FA7068-7132-4745-A9BE-49CD482EF12E/Queen%E2%80%99SSpeech (accessed 14 May 2024).

Hansard (2017a) HC Deb, 2 Nov 2017, volume 630, column 1007. Available at: https://hansard.parliament.uk/commons/2017-11-02/debates/9E75E904-9B25-475F-87C4-DD8F3C4836C4/Sentencing#1007 (accessed 14 May 2024).

Hansard (2017b) HC Deb, 2 Nov 2017, volume 630, column 1012. Available at: https://hansard.parliament.uk/commons/2017-11-02/debates/9E75E904-9B25-475F-87C4-DD8F3C4836C4/Sentencing#1007 (accessed 14 May 2024).

Hart, H.L.A. (1961) *The Concept of Law*, Oxford: Oxford University Press.

Hathaway, O. (2007) 'Why do Countries Commit to Human Rights Treaties?', *Journal of Conflict Resolution*, 51(4): 588–621.

Hawkins, A. (2015) *Victorian Political Culture: 'Habits of Heart and Mind'*, Oxford: Oxford University Press.

Hawkins, D. and W. Jacoby (2008) 'Partial Compliance: A Comparison of the European and Inter-American Courts for Human Rights', paper delivered at the Annual Meeting of the American Political Science Association, Boston, MA, 28–31 August, pp 1–60.

Hayden, R.M. (1992) 'Constitutional Nationalism in the Formerly Yugoslav Republics', *Slavic Review*, 51(4): 654–73.

Hebestreit, S. (2024) 'Statement by the Federal Government on the Proceedings at the International Court of Justice', Press and Information Office of the Federal Government, 10 January. Available at: https://www.bundesregierung.de/breg-de/aktuelles/erklaerung-der-bundesregierung-zur-verhandlung-am-internationalen-gerichtshof-2252842 (accessed 16 February 2024).

Heinrich, F. (2010) 'Deutscher Bundestag Stenografischer Bericht 49', Sitzung Plenarprotokoll 17/49, Berlin, 17 June, p 5166, para B. Available at: https://dserver.bundestag.de/btp/17/17049.pdf (accessed 14 May 2024).

Helfer, L.R. (2008) 'Redesigning the European Court of Human Rights: Embeddedness as a Deep Structural Principle of the European Human Rights Regime', *European Journal of International Law*, 19(1): 125–59.

Helfer, L.R. and A.-M. Slaughter (1997) 'Toward a Theory of Effective Supranational Adjudication', *Yale Law Journal*, 107(2): 273–391.

Henke, C. (2014) *Common Sense in Early 18th Century British Literature and Culture: Ethics, Aesthetics, and Politics, 1680–1750*, Berlin: De Gruyter.

Henkin, L. (1995) *International Law: Politics and Values*, Dordrecht: Martinus Nijhoff.

Hervey, G. (2017) 'Europe's Human Rights Court Struggles to Lay Down the Law', Politico, 20 September. Available at: https://www.politico.eu/article/human-rights-court-ilgar-mammadov-azerbaijan-struggles-to-lay-down-the-law/ (accessed 4 February 2018).

Hillebrecht, C. (2012) 'Implementing International Human Rights Law at Home: Domestic Politics and the European Court of Human Rights', *Human Rights Review*, 13(3): 279–301.

Hillebrecht, C. (2014) *Domestic Politics and International Human Rights Tribunals: The Problem of Compliance*, New York: Cambridge University Press.

Hillebrecht, C. (2021) *Saving the International Justice Regime: Beyond Backlash against International Courts*, New York: Cambridge University Press.

Hoffman, L. (2009) 'The Universality of Human Rights', Judicial Studies Board Annual Lecture, 19 March.

Home Office (1997) *Rights Brought Home: The Human Rights Bill*, London: The Stationery Office.

Hui, V.T. (2020) 'Cultural Diversity and Coercive Cultural Homogenisation in Chinese History', in A. Phillips and C. Reus-Smit (eds), *Culture and Order in World Politics*, Cambridge: Cambridge University Press, pp 93–112.

Hunko, A. (2021) 'Türkiye: Council of Europe Infringement Proceedings against Türkiye Correct', press release, 3 December. Available at: https://www.dielinke-nrw.de/parlament/bundestag/detail-bundestag/tuerkei-vertragsverletzungsverfahren-des-europarates-gegen-tuerkei-richtig/ (accessed 20 February 2024).

Hurd, I. (2003) 'Legitimacy and Authority in International Politics', *International Organization*, 53(2): 379–408.

Hurrell, A. (2005) 'Legitimacy and the Use of Force: Can the Circle Be Squared?', *Review of International Studies*, 31(S1): 15–32.

Irvine, D. (2003) 'The Impact of the Human Rights Act; Parliament, the Courts and the Executive', *Public Law*, Summer: 308–25.

Irvine, D. (2011) 'A British Interpretation of Convention Rights?', University College London Judicial Institute Lecture, London, 14 December.

Jaspers, K. (1961) *The Question of German Guilt*, translated by E.B. Ashton, New York: Capricorn Books.

Jay, Z. (2022) 'A Tale of Two Europes: How Conflating the European Court of Human Rights with the European Union Exacerbates Euroscepticism', *British Journal of Politics and International Relations*, 24(4): 563–81.

Jay, Z. and M. Killingsworth (2024) 'To Arrest or Not Arrest: South Africa, the International Criminal Court, and New Frameworks for Assessing Noncompliance', *International Studies Quarterly*, 68(2): 1–13.

Jo, H. and C.P. Thompson (2013) 'Legitimacy and Compliance with International Law: Access to Detainees in Civil Conflicts, 1991–2006', *British Journal of Political Science*, 44(2): 323–55.

Joint Committee on Human Rights (2001) 'Minutes of Evidence', 19 March. Available at: http://www.publications.parliament.uk/pa/jt200001/jtselect/jtrights/66/1031906.htm (accessed 18 April 2016).

Joint Committee on Human Rights (2008) *The Work of the Committee in 2007 and the State of Human Rights in the UK: Sixth Report of Session 2007–08*, London: The Stationery Office.

Jordan, P.A. (2003) 'Does Membership Have its Privileges?: Entrance into the Council of Europe and Compliance with Human Rights Norms', *Human Rights Quarterly*, 25(3): 660–88.

Jouet, M. (2023) 'The Abolition and Retention of Life without Parole in Europe: A Comparative and Historical Perspective', *European Convention on Human Rights Law Review*, 4: 306–54.

Jüttner, J. (2011) '"Ein unerträglicher Zustand"', *Der Spiegel*, 5 May. Available at: https://www.spiegel.de/panorama/justiz/urteil-zur-sicherungsverwahrung-ein-unertraeglicher-zustand-a-760719.html (accessed 1 April 2017).

Katzenstein, P.J. (ed) (2010) *Civilisations in World Politics: Plural and Pluralist Perspectives*, Abingdon: Routledge.

Kegel, S. (2012) 'Anatomies eines moralischen dilemmas', *Frankfurter Allgemeine Zeitung*, 24 September. Available at: http://www.faz.net/aktuell/feuilleton/kommissar-ennigkeit-zum-fall-anatomie-eines-moralischen-dilemmas-11900694-p2.html?printPagedArticle=true#pageIndex_2 (accessed 28 April 2017).

Kelemen, K. (2013) 'Dissenting Opinions in Constitutional Courts', *German Law Journal*, 14(8): 1347–8.

Keller, H. and A. Stone Sweet (eds) (2008) *A Europe of Rights: The Impact of the ECHR on National Legal Systems*, New York: Oxford University Press.

Kelsen, H. (1945) *General Theory of the Law and State*, translated by A. Wedberg, Cambridge, MA: Harvard University Press.

Keohane, R. (1997) 'International Relations and International Law: Two Optics', *Harvard International Law Journal*, 38(2): 487–502.

Kirn, T. (2012) 'Trauer, Wut und Verachtung sind geblieben', *Frankfurter Allgemeine Zeitung*, 25 September. Available at: http://www.faz.net/aktuell/rhein-main/metzler-entfuehrung-trauer-wut-und-verachtung-sind-geblieben-11903857-p2.html?printPagedArticle=true#pageIndex_2 (accessed 28 April 2017).

Klarić, J. (2017) 'Hrvatska još nije provela čak 182 presude Europskog suda', *Novilist*, 2 November. Available at: http://www.novilist.hr/Vijesti/Hrvatska/STO-UOPCE-ZNACI-SUD-U-STRASBOURGU-Hrvatska-jos-nije-provela-cak-182-presude-Europskog-suda?meta_refresh=true (accessed 3 November 2017).

Klug, F. (2010) 'Human Rights don't Belong to Political Parties', *Guardian*, 2 February. Available at: https://www.theguardian.com/commentisfree/libertycentral/2010/feb/02/human-rights-political-parties (accessed 19 January 2024).

Klug, F. and K. Starmer (1997) 'Incorporation Through the Back Door?', *Public Law*, Summer: 223–33.

Koh, H. (1997) 'Why do Nations Obey International Law?', *Yale Law Journal*, 106(8): 2599–659.

Koh, H. (1998) *1998 Frankel Lecture: Bringing International Law Home*, Yale Law School Faculty Scholarship Series, Paper 2102, pp 623–81.

Krisch, N. (2008) 'The Open Architecture of European Human Rights Law', *Modern Law Review*, 71(2): 183–216.

Krnetić, S. (2014) 'HDSSB želi promjene: Ustavni sud krši i Ustav i ljudska prava', 24stata, 10 December. Available at: https://www.24sata.hr/news/hdssb-zeli-promjene-ustavni-sud-krsi-i-ustav-i-ljudska-prava-397720 (accessed 7 September 2017).

Kroeber, A.L. (1917) 'The Superorganic', *American Anthropologist*, 19(2): 163–213.

Krook, M. and J. True (2010) 'Rethinking the Life Cycles of International Norms: The United Nations and the Global Promotion of Gender Equality', *European Journal of International Relations*, 18(1): 103–27.

Lambert Abdelgawad, E. and A. Weber (2008) 'The Reception Process in France and Germany', in H. Keller and A. Stone Sweet (eds), *A Europe of Rights: The Impact of the ECHR on National Legal Systems*, New York: Oxford University Press, pp 107–64.

Lamont, C. (2011) 'Confronting the Consequences of Authoritarianism and Conflict: The ECHR and Transition', in A. Buyse and M. Hamilton (eds), *Transitional Jurisprudence and the European Convention on Human Rights: Justice, Politics and Rights*, Cambridge: Cambridge University Press, pp 81–102.

Landale, J. (2012) 'UK Presses for European Human Rights Convention Changes', BBC News, 29 February. Available at: http://www.bbc.com/news/uk-politics-17201024 (accessed 5 February 2018).

Lautenbach, G. (2013) *The Concept of the Rule of Law and the European Court of Human Rights*, New York: Oxford University Press.

Lauterpacht, H. (1950) *International Law and Human Rights*, London: Stevens and Sons.

Leach, P. and A. Donald (2015) 'Russia Defies Strasbourg: Is Contagion Spreading?', EJIL Talk! (blog), 19 December. Available at: https://www.ejiltalk.org/russia-defies-strasbourg-is-contagion-spreading/ (accessed 30 June 2017).

Leigh, I. and R. Masterman (2008) *Making Rights Real: The Human Rights Act in its First Decade*, Portland, OR: Hart Publishing.

Lester, A. (1998) 'UK Acceptance of the Strasbourg Jurisdiction: What Really Went on in Whitehall in 1965', *Public Law*, Summer: 237–53.

Letsas, G. (2013) 'The ECHR as a Living Instrument: Its Meaning and Legitimacy', in A. Føllesdal, B. Peters, and G. Ulfstein (eds), *Constituting Europe: The European Court of Human Rights in a National, European and Global Context*, Cambridge: Cambridge University Press, pp 106–41.

Leuprecht, P. (1998) 'Innovations in the European System of Human Rights Protection: Is Enlargement Compatible with Reinforcement', *Transnational Law and Contemporary Problems*, 8(2): 313–36.

Levy, D. and N. Sznaider (2004) 'The Institutionalisation of Cosmopolitan Morality: The Holocaust and Human Rights', *Journal of Human Rights*, 3(2): 143–57.

Lindstrom, N. (2003) 'Between Europe and the Balkans: Mapping Slovenia and Croatia's "Return to Europe" in the 1990s', *Dialectical Anthropology*, 27(3–4): 313–29.

Lobba, P. (2015) 'Holocaust Denial before the European Court of Human Rights: Evolution of an Exceptional Regime', *European Journal of International Law*, 26(1): 237–53.

Loewenstein, K. (1937) 'Militant Democracy and Fundamental Rights I', *American Political Science Review*, 31(3): 417–32.

Lüdtke, A. (1993) '"Coming to Terms with the Past": Illusions of Remembering, Ways of Forgetting Nazism in West Germany', *Journal of Modern History*, 65(3): 542–72.

Lynch, C. (2014) *Interpreting International Politics*, New York: Routledge.

Madhok, S. (2021) *Vernacular Rights Cultures: The Politics of Origins, Human Rights and Gendered Struggles for Justice*, Cambridge: Cambridge University Press.

Madsen, M.R. (2018) 'Rebalancing European Human Rights: Has the Brighton Declaration Engendered a New Deal on Human Rights in Europe?', *Journal of International Dispute Settlement*, 9(2): 199–222.

Madsen, M.R., P. Cebulak, and M. Wiebusch (2018) 'Backlash against International Courts: Explaining the Forms and Patterns of Resistance to International Courts', *International Journal of Law in Context*, 14(2): 197–220.

Maier, C. (2019) 'The Weimar Origins of the West German *Rechtsstaat*, 1919–1969', *Historical Journal*, 62(4): 1069–91.

Major, J. (1996) Speech on British Constitution, Centre for Policy Studies, London, 26 June.

Mälksoo, M. (2015) '"Memory Must Be Defended": Beyond the Politics of Mnemonical Security', *Security Dialogue*, 46(3): 221–37.

March, J.G. and J.P. Olsen (2006) 'The Logic of Appropriateness', in M. Moran, M. Rein, and R.E. Goodin (eds), *The Oxford Handbook of Public Policy*, Oxford: Oxford University Press, pp 689–708.

Marcussen, M., T. Risse, D. Engelmann-Martin, H. Knopf, and K. Roscher (1999) 'Constructing Europe? The Evolution of French, British, and German Nation-State Identities', *Journal of European Public Policy*, 6(4): 614–33.

Marston, G. (1993) 'The United Kingdom's Part in the Preparation of the European Convention on Human Rights, 1950', *International and Comparative Law Quarterly*, 42(4): 796–826.

Matić, D. (2008) 'Political Culture, Socio-Cultural Values and Democratic Consolidation in Croatia', in S.P. Ramet, K. Clewing, and R. Lukić (eds), *Croatia Since Independence: War, Politics, Society, Foreign Relations*, Munich: De Gruyter, pp 171–88.

McKeown, R. (2009) 'Norm Regress: US Revisionism and the Death of the Torture Norm', *International Relations*, 23(1): 5–25.

McTague, T. (2014) 'Tory Plans to Shackle Human Rights Judges REJECTED by Europe, Leaving Britain's Membership of Court Hanging by a Thread', *Daily Mail*, 3 October. Available at: https://www.dailymail.co.uk/news/article-2779401/Tory-plans-shackle-European-human-rights-judges-REJECTED-Strasbourg-court-row-intensifies.html (accessed 8 February 2017).

Mead, D. (2015) '"You Couldn't Make it Up": Some Narratives of the Media's Coverage of Human Rights', in K.S. Ziegler, E. Wicks, and L. Hodson (eds), *The UK and European Human Rights: A Strained Relationship?*, Portland, OR: Hart, pp 453–72.

Međugorac, I. (2022) 'DOSTA JE "ČETNIČKE PROPAGANDE" O OLUJI! Pravnik iznio sve detalje: Sustavno se stvara stigma da je Hrvatska stvorena na zločinu', Dnevno.hr, 6 August. Available at: https://www.dnevno.hr/vijesti/hrvatska/dosta-je-cetnicke-propagande-o-oluji-pravnik-iznio-sve-detalje-sustavno-se-stvara-stigma-da-je-hrvatska-stvorena-na-zlocinu-2004050/ (accessed 27 February 2024).

Merkel, A. (2008) Address to the 2008 Ordinary Session of the Council of Europe Parliamentary Assembly, Strasbourg, 14–18 April. Available at: http://assembly.coe.int/Sessions/2008/Speeches/20080415_Speech-Merkel.htm (accessed 1 April 2017).

Merkel, A. (2011) Speech at the ceremony of the 60th anniversary of the Federal Constitutional Court, Karlsruhe, 28 September. Available at: https://www.bundesregierung.de/breg-de/service/newsletter-und-abos/bulletin/rede-von-bundeskanzlerin-dr-angela-merkel-802312 (accessed 29 September 2024).

Merkel, A. (2021) Speech to the Parliamentary Assembly of the Council of Europe, 20 April, video message. Available at: https://www.bundesregierung.de/breg-de/service/bulletin/rede-von-bundeskanzlerin-dr-angela-merkel-1892124 (accessed 8 February 2024).

Merry, S.E. (2004) 'Changing Rights, Changing Culture', in J.K. Cowan, M. Dembour, and R.A. Wilson (eds), *Culture and Rights: Anthropological Perspectives*, New York: Cambridge University Press, pp 31–55.

Merry, S.E. (2006) *Human Rights and Gender Violence: Translating International Law into Local Justice*, Chicago, IL: Chicago University Press.

Merry, S.E. (2012) 'What is Legal Culture? An Anthropological Perspective', *Journal of Comparative Law*, 5(2): 40–58.

Mesić, S. (2009) Address of the President of the Republic of Croatia to the Summer University for Democracy, Strasbourg, 8 July. Available at: https://www.coe.int/t/dgap/Source/Croatia_President%20Mesic-speech.doc (accessed 7 September 2017).

Michaelson, C. (2012) '"From Strasbourg, with Love" – Preventive Detention before the German Federal Constitutional Court and the European Court of Human Rights', *Human Rights Law Review*, 12(1): 148–67.

Milliken, J. (1999) 'The Study of Discourse in International Relations: A Critique of Research and Methods', *European Journal of International Relations*, 5(2): 225–54.

Ministry of Justice Office of the Agent of the Government of the Republic of Croatia (2017) *Judicial Practice: Review of Judgments and Decisions of the European Court of Human Rights*. Available at: https://uredzastupnika.gov.hr/sudska-praksa/148 (accessed 18 December 2017).

Moravcsik, A. (2000) 'The Origins of Human Rights Regimes: Democratic Delegation in Postwar Europe', *International Organization*, 54(2): 217–252.

Morgenthau, H. (1973) *Politics Among Nations: The Struggle for Power and Peace*, 5th edn, New York: Alfred A. Knopf.

Moses, D. (2021) 'The German Catechism', Geschichte der Gegenwart, 23 May. Available at: https://geschichtedergegenwart.ch/the-german-catechism/ (accessed 8 February 2024).

Mowbray, A. (2005) 'The Creativity of the European Court of Human Rights', *Human Rights Law Review*, 5(1): 57–79.

Mowbray, A. (2015) 'Subsidiarity and the European Convention on Human Rights', *Human Rights Law Review*, 15(2): 313–41.

Muižnieks, N. (2016) 'Human Rights Comment: Why Remembering the Holocaust is a Human Rights Imperative', Commissioner for Human Rights, 18 October. Available at: https://www.coe.int/en/web/commissioner/-/why-remembering-the-holocaust-is-a-human-rights-imperative (accessed 10 February 2024).

Müller, I. (1991) *Hitler's Justice: The Courts of the Third Reich*, translated by D.L. Schneider, Cambridge, MA: Harvard University Press.

Müller, J. (2006) 'On the Origins of Constitutional Patriotism', *Contemporary Political Theory*, 5(3): 278–96.

Müller, J. (2007) *Constitutional Patriotism*, Princeton, NJ: Princeton University Press.

Müller-Neuhof, J. (2010) 'Ein bisschen Folter', *Tagesspiegel*, 1 June. Available at: http://www.tagesspiegel.de/weltspiegel/magnus-gaefgen-ein-bisschen-folter/1849786.html (accessed 27 April 2017).

Murray, C.R.G. (2018) 'Magna Carta's Tainted Legacy: Historic Justifications for a British Bill of Rights and the Case Against the Human Rights Act', in F. Cowell (ed), *Critically Examining the Case Against the 1998 Human Rights Act*, Abingdon: Routledge, pp 35–51.

Murray, C.R.G. (2021) 'Prisoner Voting and Devolution: New Dimensions to an Old Dispute', *Edinburgh Law Review*, 25(3): 291–314.

N1 Zagreb (2021) 'Interior Minister: Migrant Girl's Death is "Tragic", but I Will Not Step Down', N1 News, 19 November. Available at: https://n1info.hr/english/news/interior-minister-migrant-girls-death-is-tragic-but-i-will-not-step-down/ (accessed 24 February 2024).

Nash, K. (2009) *The Cultural Politics of Human Rights: Comparing the US and UK*, Cambridge: Cambridge University Press.

Nelken, D. (2012) 'Using Legal Culture: Purposes and Problems', *Journal of Comparative Law*, 5(2): 1–39.

Neuberger, D. (2014) 'The British and Europe', Cambridge Freshfields Annual Lecture, Cambridge, 12 February. Available at: https://www.supremecourt.uk/docs/speech-140212.pdf (accessed 3 July 2017).

Neuberger, D. (2016) 'Has the Identity of the English Common Law Been Eroded by EU Laws and the European Convention on Human Rights?', speech at the National University of Singapore, 18 August. Available at: https://www.supremecourt.uk/docs/speech-160818-01.pdf (accessed 3 July 2017).

Neumann, I. (2002) 'Returning Practice to the Linguistic Turn: The Case of Diplomacy', *Millennium: Journal of International Studies*, 31(3): 627–51.

Nicol, D. (2005) 'Original Intent and the European Convention on Human Rights', *Public Law*, Spring: 152–72.

Niemann, H. and H. Schillinger (2017) 'Contestation "All the Way Down"? The Grammar of Contestation in Norm Research', *Review of International Studies*, 43(1): 29–49.

Norman, J. and P. Oborne (2009) *Churchill's Legacy: The Conservative Case for the Human Rights Act*, London: Liberty.

Noutcheva, G. (2009) 'Fake, Partial and Imposed Compliance: The Limits of the EU's Normative Power in the Western Balkans', *Journal of European Public Policy*, 16(7): 1065–84.

O'Faircheallaigh, C. (2014) 'IR Theory and Domestic Adoption of International Norms', *International Politics*, 51(2): 155–76.

O'Hara, C. (2021) 'Consensus, Difference and Sexuality: Que(e)rying the European Court of Human Rights' Concept of "European Consensus"', *Law and Critique*, 32(1): 91–114.

O'Neill, A. (2006) '"Stands Scotland Where it Did?": Devolution, Human Rights and the Scottish Constitution Seven Years On', *Northern Ireland Legal Quarterly*, 57(1): 102–37.

Omejec, J. (2009) *Legal Framework and Case-Law of the Constitutional Court of Croatia in Deciding on the Conformity of Laws with International Treaties: Report for the European Commission for Democracy Through Law (Venice Commission), Montenegro*, Strasbourg: Venice Commission.

Omejec, J. (2010a) 'The Constitutional Development of European Post-Communist and Post-Socialist States', speech delivered at the International Scientific-Practical Conference: The Constitution – A Basis of Democratic Development of the State, 27–28 August, Astana.

Omejec, J. (2010b) *Ways and Means to Recognise the Interpretive Authority of Judgments Against Other States – the Experience of the Constitutional Court of Croatia: Report to the Conference on the Principle of Subsidiarity, Skopje, 1–2 October 2010*, reproduced in Committee on Legal Affairs and Human Rights, Parliamentary Assembly of the Council of Europe (2010) *Strengthening Subsidiarity: Integrating the Strasbourg Court's Case Law into National Law and Judicial Practice*, Conference on the Principle of Subsidiarity, 1–2 October, Skopje.

Omejec, J. (2015) 'Grundrechte in Kroatien', in D. Merten and H. Papier (eds), *Handbuch der Grundrechte in Deutschland und Europa*, vol xxxiv, Hamburg: C.F. Müller, pp 331–82.

Omejec, J. (2016) 'Challenges of Implementation of the ECHR in the Post-Yugoslav Context – The Lessons of Experience of Croatian Constitutional Court', speech delivered at Regional Challenges in Implementation of the European Convention on Human Rights Conference, European Humanities University, Vilnius, 8–9 December. Available at: https://www.youtube.com/watch?v=DOVZkn3okbU&t=306s (accessed 18 August 2017).

Panke, D. and U. Petersohn (2012) 'Why International Norms Disappear Sometimes', *European Journal of International Relations*, 18(4): 719–42.

Papier, H. (2006) 'Execution and Effects of the Judgments of the European Court of Human Rights in the German Judicial System', in Council of Europe, *Dialogue between Judges*, Strasbourg: Publications Unit of the European Court of Human Rights, pp 44–56.

Parliamentary Assembly of the Council of Europe (1996a) 'Application by Croatia for Membership of the Council of Europe', Opinion 195, 24 April (12th sitting).

Parliamentary Assembly of the Council of Europe (1996b) 'Implementation by Croatia of its Commitments in the Framework of the Procedure of Accession to the Council of Europe', Resolution 1089, 29 May.

Parliamentary Assembly of the Council of Europe (2000) 'Honouring of Obligations and Commitments by Croatia', Resolution 1223, 26 September.

Parliamentary Assembly of the Council of Europe Committee on the Honouring of Obligations and Commitments by Member States of the Council of Europe (2015) *The Progress of the Assembly's Monitoring Procedure (October 2014–August 2015): Periodic Review Report of Countries not under the Monitoring Procedure sensu stricto or Engaged in a Post-Monitoring Dialogue, Croatia*, Document 13868 part 4, 14 September, Strasbourg: Council of Europe. Available at: http://assembly.coe.int/nw/xml/XRef/Xref-DocDetails-en.asp?FileID=22028&lang=en (accessed 12 November 2015).

Percival, J. (2009) 'Abu Qatada gets £2,500 Compensation for Breach of Human Rights', *Guardian*, 20 February. Available at: https://www.theguardian.com/world/2009/feb/19/abu-qatada-compensation-european-court (accessed 20 January 2017).

Pešelj, B. (1963) 'Socialist Law and the New Yugoslav Constitution', *Georgetown Law Journal*, 51(4): 651–705.

Phillips, A. and J.C. Sharman (2015) *International Order in Diversity: War, Trade and Rule in the Indian Ocean*, Cambridge: Cambridge University Press.

Phillips, A. and C. Reus-Smit (eds) (2020) *Culture and Order in World Politics*, Cambridge: Cambridge University Press.

Polak, K. (1946) 'Gewaltteilung, Menschenrechte, Rechtsstaat: Begriffsformalismus und Demokratie', *Einheit*, 7 December.

Pouliot, V. (2008) 'The Logic of Practicality: A Theory of Practice of Security Communities', *International Organization*, 62(2): 257–88.

Poznansky, M. (2019) 'Feigning Compliance: Covert Action and International Law', *International Studies Quarterly*, 63(1): 72–84.

Presidency of the Republic of Namibia (2024) 'Namibia Rejects Germany's Support of the Genocidal Intent of the Racist Israeli State against Innocent Civilians in Gaza', media release dated 13 January, Twitter/X. Available at: https://x.com/NamPresidency/status/1746259880871149956?s=20 (accessed 16 February 2024).

Rackow, J. (2015) 'From Conflict to Cooperation: The Relationship between Karlsruhe and Strasbourg', in K.S. Ziegler, E. Wicks, and L. Hodson (eds), *The UK and European Human Rights: A Strained Relationship?*, Portland, OR: Hart Publishing, pp 379–99.

Rasza, M. and N. Lindstrom (2004) 'Balkan is Beautiful: Balkanism in the Political Discourse of Tuđman's Croatia', *East European Politics and Societies*, 18(4): 628–50.

Raustiala, K. (2000) 'Compliance and Effectiveness in International Regulatory Cooperation', *Case Western Reserve Journal of International Law*, 32(3): 387–440.

Reckwitz, A. (2002) 'Toward a Theory of Social Practices: A Development in Culturalist Theorising', *European Journal of Social Theory*, 5(2): 243–63.

Reus-Smit, C. (1999) *The Moral Purpose of the State: Culture, Social Identity, and Institutional Rationality in International Relations*, Princeton, NJ: Princeton University Press.

Reus-Smit, C. (2003) 'Politics and International Legal Obligation', *European Journal of International Relations*, 9(4): 591–625.

Reus-Smit, C. (ed) (2004) *The Politics of International Law*, Cambridge: Cambridge University Press.

Reus-Smit, C. (2011) 'Obligation Through Practice', *International Theory*, 3(2): 339–47.

Reus-Smit, C. (2017) 'Cultural Diversity and International Order', *International Organization*, 71(4): 851–85.

Reus-Smit, C. (2018) *On Cultural Diversity: International Theory in a World of Difference*, Cambridge: Cambridge University Press.

Richardson-Little, N. (2014) 'Dictatorship and Dissent: Human Rights in East Germany in the 1970s', in J. Eckel and S. Moyn (eds), *The Breakthrough: Human Rights in the 1970s*, Philadelphia, PA: University of Pennsylvania Press, pp 49–67.

Riexinger, B. (2018) 'On the ECHR Judgment on Demirtas/Türkiye', press release, 20 November. Available at: https://www.bernd-riexinger.de/aktuell/detail/bernd-riexinger-zum-egmr-urteil-zu-demirtas-tuerkei/ (accessed 20 February 2024).

Risse, T. (2000) '"Let's Argue!": Communicative Action in World Politics', *International Organization*, 54(1): 1–39.

Risse, T. (2001) 'A European Identity? Europeanisation and the Evolution of Nation-State Identities', in M.G. Cowles, J. Caporaso, and T. Risse (eds), *Transforming Europe: Europeanisation and Domestic Change*, Ithaca, NY: Cornell University Press, pp 198–216.

Risse, T. and K. Sikkink (1999) 'The Socialisation of Human Rights Norms into Domestic Practices: Introduction', in T. Risse, S. Ropp, and K. Sikkink (eds), *The Power of Human Rights: International Norms and Domestic Change*, Cambridge: Cambridge University Press, pp 1–38.

Risse, T., S.C. Ropp, and K. Sikkink (eds) (1999) *The Power of Human Rights: International Norms and Domestic Change*, Cambridge: Cambridge University Press.

Rodin, S. (1999) 'Application of the European Human Rights Convention in the Republic of Croatia – an Element of Constitutional Checks and Balances', *European Studies*, 36(5): 93–108.

Rodin, S. (2005) 'Discourse and Authority in European and Post-Communist Legal Culture', *Croatian Yearbook of European Law and Policy*, 1(1): 1–16.

Rodin, S. (2012) 'Croatia', in L. Hammer and F. Emmert (eds), *The European Convention on Human Rights and Fundamental Freedoms in Central and Eastern Europe*, The Hague: Eleven International Publishing, pp 135–62.

Rodin, S. (2013) 'Croatia: Developing Judicial Culture of Fundamental Rights', in R. Arnold (ed), *The Universalism of Human Rights*, Dordrecht: Springer, pp 391–404.

Rothberg, M. (2022) 'Lived Multidirectionality: "*Historikerstreit 2.0*" and the Politics of Holocaust Memory', *Memory Studies*, 15(6): 1316–29.

Rudolf, B. (2016) 'Human Rights in Germany – A View from Germany's National Human Rights Institution', *International Journal of Legal Information*, 44(1): 50–8.

Ruggie, J.G. (1998) 'What Makes the World Hang Together? Neo-Utilitarianism and the Social Constructivist Challenge', *International Organization*, 52(4): 855–85.

Ryssdal, R. (1996a) 'The Coming of Age of the European Convention on Human Rights', *European Human Rights Law Review*, 1: 18–29.

Ryssdal, R. (1996b) 'The Enforcement System Set Up under the European Convention on Human Rights', in M.K. Bulterman and M. Kuijer (eds), *Compliance with Judgments of International Courts: Proceedings of the Symposium Organised in Honour of Professor Henry G. Schermers by Mordenate College and the Department of International Public Law of Leiden University*, The Hague: Martinus Nijhoff, pp 47–79.

Samudzi, Z. (2020) 'Paradox of Recognition: Genocide and Colonialism', *Postmodern Culture*, 31(1&2): 1–13.

Sandholtz, W. (2017) 'Expanding Rights: Norm Innovation in the European and Inter-American Courts', in A. Brysk and M. Stohl (eds), *Expanding Human Rights: 21st Century Norms and Governance*, Cheltenham: Edward Elgar Publishing, pp 156–76.

Scharpf, F. (1999) *Governing Europe: Effective and Democratic?*, Oxford: Oxford University Press.

Schattauer, G. (2019) 'Umfrage-Desaster: Nicht einmal 39 Prozent der Deutschen vertrauen unserer Justiz', Focus, 19 December. Available at: https://www.focus.de/politik/gerichte-in-deutschland/exklusive-erhebung-umfrage-desaster-nicht-einmal-39-prozent-der-deutschen-vertrauen-unserer-justiz_id_11474205.html (accessed 1 April 2020).

Schimmelfennig, F. (2005) 'Strategic Calculation and International Socialisation: Membership Incentives, Party Constellations, and Sustained Compliance in Central and Eastern Europe', *International Organization*, 59(4): 827–60.

Schlieben, M. (2012) 'Großes Vertrauen in Karlsruhe, wenig in die Regierung', *Zeit Online*, 9 July. Available at: https://www.zeit.de/politik/deutschland/2012-07/umfrage-institutionen-karlsruhe (accessed 1 April 2020).

Schröder, G. (2003) Speech at the joint meeting of the German Bundestag and the Assemblée Nationale on the 40th anniversary of the signing of the Elysée Treaty, 22 January, Versailles. Available at: https://www.bundesregierung.de/breg-de/service/bulletin/rede-von-bundeskanzler-gerhard-schroeder-789522 (accessed 8 February 2024).

Scott, J. (2024) 'Rwanda Bill: Rishi Sunak "Crystal Clear" He will Ignore International Law to Ensure Asylum Seekers are Deported', SkyNews, 18 January. Available at: https://news.sky.com/story/rishi-sunak-crystal-clear-he-will-ignore-international-law-to-get-asylum-seekers-sent-to-rwanda-13050781 (accessed 23 January 2024).

Searle, J.R. (1995) *The Construction of Social Reality*, New York: Free Press.

Silbey, S. (2001) 'Legal Culture and Legal Consciousness', in N.J. Smelser and P.B. Baltes (eds), *International Encyclopedia of Social and Behavioural Sciences*, Oxford: Pergamon Press, pp 8623–9.

Simmons, B. (2000) 'The Legalisation of International Monetary Affairs', *International Organization*, 54(3): 573–602.

Simmons, B. (2009) *Mobilizing for Human Rights: International Law in Domestic Politics*, New York: Cambridge University Press.

Simpson, A.W.B. (2004) *Human Rights and the End of Empire: Britain and the Genesis of the European Convention*, Oxford: Oxford University Press.

Sims, A. (2015) 'Vladimir Putin Signs Law Allowing Russia to Ignore International Human Rights', *Independent*, 15 December. Available at: http://www.independent.co.uk/news/world/europe/vladimir-putin-signs-law-allowing-russian-court-to-overthrow-international-human-rights-rulings-a6773581.html (accessed 5 February 2018).

Slaughter, A.-M. (1995) 'International Law in a World of Liberal States', *European Journal of International Law*, 6(3): 503–38.

Slotte, P. and M. Scheinin (2011) 'Captain, Fire Brigade or Icebreaker? Political Legitimacy as a Rationale in Human Rights Adjudication', in T. Kurtén and L. Hertzberg (eds), *Legitimacy: The Treasure of Politics*, Frankfurt am Main: Peter Lang, pp 89–127.

Smerdel, B. (2014) 'In Quest of a Doctrine: Croatian Constitutional Identity in the European Union', *Zbornik Pravnog fakulteta u Zagrebu*, 64(4): 513–34.

Soley, X. and S. Steininger (2018) 'Parting Ways or Lashing Back? Withdrawals, Backlash and the Inter-American Court of Human Rights', *International Journal of Law in Context*, 14(2): 237–57.

Sozialdemokratische Partei Deutschlands (2013) *Das Wir Entscheidet, Das Regierungsprogramm 2013–2017*, Berlin: SPD-Parteivorstand.

Spano, R. (2014) 'Universality or Diversity of Human Rights? Strasbourg in the Age of Subsidiarity', *Human Rights Law Review*, 14(3): 487–502.

Spiegel Online (2001) 'Sexualstraftäter lebenslang wegsperren', Spiegel Politik, 8 July. Available at: http://www.spiegel.de/politik/deutschland/gerhard-schroeder-sexualstraftaeter-lebenslang-wegsperren-a-144052.html (accessed 1 April 2017).

Spiegel Online (2010) 'Kay Nehm fordert radikale Verschärfung der Sicherungsverwahrung', Spiegel Panorama, 12 May. Available at: http://www.spiegel.de/panorama/justiz/urteil-des-europaeischen-menschenrechtsgerichts-kay-nehm-fordert-radikale-verschaerfung-der-sicherungsverwahrung-a-694486.html (accessed 20 December 2017).

Spielmann, D. (2013) 'Allowing the Right Margin: The European Court of Human Rights and the National Margin of Appreciation Doctrine: Waiver or Subsidiarity of European Review?', speech at the Max Planck Institute for Comparative Public Law and International Law, Heidelberg, 13 December.

Spielmann, D. (2014) 'Whither the Margin of Appreciation?', UCL Current Legal Problems Lecture, London, 20 March.

Spruyt, H. (2020) *The World Imagined: Collective Beliefs and Political Order in the Sinocentric, Islamic and Southeast Asian International Societies*, Cambridge: Cambridge University Press.

Statista Research Department (2020) *Umfrage in Deutschland zum Vertrauen in Justiz und Rechtssystem 2019*, 9 March. Available at: https://de.statista.com/statistik/daten/studie/153813/umfrage/allgemeines-vertrauen-in-die-justiz-und-das-rechtssystem/ (accessed 1 April 2020).

Sternberger, D. (1980) *Staatsfreundschaft [Schriften IV]*, Frankfurt am Main: Suhrkamp.

Stiansen Ø. and E. Voeten (2020) 'Backlash and Judicial Restraint: Evidence from the European Court of Human Rights', *International Studies Quarterly*, 64(4): 770–84.

Stojic, M. (2006) 'Between Europhobia and Europhilia: Party and Popular Attitudes Towards Membership of the European Union in Serbia and Croatia', *Perspectives on European Politics and Society*, 7(3): 312–35.

Stone, J. (2015) 'Scottish Government will Block Human Rights Act Repeal for the Whole UK, says Nicola Sturgeon', *Independent*, 23 September. Available at: http://www.independent.co.uk/news/uk/politics/scottish-government-will-block-human-rights-act-repeal-for-the-whole-uk-says-nicola-sturgeon-10514015.html (accessed 11 August 2017).

Straw, J. and P. Boateng (1997) 'Bringing Rights Home: Labour's Plans to Incorporate the European Convention on Human Rights into UK Law', *European Human Rights Law Review*, 1: 71–80.

Sturge, G. (2023) *Research Briefing: UK Prison Population Statistics*, London: House of Commons Library. Available at: https://commonslibrary.parliament.uk/research-briefings/sn04334/ (accessed 23 March 2024).

Subotić, J. (2011) 'Europe is a State of Mind: Identity and Europeanisation in the Balkans', *International Studies Quarterly*, 55(2): 309–30.

Subotić, J. (2013) 'Stories States Tell: Identity, Narrative and Human Rights in the Balkans', *Slavic Review*, 72(2): 306–26.

Subotić, J. (2014) 'Legitimacy, Scope, and Conflicting Claims on the ICTY: In the Aftermath of *Gotovina, Haradinai* and *Perišić*', *Journal of Human Rights*, 13(2): 170–85.

Subotić, J. (2019) *Yellow Star, Red Star: Holocaust Remembrance after Communism*, London and Ithaca, NY: Cornell University Press.

Subotić, J. and A. Zarakol (2012) 'Cultural Intimacy in International Relations', *European Journal of International Relations*, 19(4): 915–38.

Suchman, M. (1995) 'Managing Legitimacy: Strategic and Institutional Approaches', *Academy of Management Review*, 20(3): 571–611.

Süddeutsche Zeitung (2010) 'Folterverbot gilt absolut', *Süddeutsche Zeitung*, 1 June. Available at: http://www.sueddeutsche.de/politik/erfolg-fuer-kindesmoerder-strassburg-gibt-gaefgen-recht-1.952672 (accessed 27 April 2017).

Süddeutsche Zeitung (2011) 'Bundesverfassungsgericht kippt Sicherungsverwahrung', *Süddeutscher Zeitung*, 4 May. Available at: http://www.sueddeutsche.de/politik/urteil-aus-karlsruhe-bundesverfassungsgericht-kippt-sicherungsverwahrung-1.1092944 (accessed 1 April 2017).

Swidler, A. (1986) 'Culture in Action: Symbols and Strategies', *American Sociological Review*, 51(2): 273–86.

Sydow, G. (2007) 'Independence of the Judiciary in Germany', in K.S. Ziegler, D. Baranger, and A.W. Bradley (eds), *Constitutionalism and the Role of Parliaments*, Portland, OR: Hart Publishing, pp 225–38.

Talmon, S. (2024) 'Germany Rushes to Declare Intention to Intervene in the Genocide Case brought by South Africa against Israel before the International Court of Justice', GPIL – German Practice in International Law, 15 January. Available at: https://gpil.jura.uni-bonn.de/2024/01/germany-rushes-to-declare-intention-to-intervene-in-the-genocide-case-brought-by-south-africa-against-israel-before-the-international-court-of-justice/ (accessed 16 February 2024).

Tanner, M. (2010) *Croatia: A Nation Forged in War*, 3rd edn, New Haven, CT: Yale University Press.

Terman, R. (2020) 'The Positive Side of Negative Identity: Stigma and Deviance in Backlash Movements', *British Journal of Politics and International Relations*, 22(4): 619–30.

Theilen, J. (2021) *European Consensus between Strategy and Principle: The Uses of Vertically Comparative Legal Reasoning in Regional Human Rights Adjudication*, Baden: Nomos Verlagsgesellschaft.

Tomuschat, C. (2010) 'The Effects of the Judgments of the European Court of Human Rights According to the German Constitutional Court', *German Law Journal*, 11(5): 513–26.

Travis, A. (2005) 'Worst Criminals will Not get Vote in Jail Despite European Court Ruling', *Guardian*, 7 October. Available at: https://www.theguardian.com/uk/2005/oct/07/constitution.ukcrime (accessed 3 July 2017).

Travis, A. (2013) 'Theresa May Criticises Human Rights Convention after Abu Qatada Affair', *Guardian*, 9 July. Available at: http://www.theguardian.com/world/2013/jul/08/theresa-may-human-rights-abu-qatada (accessed 9 May 2016).

Tully, J. (1995) *Strange Multiplicity: Constitutionalism in an Age of Diversity*, Cambridge: Cambridge University Press.

Tully, J. (2008) 'The Unfreedom of the Moderns in Comparison to their Ideals of Constitutionalism and Democracy', *Modern Law Review*, 65(2): 204–28.

Turković, K. and J. Omejec (2016) 'Commitment to Reform: Assessing the Impact of the ECtHR's Case Law on Reinforcing Democratisation Efforts in Croatian Legal Order', in I. Motoc and I. Ziemele (eds), *The Impact of the ECHR on Democratic Change in Central and Eastern Europe*, Cambridge: Cambridge University Press, pp 110–35.

Utley, T. (2005) 'We Need Common Sense and Justice – not "Human Rights"', *Telegraph*, 4 March. Available at: http://www.telegraph.co.uk/comment/columnists/tomutley/3615318/We-need-common-sense-and-justice-not-human-rights.html (accessed 9 May 2016).

Uzelac, A. (2010) 'Survival of the Third Legal Tradition?', *Supreme Court Law Review*, 49: 377–96.

Voltner, K. and C. Eilders (2003) 'The Media Agenda: The Marginalisation and Domestication of Europe', in K. Dyson and K. Goetz (eds), *Germany, Europe, and the Politics of Constraint*, Oxford: Oxford University Press/British Academy, pp 173–97.

von Staden, A. (2018) *Strategies of Compliance with the European Court of Human Rights: Rational Choice within Normative Constraints*, Philadelphia, PA: University of Pennsylvania Press.

Voßkuhle, A. (2010a) 'Multilevel Cooperation of the European Constitutional Courts: *Der Europäische Verfassungsgerichtsverbund*', *European Constitutional Law Review*, 6(2): 175–98.

Voßkuhle, A. (2010b) 'Protection of Human Rights in the European Union. Multilevel Cooperation on Human Rights between the European Constitutional Courts', lecture at Our Common Future, Hannover, 4 November.

Weber, M. (1964) *The Theory of Social and Economic Organisation*, translated by T. Parsons, New York: Oxford University Press.

Weber, R. and L. Wittmann (2022) 'The Role of Precedents and Case Law in the Jurisprudence of the German Federal Constitutional Court', in M. Florczak-Wator (ed), *Constitutional Law and Precedent: International Perspectives on Case-Based Reasoning*, London: Routledge, pp 83–105.

Weiler, J.H.H. (2004) 'The Geology of International Law – Governance, Democracy and Legitimacy', *Zeitschrift für ausländisches öffentlisches Recht und Völkerrecht*, 64: 547–62.

Weiss, N. (2003) 'The Impact of the European Convention on Human Rights on German Jurisprudence', in E. Örücü (ed), *Judicial Comparativism in Human Rights Cases*, London: British Institute of International and Comparative Law, pp 49–61.

Wendt, A. (1999) *Social Theory of International Politics*, New York: Cambridge University Press.

Wenger, E. (1998) *Communities of Practice: Learning, Meaning, and Identity*, Cambridge: Cambridge University Press.

Welt (2010) 'Kindermörder ist Folteropfer – Kein neuer Prozess' [Child murderer is torture victim – no new trial], *Welt*, 1 June. Available at: https://www.welt.de/aktuell/article7869770/Kindermoerder-ist-Folteropfer-Kein-neuer-Prozess.html (accessed 29 September 2024).

Whitehead, T. (2012) 'David Cameron Urged to Stand Up to Europe over Prisoner Vote Row', *Telegraph*, 22 May. Available at: http://www.telegraph.co.uk/news/politics/9283297/David-Cameron-urged-to-stand-up-to-Europe-over-prisoner-vote-row.html (accessed 3 July 2017).

Wicks, E. (2000) 'The United Kingdom Government's Perceptions of the European Convention on Human Rights at the Time of Entry', *Public Law*, Autumn: 438–55.

Wiener, A. (2004) 'Contested Compliance: Interventions on the Normative Structure of World Politics', *European Journal of International Relations*, 10(2): 198–234.

Wiener, A. (2008) *The Invisible Constitution of Politics: Contested Norms and International Encounters*, Cambridge: Cambridge University Press.

Wiener, A. (2014) *A Theory of Contestation*, Heidelberg: Springer.

Wiener, A. and U. Puetter (2009) 'The Quality of Norms is What Actors Make of it: Critical Constructivist Research on Norms', *Journal of International Law and International Relations*, 5(1): 1–16.

Wildenthal, L. (2013) *The Language of Human Rights in West Germany*, Philadelphia, PA: University of Pennsylvania Press.

Wittgenstein, L. (1967) *Philosophical Investigations*, 3rd edn, Oxford: Blackwell.

Woodhouse, C. (2012) 'Prison Paedos "Will Get Vote"', *Sun*, 23 December, p 2.

Worley, W. (2016) 'Theresa May "Will Campaign to Leave the European Convention on Human Rights in 2020 Election"', *Independent*, 29 December. Available at: http://www.independent.co.uk/news/uk/politics/theresa-may-campaign-leave-european-convention-on-human-rights-2020-general-election-brexit-a7499951.html (accessed 20 January 2017).

Young, A. (2005) 'A Peculiarly British Protection of Human Rights?', *Modern Law Review*, 68(5): 858–72.

Young, O. (1979) *Compliance and Public Authority: A Theory with International Applications*, Baltimore, MD: Johns Hopkins University Press.

Zarakol, A. (2020) 'The Ottomans and Diversity', in A. Phillips and C. Reus-Smit (eds), *Culture and Order in World Politics*, Cambridge: Cambridge University Press, pp 49–70.

Ziegler, K. (2007) 'The Princess and the Press: Privacy after *Caroline von Hannover v Germany*', in K. Ziegler (ed), *Human Rights and Private Law: Privacy as Autonomy*, Oxford: Hart Publishing, pp 189–208.

Ziegler, K., E. Wicks, and L. Hodson (eds) (2015) *The UK and European Human Rights: A Strained Relationship?*, Portland, OR: Hart Publishing.

Zimmermann, A. (2001) 'Germany', in R. Blackburn and J. Polakiewicz (eds), *Fundamental Rights in Europe: The European Convention on Human Rights and its Member States, 1950–2000*, New York: Oxford University Press, pp 335–54.

Zimmermann, L. (2016) 'Same Same or Different? Norm Diffusion Between Resistance, Compliance, and Localisation in Post-Conflict States', *International Studies Perspectives*, 17(1): 98–115.

Zimmermann, L. (2017) *Global Norms with a Local Face: Between Global Norms and Local Translation*, Cambridge: Cambridge University Press.

Index

References to footnotes show both the page number and the note number (111n117).